Toward a Philosophy of Religious Studies

Toward a Philosophy of Religious Studies
Enecstatic Explorations

JIM KANARIS

Published by State University of New York Press, Albany

© 2023 State University of New York

All rights reserved

Printed in the United States of America

No part of this book may be used or reproduced in any manner whatsoever without written permission. No part of this book may be stored in a retrieval system or transmitted in any form or by any means including electronic, electrostatic, magnetic tape, mechanical, photocopying, recording, or otherwise without the prior permission in writing of the publisher.

For information, contact State University of New York Press, Albany, NY
www.sunypress.edu

Library of Congress Cataloging-in-Publication Data

Name: Kanaris, James, author.
Title: Toward a philosophy of religious studies : enecstatic explorations / James Kanaris.
Description: Albany : State University of New York Press, [2023] | Includes bibliographical references and index.
Identifiers: ISBN 9781438494548 (hardcover : alk. paper) | ISBN 9781438494562 (ebook) | ISBN 9781438494555 (pbk. : alk. paper)
Further information is available at the Library of Congress.

10 9 8 7 6 5 4 3 2 1

To my students, past and present.
Sine qua non.

Contents

Preface ix

Acknowledgments xvii

Introduction 1

Part I.
Delimiting Enecstasis

Chapter 1 Enecstasis: A Disposition for Our Times? 11

Chapter 2 The Enecstatic Jig: Personalizing Philosophy of Religion 23

Part II.
Contouring Enecstatic Philosophy of Religious Studies

Chapter 3 Philosophy of Religious Studies: The Changing Face of Philosophy of Religion 39

Chapter 4 Philosophy of Religion Religious Studies Style 55

Chapter 5 Derrida's Philosophy of Religion for Religious Studies 77

Part III.
The Heritage and Modus Operandi of Enecstasis

Chapter 6 Theorizing Religion Enecstatically: The
Transcendental Gesture in a New Key 93

Chapter 7 Enecstatic Philosophy of Religious Studies:
A Sidelong Bow to Self-Appropriation 105

Chapter 8 The Normative Impetus of Enecstatic Philosophy of
Religious Studies: Dialectic and Foundations 115

Conclusion 131

Postscript 139

Notes 161

References 187

Index 199

Preface

> Whoever wishes to philosophize about religion must know what it is concerned with; he should not presuppose this as self-evident.
>
> —Gerardus van der Leeuw ([1938] 1986)

The title of this book speaks to certain idiosyncrasies that would be good to address at the outset. *Toward a Philosophy of Religious Studies?* The only thing to be said about the overworked term "toward" in the title is that it is merited here, complementing the slightly less overworked term "explorations" in the subtitle. But what about "philosophy of *religious studies*"? Why introduce another designation when a similar term (philosophy of religion) is in vogue already? My answer: connotation is a luxury that would be unwise to neglect. I should like to keep my proposal simple by calling it philosophy of religion. However, the convention that goes by that name is complex, far more complex even than what I discuss in chapter 3, which is a token appreciation of philosophy of religion as a discipline. The treatment there, besides being based on what now will strike some as a dated "ethnography" of the two main species of philosophy, analytic and continental, merely pinpoints still extant stylistic differences that beg a new configuration in the field of religious studies. Analytic philosophers of religion will find my exposition about as illuminating as the proverbial deaf person attending a lecture on auditory oscillation; I fail to adequately describe their discipline or tradition. Bits of my narrative may resonate with continental philosophers of religion, but a struggle will ensue to see their main orientation represented or, for that matter, the litany of issues currently directing their gaze. In the book I identify the latter in terms of a specialized object-constitutive preoccupation.

My analysis has the student in mind but, in its current form, a generic kind of student, one beleaguered by, if even aware of, the problems surrounding theory selection in religious studies. This type of student may have a foggy memory of some traditional themes covered in undergraduate courses that overlap philosophy and religion, the famous ones being arguments for the existence of God and the conundrums that follow such arguments as topics of evil and suffering. The student may even recall select concerns attending the European and North American "turn to religion" in philosophy, say, in phenomenology, genealogy, and deconstruction. The idiosyncrasy here is twofold: first, the burden of my project, which is intended predominately for students of philosophy, religion, and theology, and second, the fact that this adumbration may prove to be demonstratively ineffective toward that aim, as with our proverbial deaf person. Is this a work for students? It is important to keep in mind that the burden of this work does not necessarily equate with its form. As I note in the postscript, it recounts a journey, my journey, as a catalyst for this aim. It is a propaedeutic to reengaging philosophical inquiry vis-à-vis religion sutured to what in the introduction I describe by the Greek *meráki*, the performance of an activity (in this case thinking, philosophy) with soul, creativity, and love. Unlike John Wisdom's two individuals in the celebrated parable "Gods" (1944), who are fixated on explaining the presence of plants amid weeds in their neglected garden, I fuss with the weeds that barricade my appreciation of there even being a garden. The following recounts the twists and turns that plunged me onto Wisdom's "clearing in the jungle," to put it in the terms of Anthony Flew (1971). *Meráki* and desire to facilitate the existential needs and wants of students inspired the entire expedition, however circuitous and formalistic this looks bookended.

It took this expedition to conceive an approach to the clearing I wish to continue to nominate—controversially, perhaps—as philosophy of religion. However, to distinguish it from what usually passes as such, without the hint of surpassing it, I prefer the term "philosophy of religious studies." The designation flags the more general preoccupation of how the general inquirer interested in religion, especially the philosophically inclined individual, can engage in the study of religion without the imprimatur of a philosophical area of specialty. The invitation instead is a consideration of the issues, theories, and methods that form a second-order tradition, a tradition of studying a phenomenon that, conveniently, though not insignificantly, came to be designated by the catchall "religion." Historically the inclination stretches back to the cultural revolutions to which Karl Jaspers assigned the term "axial period" (eighth century BCE) all the way to contemporary "postmodern" developments. It has configured and continues to configure understandings of this peculiar phenomenon. The feature of this inclination, in other words, exemplifies, without necessarily endorsing wholesale, the now well-known provocation of J. Z. Smith (1982, xi) that "religion is solely the creation of the scholar's study." I would volunteer that the normative reflection of insiders be included as well to avoid the assumption of an extraneous imposition of a category that came into technical prominence in the eighteenth and nineteenth centuries with the creation of comparative religion. What is truly wonderful about Smith's suggestion may also be unintended. The association of religion with this inheritance bears witness to the tenuousness of the scholarly activity. The scholar takes away what necessarily surfaces in their observations. "Religion" is tenuous in this way and so, the suggestion seems to be, we must be vigilant when heedlessly invoking the term. And how! However, and this is where I think Smith's suggestion may be unintended, the so-called creation of that category drags with it a dimension of normativity the coping mechanism of which is inextricably bound up with the mediation of that phenomenon.

Perhaps an illustration may be useful. Grace advocates for the exclusion of a belief-practice in her observation to ensure that her assessment is unbiased, that is, does not presuppose or reiterate the belief-practices under consideration. (I hyphenate the terms to signal their oftentimes inextricable nature, whether considered in terms of their materiality or ideality, their function or presumed diffusion.) All checks and balances are put into place for a dispassionate mediation of what qualifies as significant in the observation. I do not spurn the posture. It accentuates aspects of the phenomenon that have gone into the creation of the category of religion ever since German idealism bifurcated inquiry into humanistic and social-scientific pathways. Grace pinpoints the quantifiable, giving us insight into that dimension of religious behavior *while configuring our proximity toward it to the degree to which we value such posturing.* This is where things get tricky. What is mediated is an other, an object, according to which in our othering may be a well-intentioned desire "merely" to explain or describe that other. In such a circumstance, Grace's role is, in my estimation, exemplary. She adds to our understanding of the phenomenon in question. We may quibble with Grace if the data is misdirected on this or that point, this or that assumption, and so forth. "It does not add up," we say. Her point is revised or dismissed, according to the rules and regulations guiding this specific management of data in our shared value set, framework of inquiry. We engage in what philosophers call dialectic, a procedure of argumentation that negotiates contrary claims. However, this is not the truly menacing part of this activity of categorization. It can go in one of several different directions, but for purposes of convenience I limit myself to two.

Grace's procedure can protract the category of religion as described. This involves a perfunctory level of engagement with religion signaled, I believe, in Smith's provocation. But Grace's procedure can also configure that category by the shared value set of inquiry, deciding a, if not the, proper role of engagement. And it is thus decided because the framework supplies the legitimacy, the touchstone of what qualifies as true and what is tolerated as epiphenomenal. A strong and weak sense exists in the decision. The reflex that assumes it or slightly consciously considers it an important rule of thumb (i.e., methodologically requisite) is the weak sense. The strong sense lassoes the category into an ontology where various jurisdictional, educational restrictions apply. It will become clear to the reader soon enough what philosophy, group, individuals I associate with these different versions of a light- or heavyweight Grace. Important to note now is (1) how philosophy is both implicated in and summoned by this investigation and (2) how engagement with the category of religion protracts a "religious" inclination we might better nominate as "metaphysical" or, as I prefer, "ideological" qua "ideology critique." The second-order *tradition* of religious studies (see discussion in chapter 4).

In effect, what I have been describing pertains to the three types of criticism (analysis) the late Tyler Roberts (2018, 192–193) itemizes in his elucidation of a fourth type, "reverence as *critical* responsiveness," which I endorse, though qualify. Roberts's outline of these three types of criticism is worth quoting in full before moving to an exposition of the fourth.

> First, critical thinking is reflexively analytic. On a very basic level, all critical thinking is grounded in analysis that makes useful and illuminating distinctions with respect to the constitutive elements of concepts, arguments, literary works, practices, etc. Such thinking becomes properly critical when it becomes *reflexive*, that is, when one reflects on one's own stance or perspective in relation to the object of analysis and the distinctions one employs. Second, critical thinking is "critique"—in the

Kantian sense of the term—when it identifies the conditions of possibility and the limits of particular concepts and experiences. Third, there is "critique" as a demystifying procedure, originating with Marx and developing in many directions since, that employs historical, psychological, sociological, and linguistic methods to expose the workings of desire and power in the construction of concepts, values, and social relations.

This is an effective way to make my earlier point concerning how philosophical traditions combine to provide for the various methodological commitments embodied in the example of Grace: study, analysis, critique, criticism, and so on—in a word, dialectic, philosophically engaged study of religion.

Roberts's fourth type of criticism speaks to my second point about protracting the "religious" (metaphysical, ideological) *into* the differentiated category of religion, "the creation of the scholar's study": "The fourth kind of intellectual operation that we associate with the "critical" . . . refer[s] to critical thinking directed to the appreciation of cultural phenomena or, more generally, to the synthetic and constructive work of evaluation that makes judgments, negative and positive, about *our aesthetic, moral, political, and religious commitments and values*" (Roberts 2018, 193, italics added). Grace's framework enframes, to put it in Heidegger's ontological terms. That framework is different from what it seeks to explain or describe—in our case, religion. However, in its relationship to this object, Grace's framework "brings forth" what is conceived as its proper essence or function. Religion, in a very real sense, is not "really" religion without it. That is, the framework delivers both sense and (reconfigured) object. Smith's invocation of "creation" is effective in getting this across. Moreover, the process does not take place in a vacuum. Assumptions, many of them good and true, are of a (second-order) tradition extended and modified in this and that way by a subject, the scholar, guided by the various commitments and values that Roberts names. This kind of engagement crosses the threshold of critique as reflexive, transcendental, and demystifying (dialectic) into a deeper level of normativity, a philosophical horizon of self-care (foundations).[1]

Having addressed the paradoxical and idiosyncratic nature of my idea of philosophy of religion, it may be useful to close with some thoughts on an expression the reader will encounter in chapter 2: "personalizing philosophy of religion." This ties in with the element of self-care just mentioned. "Self-discovery" can also be invoked since it goes—or should go—hand in hand with the quest of knowledge acquisition.

The personal nature of this type of philosophy of religion is a reference to the practicum of what I earlier called the *burden* of my project. It is to be distinguished, as I also said, from its current *form*, which paradoxically is specialized. This is what the neologism in the subtitle, *enecstatic*, intimates. In this respect, the explorations gathered here in thematically disparate chapters recount my personal journey *toward* that practical aim. It involves a technical preoccupation with select theories that I had to personally negotiate in order to (re)discover and meet that aim; the postscript explains this further. Personal in this sense, then, is rather banal and admittedly self-serving. It is not a direct reference to the ethos of a school of thought popular in the early twentieth century dubbed personalism, which included distinguished figures such as Ferdinand Ebner (1882–1931), Franz Rosenzweig (1886–1929), and Eugene Rosenstock-Huessy (1888–1973). The thought of Martin Buber (1878–1965) and Emmanuel Levinas (1906–1995) also tend to be associated with personalism, albeit as idiosyncratic forms. While enecstatic philosophy of religion echoes certain emphases found in these celebrated thinkers, the centrality of persons and personal relationships at the heart of theory and practice being principal among them, the properly basic role of moral categories in that orientation is not an essential feature of the "critical" work I am advancing. It is, of course, not inimical to it either. The scope of the irreducible primacy of the category of the personal in enecstatic philosophy of religion exceeds what is advocated in personalism, or perhaps more adequately stated, serves a more general purpose. In terms of this book, it describes my personalization of philosophy of religion, my journey to make it, in the broader context of studying religion, personalizable. *Enecstasis*, which I outline in the book, is the term proposed as an opening to aid those caught in the throes of self-discovery to personalize it for themselves. That is why I give so much traction to the notion of singularity in my exposition. Singularity of the self, in a word, refers to an irreducible complexity, the generalizations of which can never satisfy the demands of individual applications and their necessity.

All of this, personalizing philosophy of religion qua philosophy of religious studies, enecstaticizing philosophy of religion, if you will, is my implementation of the very laudable advice encapsulated in the epigraph by the doyen of phenomenology of religion. Indeed, it is a response to a desideratum announced by Ninian Smart (1996, 24) over two decades ago that we need a general theory in the science of religion approximating the style of Gerardus van der Leeuw. Smart names Nathan Söderblom as well, but I prefer his first-named choice in the detour to "being 'Smart' about bringing 'Religion' back in[to religious studies]" (Strenski 2015, 241–253).

Jim Kanaris
Montreal, QC
August 2022

Acknowledgments

As I complete this journey, I am reminded of the revelation of Martin Buber ([1923] 1986) that appears to run contrary to a key trope in the argument presented here: "There is no *I* taken in itself, but only the *I* of the primary word *I-Thou* and the *I* of the primary word *I-It*" (4). A correlative truism if ever there was one. In this work, I struggle with one of the basal aspects of the inextricable relationality Buber has no qualms calling primary: *I-*. The hyphen is presupposed in my utterance of "it." The reader would be remiss to imagine the *I-* proffered in these pages as a retrieval of the isolated ego that twentieth-century philosophies were only too happy to proclaim dead. Perhaps better would be to see my accent as reiterating Buber's insight about the constancy of the *I-* in his relativizing configuration, primarily with respect to *-Thou* as he critiqued the predominant *-It* relationality championed by modernity. What better way than acknowledgments to demonstrate this concretely? Hopefully, it offsets what my accent unwittingly conveys.

Several times in this study I use the term "personal journey" to describe the output of this collection. While true, it would not have taken the shape it did without *Thou* said along with it, namely, the individuals helping me steer my course. Ruinous whirlpools were avoided thanks to them. Aaron Simmons stands out for special acknowledgment. His key recommendations to change the title and to reorganize the essays, replacing an older version of the preface (now postscript) with a much shorter, more reader-friendly one, were paramount. It changed the whole tenor and cadence of the volume, making it less perplexing on account of its idiosyncrasies. Aaron was a beacon of light leading me to calmer straits. Elyse MacLeod, my graduate student, is another. Without her research assistance and "eagle eye," this book, already tardy in gestation, would not have seen the light of day for several years hence. I owe to them both a great debt of gratitude, and to Garth Green as well, whose friendship and support since joining me at McGill have been simply incalculable. I am grateful, too, to McGill's School of Religious Studies, under Green's directorship, which provided funds toward the speedier completion of this volume. State University of New York Press also deserves my profound thanks, for backing not only this project but my other projects as well. Their flexibility and courage to publish unique research is second to none, which is why I proudly continue to bear the press's insignia.

And now a special word of thanks to my children, Maria and Sophia Kanaris, and to my partner, Jennifer Der. Their support and love have been my mainstay. They alone understand how personal this personal journey has been, how it parallels my existential journey and what its completion signifies in the form of a book. Finally, my *It*, in which strangely is also a *Thou*: Betsy (RIP), Glenda (RIP), and Maddy, my road bikes! Trivial as this sounds, cyclists know exactly what I mean. The ridiculous amount of time spent in their saddle accounts for whatever equilibrium I maintained just before, during, and up to this point. Without them, I doubt I would have survived the chaos that forced enecstasis from me.

Introduction

A voice within whispers strangeness. We all experience it. It elevates the Prufrockian. "That is not it at all." What confronts us strikes us as reasonable, but it somehow eludes the effluence stirring within. This study gives personal voice to that experience. It has been with me ever since I started reading works of philosophy and theology as an undergraduate. It has intensified over the years of teaching a broad demographic in religious studies, with backgrounds and interests in religion figuratively and literally worlds apart from my own. No one work or combination of works that influenced me formatively could facilitate this yawning chasm. Not unlike many colleagues, I faced this situation daily in my professional life. As a result, I set myself the rather solitary task of revoicing the voices that helped me to listen to my own, a practice colleagues are familiar with and which "comes with the territory." The challenge was to do this without (completely) alienating those curious enough to lend an ear, students and colleagues alike. The present work is a result of that exercise—perhaps better: anguish, a form of philosophizing religion that accents the irreducible experience of self-discovery in deference to systems too specialized and determinate to form my teaching curriculum.

This is neither a comprehensive nor an erudite work in the philosophy of religion. It develops a hunch induced painfully through trial and error. It can, in principle, serve such works, but its cluster of points, if deemed valid, is applicable no matter the overview. The research, then, is selective, there to facilitate a discussion correlating a personal insight with a stream of relevant literature that sets a problematic in disparate configurations of philosophy, religious studies, and theology. The chapters are independent entities written for different occasions that exemplify my basic theme. ("Variations on a theme" was a tempting subtitle vetoed on account of being prosaic.) Together they flesh out a perspective to which each chapter contributes in its own way. The theme is personalizing philosophy of religion. The context is eclecticism in the academic study of religion, which can be beneficial in furnishing a rich horizon. It can also be precarious when the reflex stifles attention to self. "Enecstasis" is my term to mark out an interstice in this binary of circumstance. As will be evident to readers familiar with the history of philosophy, the term itself contains fragments reminiscent of perspectives in the transcendental tradition that are radically critical of notions of personhood qua the notion of the subject. Clearly "personal" and "subjective experience" will mean something different and yet necessarily related in this exposition.

The chapters are reworked essays produced over roughly a decade. This is important to index for the simple reason that the chapters are separate inscriptions formulated at different times addressing diverse, though related, pressing issues as I understood them. They are inscriptions, in other words, that develop a momentum addressing a specific situation at different times and in different contexts. The covers of this project close on a personal venture. It began formally in 2010 with chapter 1 ("Enecstasis: A Disposition for Our Times?") of part 1 ("Delimiting Enecstasis"), when I threw my proverbial hat into the philosophical ring. The context was poststructuralism and the death of the subject. The burden was my conviction that, although dead, the subject, phoenixlike, was rising from a peculiar ash heap.

In this inaugural chapter, I begin to delimit my principal theme coined enecstasis. I provide background information concerning its general nature, etymology, and basic form. Heidegger is the key figure. His critique of the Cartesian tradition and his answer to the disengaged analysis of representational thinking is a basic presupposition of the post-Heideggerian context after which enecstasis models itself and aims to address. While I turn to the Heidegger of *Sein und Zeit*—which the later Heidegger finds too transcendental for an appreciation of the unity, singularity, and commonness of Being—his thoughts on ecstatic *Dasein* nonetheless embody a notion of care consonant not only with programs of philosophy that seek to cultivate the self, but also, incidentally, with the entirety of Heidegger's thought (see Olafson 1993). Noteworthy, too, is that Foucault, that great modern exponent of "care of the self," numbered Heidegger among his chief influences. The prefix "en" in enecstasis is meant to summon this sensibility as apropos to present-day thinking and scholarship, that is, it brings with it the practical underpinnings of Heidegger's ontology to shape an orientation befitting an ontic practice for our times. I cannot be sanguine about completing the movement of return, as Ricoeur wished, from fundamental ontology "to the properly epistemological question of the status of the human sciences" (1981, 59). My project is less ambitious while maintaining ties with this wish. Enecstasis provides, necessarily perhaps, a rough outline of one particular aspect within this return as it pertains to the human sciences of philosophy and religious studies. It seems apropos to examine another word from the national heritage of *en-ec-stasis* to flesh out this aspect further.

Greeks have an untranslatable expression that communicates an activity performed with soul, creativity, or love. The term is *meráki* (μεράκι). According to linguist Christopher J. Moore (2004, 156), it means putting "'something of yourself' into what you're doing, whatever it may be." It is "often used to describe cooking or preparing a meal, but it can also mean arranging a room, choosing decorations, or setting an elegant table."[1] While the quality of the form is not ignored, the proper referent in *meráki* is the "spirit" of the act, how one identifies with whatever one is doing. In other words, when one does something with *meráki* the defining element is not whether one does it well, according to accepted standards, but whether one does it lovingly, wholeheartedly. Of course, the two go together. If something is done with *meráki*, it is the skill with which it is executed that typically draws attention. However, in devising this contrast I distinguish *meráki* from the skill that happens to manifest it. *Meráki* is defined by a state of being or quality of disposition, not the skill with which it is engineered. One can, for instance, be an accomplished artisan but lack *meráki*. Conversely, one can practice one's art with *meráki* but be a subpar artisan. An act of personal investment is essentially what is at stake in *meráki*, and it is this element that I conjoin with the thinking implied in enecstasis.

It seems to me that *meráki*, in conjunction with enecstasis, captures the classical significance of philosophy according to which one pursues knowledge as an integral part of oneself, as a way of caring for the self and, by extension, others interested in thinking. Rather than simply communicating a craft, a specialty, or facilitating a disengaged acquisition of knowledge, enecstasis embodies a thinking that possesses soul, creativity, or love. Without *meráki*, thinking is like body without soul: necessary, perhaps, but lifeless. It is not too surprising, then, to discover scholars identifying philosophy with *meráki* in ancient Greece in terms of an "art of living" or "way of life" (see Nehamas 1998; also Hadot 1995 and Foucault

1999). This lies behind the whimsical reference to the "jig" of enecstasis in chapter 2. Nietzsche is the more immediate referent here, whose love of this artistic metaphor, let alone his love of the ancient Greeks, is not among his best-kept secrets. "I should only believe in a God that would know how to dance" (Nietzsche [1883–1891] 1999, I.7).

In chapter 2, then, these themes come together with explicit developments in religious studies that negotiate the element of the personal that has been spearheaded by certain phenomenologists of religion. The basic proposal of enecstasis in this context emerges in critical sympathy with phenomenologists but as philosophy of religious studies, which is something altogether different from phenomenology of religion properly so called and, incidentally, what typically passes as philosophy of religion, a bewitching designation simple only in form. In a pointed overview of current trends in philosophy of religion and academic theology, discussed in chapter 1, I further delimit enecstasis in solidarity with these trends but also in its difference from them. The enecstatic jig consists of a supple movement that guards the scholarly integrity desirous of meeting the particular aims of a research program while simultaneously embracing, in self-critical reflexivity, the ideological underpinnings of such aims as they pertain to religion. This movement, on my reading, is what philosophy of religious studies is fundamentally about. It is taken captive to the view that one's methodological commitment can not only enrich a research program but also become a potentially cancerous metaphysics that metastasizes into one.

In the subsequent chapters of part 2 ("Contouring Enecstatic Philosophy of Religion"), I configure enecstasis in conversation with different philosophical postures that overlap in their interest with religion. Highlighted is the connection to continental philosophy. As I explain in the conclusion, enecstatic thinking is not averse to philosophical theology and the analytic tradition that informs it. However, as incited by issues and concerns arising out of the continent, enecstasis has a special relation to the philosophizing birthed by Immanuel Kant and G. W. F. Hegel. It also stands to reason that the search for a philosophy of *religious studies* would turn to philosophical styles that root early "comparative" religion and subsequent schools of phenomenology. An enecstatic philosophy of religion, then, which addresses traditional analytic concerns, will, de jure, betray continental leanings. The new face of philosophy of religion, to embellish the title of chapter 3, forges a rapprochement between the two traditions but at the level of personal involvement. It complements the equivalent concern in phenomenology of religion by reconstructing the dimension of the personal according to "postmodern" complaints voiced against phenomenology. And yet enecstasis signals a space different from what both advocate in the study of religion. In effect, enecstasis means to complement systems in its difference.²

Chapter 4 ("Philosophy of Religion Religious Studies Style") is an example of philosophy of religious studies in action. It represents issues broached in my graduate seminars, which treat key figures when tackling religion in the second-order tradition of religious studies. While the issues are methodological in nature, they nonetheless presuppose a manner of philosophical inquiry that causes scholars of religion to look askance at "philosophy of religion" or the discipline typically identified as such. I am not making the case that philosophy of religious studies, the trope depicted in this chapter, is true philosophy of religion. Rather, enecstatic involvement, focused on such issues, is a propaedeutic for a fuller appreciation of it.

Enter Jacques Derrida. Chapter 5 is a pivotal chapter in this regard. In it, I examine the philosophy of religion of the great *philosophe* who mastered the art of suspicion wholly constructively, in my opinion. Derrida frames the basic comportment of enecstasis described in earlier chapters, bridging its explicit formulation in the programmatic outlined in later chapters. He offers the philosophical sources for the differance in (the tradition of) *le souci de soi* that Michel Foucault, his fellow countryman, spins more historically. Enecstasis is a tribute to the view that the self is different from itself, a singularity that necessarily eludes the necessary singularizations of a system. This conundrum puts Derrida above interpreters who read him as though he were offering more than a self-critically reflexive strategy. Once this is grasped one sees immediately why in later chapters I do not seek an escape route from particular transcendental methods, but rather contextualize their shaping import on enecstasis in its difference.

This launches the third and last part of my discussion ("The Heritage and Modus Operandi of Enecstasis") concerned with the inheritance and basic procedure of enecstasis. The cluster of chapters (6–8) formulates my version of what John D. Caputo (2000) calls "hyper-realism" and the releasing of "the possibility of the impossible" in thinking. As Caputo discovered hyperrealism in Derrida, who fashioned it out of his early interest in the rigorous phenomenology of Edmund Husserl, I discovered the hyperrealism of enecstasis, as it were, through the range of scholarship discussed in this study. Notable in this connection is my critical conversation with the equally rigorous "phenomenology" (rather: generalized empirical method) of Bernard Lonergan. Enecstasis bears the stamp of Lonergan, even if Heidegger, Foucault, and Derrida shape its form. If this study is unique, it is owed in great part to Lonergan's influence, which many overlook in metamethodological discussions of philosophy of religion like this one. Charles Winquist is among the few notables in the conversation that considers Lonergan, which is why he factors into my discussion (see chapter 6).[3]

Lonergan's idea of self-appropriation is key to understanding the path to enecstasis. Self-appropriation is the inner lining of Lonergan's model of understanding, which he states aims to effect "the appropriation of one's own rational self-consciousness" (Lonergan [1957] 1992, 22). This is a target interest of enecstasis. Lonergan further goes on to state that self-appropriation is a "necessary beginning" in a quest that "heads through an understanding of all understanding to a basic understanding of all that can be understood." He puts it famously as follows in his defining work *Insight: A Study of Human Understanding* (1957): "*Thoroughly understand what it is to understand, and not only will you understand the broad lines of all there is to be understood but also you will possess a fixed base, an invariant pattern, opening upon all further developments of understanding*" (Lonergan [1957] 1992, 22, italics his). In Lonergan's procedure, I discovered a clue for inciting a hyperrealism indwelling his "critical realism." It is fixed by his own peculiar transcendental method, which involves a series of mental "exercises" in the examination of what Lonergan calls operations immanent in consciousness. The main objective is to get readers to personally encounter and appropriate their own intellectual foundations, which is a wonderful opportunity for thinking with *meráki*.

This program of self-appropriation, understandably, however, "is not an end in itself but rather a beginning" (Lonergan [1957] 1992, 22). The editors of the critical edition of *Insight* (1992) highlight this sentiment by connecting it to a similar point Lonergan makes several years later in *Method in Theology* (1972b). Significant for us is the editors' observation that the reaffirmation in *Method* is "useful for perspective on Lonergan's long-range strategy" (Lonergan [1957] 1992, 780m): " 'The withdrawal into interiority is not an end in itself' [Lonergan 1972b, 83], and 'withdrawal is for return' [Lonergan 1972b, 342]."

Lonergan had a determinate plan for his generalized empirical method. It coalesced with many of his overlapping concerns regarding the classist notion of culture embodied in scholasticism, the view that takes culture to be universal and permanent (see Kanaris 2005b, 330-334; Lonergan 1972b, xi). This is captured in a hyperbolic statement by Lonergan that "all [his] work has been introducing history into Catholic theology" (Lonergan as quoted in Crowe 1992, 98). It is wise not to reduce the significance of self-appropriation—which takes up only the first of two parts in *Insight*—to this aim. However, we risk the ahistorical metaphysics Lonergan sought to overcome by thinking that his empirical method and accompanying empirical notion of culture—"the set of meanings and values that informs a way of life" (Lonergan 1972b, xi)—are incidental to his subordination of self-appropriation to its proper objective qua the pure desire to know: the universe of proportionate being (Lonergan [1957] 1992, 373-374). This "return" virtually becomes an end in itself in the exposition of self-appropriation. Moreover, and also not incidentally, the return is mediated most satisfactorily (one quickly gathers reading *Insight*) by the explanatory mode of the intellectual pattern of experience exemplified in science (see Lonergan [1957] 1992, 204-212, 397-409, 512-552, 657-708).

I do not wish to dispute the legitimacy of Lonergan's delineation. Enecstasis merely displaces it for reasons provided in this last part of my exploration. I summarize these reasons along the lines of hyperrealism, my spin on which is to see it as a virtue of releasing the possibility of the impossible—specifically the peculiarity of thinking the impossible, the irreducible, that is, the singularity of an appropriating self—for ontic purposes. Enecstasis emphasizes the withdrawal of self-appropriation *as an end in itself*. The return it envisions remains a "knowledge" *strategy* under the constancy of the hyperrealist problematic. If we imagine this in the terms introduced in chapter 6, which are Lonergan's own, it is to trump explanation in the intellectual pattern by the exigencies of an artistic thinking pattern (see chapters 7 and 8). Briefly, the artistic pattern of experience is one in which one experiences, understands, and judges differently from the pattern driven by intellectual concerns, that is, differentiated knowledge commensurate with and immanent in scientific generality concerning reality. The artistic pattern, by contrast, consists of a differentiation of concerns whose aesthetic manner of thinking is absorbed by a world that is "other, different, novel, strange, remote, intimate" (Lonergan 1993, 216). It underscores a conscious decision to live accordingly based on such "knowledge." The sensibility, in other words, can be found in hyperrealism, which as a matter of course problematizes the rationality that the intellectual pattern features.[4] We might want to call it "alterity thinking," which is admittedly clumsy. However we wish to nominate it, the point is to recognize that such thinking is disruptive of the effective historical consciousness that equates knowledge with science and analytic philosophy. By calling it a thinking, I am clearly elevating alterity thinking, in solidarity with enecstasis, to the status of knowledge, albeit a form many would struggle to see as such. I acknowledge this earlier by placing the term knowledge in scare quotes.[5]

My sense is that the specificities surrounding Lonergan's formulation of self-appropriation—that he was Catholic, that he wished to usher his Church into the modern era of historical consciousness and empirical science—not only bias the withdrawal of the enecstatic dimension of self-appropriation *for* return, for determinate generalized expression, but also bias the return in favor of the explanatory, intellectual pattern of experience. Invoking Charles Winquist in chapter 6, both a sympathizer and critic of Lonergan, is intended to this end. He serves as a notable example of one reacting specifically to this tendency in Lonergan and managing a view of self-appropriation (although not in word) as an end in itself. Winquist does this based on a reconstituted understanding of the general principles that underlie transcendental method. Whether Winquist's alternative biases another return route, I leave to the reader. My only purpose here is to show that Lonergan's otherwise laudable bias is a historical accident, not an integral, necessary presupposition of his notion of self-appropriation and perhaps even his philosophy. Indeed, I do not see anything in Lonergan that biases self-appropriation when treated strictly phenomenologically, for us enecstatically, as an end in itself; the emphasis on the self-appropriating venture in its singularity requires this. In the final chapters I discuss ways in which this is true, the ways in which the pragmatics of this possibility of the impossible further contours philosophy of religion for religious studies. While the overall framework is enecstatic philosophy of religious studies, in the conclusion I pinpoint how my main argument also applies to the various branches of religious studies, including philosophical theology and academic theology. If this does not resonate with readers, if "that is not it at all," I can only beg their pardon and wish them well.

Part I

Delimiting Enecstasis

Chapter 1

Enecstasis

A Disposition for Our Times?

The assault on subjectivity and transcendental reflection from Nietzsche to Derrida has done much to assuage the appetite for certainty. Non-agential language has superseded "foundationalism," and hypervigilant reflective strategies have managed to stem the tide of system building. Some thinkers have used this critique of modernity to further disenfranchise "individualism" from the university, revalorizing objectivity for the public square. In religious studies this translates into an overt attack on phenomenology of religion, understood by critics to be especially sinister for masking subjectivist ideology in a false pretense of objectivity (sui generis religion). One reaction has been to disassemble this critique from the perspective of what is called "academic theology." Another has been more overtly philosophical, blending deconstructive and semiological themes. Although both reactions assume the postmodern critique, they do so in appreciation of singularity and engaged discourse For this reason, particularly with respect to the element of engaged agency, I adumbrate the development in Heideggerian terms while earmarking its post-Heideggerian emphasis on deconstructive and constructive forms of agential self-possession.

This is a reworked version of a chapter that appeared originally in proceedings from a symposium, "Polyphonic Thinking about the Divine," held in honor of Dr. Maurice Boutin at McGill University in 2010 (Kanaris 2013, 97–104).

The Contours of Enecstasis

Melford Spiro, relying on Carl Gustav Hempel, distinguishes between nominal and real definitions (see Spiro 1966, 85–87). What Spiro writes about nominal definitions is how I would like to begin. Unlike real definitions, which aim to be true statements about entities or things, nominal definitions have the more pragmatic aim of communicating ideas efficiently and unambiguously. It is the device of scholars and teachers, Spiro tells us, according to which arbitrary meaning is assigned to linguistic symbols.

Nominal definitions are our stock and trade. Tenuousness exists in the invention of nominal definitions, which for my purposes is attractive. Nominal definitions circumscribe meaning without too much care given to their semantic adequacy. The term I wish to register is one I mention in the introduction: "enecstasis." Its nominal definition will be my focus. Enecstasis is tied to a cluster of terms in Heidegger that I may be at cross-purposes employing. What I aim to signal by enecstasis is not altogether unlike Heidegger's early ontological preoccupation with Selfhood, "which belongs to the essential attributes of Dasein" (Heidegger [1927] 1962, 365). But my aim is not altogether consonant with Heidegger's. His concern is with the quotidian existential structure of the Self qua *Dasein* and its peculiar *Jemeinigkeit* (self-possessive beingness, or "mineness") that is grounded in care.

My concern is with agential self-possession as ontical reflection—put otherwise: ontical reflective selfhood. The issue, in other words, is not one of addressing an object as the Self as the positive sciences do. Were that the case I would settle on a term less Heideggerian in form. Nor is the issue one of recalling what precedes or is more fundamental than ontical representations, otherwise my present qualifications would be unnecessary. My concern rather is with the singularity of Selfhood, an incalculable je ne sais quoi sensed and partially known in and through ontical reflection. Students of Heidegger might see the move as confused and, admittedly, may be right to do so. But I should find it odd (and I like to think Heidegger would too) if I should be committed to Heidegger's sensibility about ontological inquiry as incontrovertibly exclusive. The sensibility in Heideggerian discourse can be so total and complete at times that any discussion of subjectivity is substandardized in terms of *hypokeimenon* or *Subjectum*. The *Subjectum* is something of a necessary tragic figure in Heideggerian discourse, despite Heidegger's many admissions concerning the importance, eventfulness, of this figure. What I am saying may echo a complaint Ricoeur once voiced about Heidegger concerning a shift that needs to be made to epistemology from ontology (see Ricoeur 1981, 59). Bernard Lonergan voiced a similar complaint when he noted that Kant remains unfinished business even after Heidegger (see Kanaris 2002, 158n27). But allow me to say a little more about how enecstasis relates to Heidegger's concerns.

The operative term is *ekstatikón*, literally "standing outside." According to John Macquarrie and Edward Robinson, the general use of the Greek term describes an action of "removal' or "displacement," which suggests a position of disengagement or detachment. Thus "it came to be applied to states-of-mind which we would now call 'ecstatic' " (Heidegger [1927] 1962, 377). Heidegger changes the spatial tapestry of the term by associating it with the root meaning of the word "existence." As a result, the function of ecstasis takes on an ontologically engaged significance that simultaneously connects with *Dasein*'s tenuous primordial temporality, *Dasein*'s projecting "towards oneself" (Heidegger [1927] 1962, 378–379). Enecstasis connotes this ontological readjustment by prefixing the Greek preposition "en" to ecstasis. This is brought out clearly and summarily in a post–*Being and Time* paper by Heidegger.

In "The Way Back into the Ground of Metaphysics," Heidegger enriches the meaning of "existence" qua "standing out" by extending the terms of the phrase respectively to *Dasein* and *Sein*. This highlights not only the ontological difference of *Sein* and *Dasein* but also their equiprimordial relation. The "out" of the essence of existence pertains to the openness of Being itself. The standing pertains to *Dasein*'s enduring Being, another term for which is "care" (*Sorge*). In this way both the "ek" and "stasis" of existence is accounted for in its primordial significance, ontologically. Heidegger says as much when he attributes the meaning of "out," in terms of "away from," to the inadequate understandings of ontotheology. The ecstatic essence of existence in ontotheology is properly speaking a standing out and does not contain the primordial significance of ecstasis understood ontologically, which is a "standing in" in the openness of Being, "of enduring and out-standing this standing-in (care), and of out-braving the utmost (Being-toward-death)" (Heidegger [1949] 1992, 255).

A little more now on enecstasis but in terms of how it differs from Heidegger's concerns, which the "en" added to Heidegger's ecstasis serves to differentiate. Enecstasis, like Heidegger's ecstasis, signals a disposition of personal involvement. However, it is not tied to Heidegger's existential analytic. I use it to flag a sensibility in contemporary thought and debates that are ontical in nature. This sensibility is clearly indebted to philosophies of consciousness, which have tried to ground objectivity in subjective operations. But it transcends these philosophies in the recognition that subjectivity is necessarily tenuous and can never serve as its own ground. The essence of subjectivity, irreducible and singular, is forever concealed from the discourse on subjectivity, even when, and perhaps especially when, aware of this irreducible essence. The essence "perdures" (*austragt*), to invoke Heidegger again: the essence of subjectivity is grounded in a difference that simultaneously binds and distinguishes subjectivity as enecstatic from a discourse *about* it. Heidegger, of course, managed the difference by thinking the clearing of Being. However, post-Heideggerian forms exist in philosophy of religion that have rearranged the Heideggerian furniture, so to speak, thanks to poststructuralist thought. "Enecstasis" earmarks this current.

The dismantling gesture of Heidegger is evident in these contemporary forms of thought while remodeled by deconstructive and constructive phases of what I take to be an ontical preoccupation. This, I see, in terms of agential self-possession. In chapter 7 I discuss this feature at some length in connection with Bernard Lonergan's notion of self-appropriation. Its potential as a category of analysis is exploited there in terms of the principal problematic of enecstasis. My main purpose here is more general, which is to identify a locus in religious studies that holds out promise for such an explicit programmatic.

Phenomenology of Religion: The Problematic

My launching pad is current debates surrounding the academic status of religious studies. There has been little consensus as to what constitutes the proper subject matter of the study of religion and a fortiori the proper manner in which students of religion are to approach the subject matter. Obviously, the discussion of the academic status of anything presupposes notions of objectivity, which also naturally involves assumptions about subjectivity, the good old problem of the subject-object relation. The latter in particular conveniently connects with my topic. For our purposes I will ignore the often tacit ideas about both these terms and concentrate instead on what I take to be enecstatic developments in current discussions.

In a concerted effort to dissociate from theology, scholarship in the nineteenth century toed a hard line with respect to descriptions of religion that tended to sequester religion from its socioeconomic and psychological conditions. Social scientists rooted religion on the terra firma of material existence. Social mores, economic constraints, and psychological dispositions would be seen as the indispensable conditions of religion that would explain the origin and persistence of religion in society. Anthropologists were concocting genetic explanations of "primitive" and "advanced" belief systems in the milieu of human evolution. *Religionswissenschaft*, the science of religion, was mated to this development as it formulated historical-critical understandings documenting the unwieldy phenomena of religion.[1]

Phenomenology of religion in particular sought to complement these developments by reinstating analysis of the specifically religious dimension as academically viable. Distinct from theology and historical-naturalistic approaches, some phenomenologies of religion hunt instead for universal structures of religious consciousness by decoding religious symbol systems (as in the case of Mircea Eliade). Others, notably Wilfred Cantwell Smith's offering, center religion in persons, honoring the "cumulative tradition" and the dimension of "faith." I spell this out more in the next chapter. A simple point to note presently is that, however different, a unity of intent binds approaches as these in their respective differences, which is that the study of religion ought to include serious consideration of the religious, its symbolic meanings and the faith dimension that garners these meanings.

Not all are convinced by the phenomenological case. In recent decades, for instance, scholars have seen fit to describe phenomenology derogatorily as crypto-theology. The object phenomenologists seek, it is argued, is created and manufactured by phenomenologists themselves. It legitimizes a class of interpreters eager to comply with the methodological rules instituted by phenomenologists. The ideological implications are then glossed over by appealing to common sentiments about the estranged mediation of scholars out of touch with faith communities and/or of scholars lacking religious sensibility. The result is a protective strategy that does double duty, first to guard the object and field of phenomenology of religion from the social-scientific (read: reductionist) gaze, and second to promote some form of faith as integral to the *objective* study of religion. The catchall to describe this strategy is sui generis religion. For this new critical wing in religious studies, the strategy of phenomenology of religion protracts a common confusion between private and public sectors of knowledge, experiential and empirical study, personal and objective analysis, theological and scientific explanation (see McCutcheon, 1997, for more on this critique).

The claim is really quite simple. One is not engaged in the study of religion when, in the name of irreducibility, one hedges off religion from scientific explanation. One is engaged rather in a form of theology, which scholars such as Russell T. McCutcheon and Robert A. Segal recognize as too normative and partisan to qualify as strictly academic. Objectivity only manages observable behavior and what motivates behavior; it cannot discern experiential, subjective states qua subjective. That would be, in their estimation, to do religion rather than to study it.

Postphenomenological Developments

A countercurrent, with no desire to justify phenomenology, has argued that anti-phenomenologists, such as Segal and McCutcheon, have misrepresented theology in their diatribe against phenomenology. What this means for us is that the thinking of religion is, like it or not, an act of involvement in the construction of meaning. Two ways of attacking the issue are typically proposed, one theological (Ninian Smart [1996, 15–25] once described it as "pluralizing theology"), the other philosophical.

The theological response, based on developments in cultural studies, bemoans the typical move of confusing "academic theology" with partisan forms of theology. Pluralizing or academic theology is neither Christian nor Buddhist. Moreover, it is argued, the case for neutral empirical study, spearheaded by critics of all theologies, cryptic and otherwise, overlooks the fact that objectivity itself is implicated in cultural interactions—a surprising oversight given the postmodern literature relied on. It is naive to argue that religious studies can or should exclude personally engaged thought in the analysis of frameworks of meaning. The point is to enter the study of religion cognizant of the multicultural and pluralistic interactive contexts as academic theologians make and unmake the central symbols of religion such as God, Goddess, Brahman, Nirvana, Sunyata, and the Tao (Cooey 2002, 178–179). What this means for proponents of academic theology is that theologians in the university should engage students and greater society concerning the norms and symbols that inform university patronage.

The other side of the debate is, as I said, more explicitly philosophical. The point of contention tends to be theory, its use and misuse. McCutcheon, for example, identifies the dismal state of the religious academy as a result of the field's rejection of theory, specifically theories with a naturalistic-historicist frame. Phenomenology of religion is a case in point. Making theory central to religious studies, McCutcheon argues, would replace the academically suspect search for "skyhooks" with the more feasible investment into "cranes."[2] Although industrious, one has to wonder whether McCutcheon himself doesn't have a soft spot for skyhooks. He seems to think that a *non-ideological* site exists for contesting what he calls the protectionism of sui generis religion and theological discourse. Tyler Roberts (2004, 2005, 2013) and Paul Griffiths (1997) rightly see this as a new protectionism, one that excludes as academically viable any discourse that would explain religion on grounds other than the social-political, naturalist-historical. In this respect, the complaint of philosophers of religion resonates with those making a case for academic theology but in more rhythmically postmodern terms. The proposals of Carl Raschke, for example, mimic a form of deconstruction in outlining the contours of a semiotics of representation.

Representation, in Raschke's sense, does not consist in the traditional idea of mimesis: re-presenting the real in one form or another. Rather, representation is an act of reference that paradoxically overcomes the referent. Religion, considered with an accent on theory, denotes a semiotic relation where the "sacred" has no entitative status. What the sacred implies is a movement or mutation of signs whose signifying constituents are asymmetrical. "It is this unique asymmetry of religious semiosis, wherein the 'object' signified is neither visible nor recognizable . . . that produces the mythical, or the numinous" (Raschke 1999, 8). More recently, Raschke has described this "object" of study, indebted to Paul Tillich for his insight that religion is the "form" of culture, as "postmodern religion,"

> a vast, and de-differentiated, circuit of cultural signs and metaphors that do not add up to anything resembling what religious studies scholars in the past have identified as "movements" or "traditions." Postmodern religion is the motivational underlay of postmodern culture as a whole. Whether we are talking about metaphysical seekers who chant to the "ascended masters" using quartz crystals, or urban Pentecostals who find "gold dust" on themselves after having received "miraculous healings," or Christian rock singers who can hardly be distinguished in their demeanor or music from other pop musicians, we are no longer entering into some arcane, academic discourse about "dialogue" among Buddhists, Hindus, Jews, and Christians We are no longer even talking about "religion" as conventionally construed. (Raschke 2012, 25–26)

While I would beg to differ about the demeanor of Christian rock singers—the so-called rock community at least would and do consider it highly irregular—Raschke denudes traditional, academic conceptions of religion inspired by a century-long identitarian shift of religious studies from Protestant thinking. Needless to say, traditional theology is no better off in directing the thinking that he has in mind. What is needed, according to Raschke, is a semiotic turn, one modeled on or at least taking inspiration from Derrida's commendable deconstruction of the conceit of referentiality and its grand narratives. Such a form of semiology is promising for the delineation of the "form of culture" Raschke is after, the way toward its ontology being sourced through reflection on such thinkers as Georges Bataille, Thomas Altizer, Emmanuel Levinas, Slavoj Žižek, and Alain Badiou.

Tyler Roberts is less ambitious in terms of religious theory. Raschke's reconfiguration is total in scope, evacuating theoretical consideration of the religious referent from religious studies altogether—or at least from an understanding of religious studies he considers apropos to postmodern culture and faith. Raschke follows Richard Murphy (1999) in calling it a "counterdiscourse [that] is no longer about the 'disciplinary object' we know as religion. It is not 'about' anything at all, in fact, but amounts to a second order of simulation—the retextualizing, or developing, of an interpretive code for the play of performances and iconic showings that make up 'religious culture'" (Raschke 2012, 26). While Roberts is deeply aware of the conceits of referentiality, he is not committed per se to the elimination of religious referents, their consideration, from a robust philosophy of religion in religious studies. In fact, he accedes to its potential once simplistic assumptions about such reflection have been weeded out. He singles out proponents of "new materialism" in religious studies—not to be confused with the contemporary philosophic form—who caricaturize such reflection, "theology," as mystifying discourse in the service of identity, stability, and cohesion. He does not deny that this occurs, but he has successfully shown the charge to be both too general and self-serving, missing how theology can and sometimes does function "to relativize, interrupt, or transgress discourses, including its own" (Roberts 2004, 160). He turns to the work of Jacques Derrida, Charles Winquist, and Hent de Vries, among others, to inform his magnanimous treatment of religious insights, albeit, as was said earlier, in a way and with aims that differ from Raschke's.

Roberts conceives theology as a discourse of singularity that simultaneously gestures toward and away from God, *à dieu* and *adieu* respectively.

As such, theology is taken to be a critical practice of attuning itself interminably to singularity. When doing so, theology resists homogenization, abstraction, and universalization. Invoking God, then—contrary to what scholars such as McCutcheon fears is a mystifying and authorizing practice based on what is arguably a modernist agenda of excluding theology— signals the representational incompleteness of its own discourse. Theology on this score is understood with Winquist and de Vries as interruptive and critical rather than systematizing and stabilizing.

The Enecstatic Preoccupation

Whether it is "academic" theologians sensitized to the relativizations of culture theorists, or philosophers of religion revisioning the role of theory in religious studies, a key preoccupation is with personally engaged reflection, loosely identified here as "religious." Classical phenomenology of religion was no less driven by the concern. Its protectionist strategy, guided by an essentialistic reduction of religious symbology, is what sullied its otherwise admirable intention: it distracted individuals spearheading the hunt for academic neutrality while pouring far too much contempt on the important role of the social sciences in the study of religion. Academic theologians and philosophers of religion have been more discriminate. They separate the phenomenological husk from the phenomenological core. One detects this in the way in which these constructive postphenomenological thinkers generally abstain from critiquing a self-alert sensibility in certain forms of phenomenology of religion. It is to the great credit of studies such as Steven M. Wasserstrom's (1999) on Gershom Scholem, Mircea Eliade, and Henry Corbin that have alerted a generation of scholarship to the creative, even if flawed, potential of the phenomenological treatment of the *Totaliter Aliter*.

But where is the enecstatic in all this? We find it, I believe, in the call of Paula Cooey to intervene *in* the systems of thought we study, as poets and fiction writers who teach English, as composers who teach music, as clinicians who teach psychology. The admonition is to become "critics and construers of culture," to develop theological anthropologies, cosmologies, and ethics, just "as philosophers intentionally construct theories of human moral life and practice, of justice, of aesthetics, of nature, and of language" (Cooey 2002, 179–180).

We find it in the concern of Tyler Roberts, and the chorus of thinkers he relies on, to take seriously questions about the value of the pursuit of knowledge, religious knowledge included. Roberts calls us to be receptive to the disruptive potential of theological language—the aporetic sign "God," for instance—that opens us up to the excess of language and to ourselves, selves who are not, as Eric Santner writes, exhausted by the predicates that form our identity: "that there is to each of us, beyond those characteristics, 'a surplus of being, this existential exaggeration that is called being me'" (Santner as quoted in Roberts 2004, 162). The condition of possibility of authentic self-engagement, it is suggested, is premised on reflective preoccupation with the impossible singularity of the divine other. The disruptive force of this singularity refracts the singularity of our selves as though in a hall of mirrors.

A trauma of sorts seems to be implied. But this trauma has revelatory implications and potential. It does not substitute a new identity for an old one but, rather, disrupts identity, "disorienting us in a way that productively unloosens the bonds of identification and ideology, opening us to the world and others in a way that is not constrained by our own fantasies, needs, and neuroses" (Roberts 2004, 164).

We find the enecstatic, too, in Carl Raschke, who couches a similar concern in his condemnatory postmodern remarks on postmodernism. Why else would Raschke pour so much contempt (markedly in his earlier writings) on deconstructive systems that, in his opinion, disenfranchise the general public expressed in popular culture? And so Raschke valorizes the *cri de coeur* of the disenfranchised through a decentering of the sign-performances of popular culture.[3] This hermeneutical move, it is true, does not necessarily legitimate the moral or ontological character of these sign-performances. However, it does "[*reframe*] their purpose, primarily in terms of the categories of regimentation, subversion, 'ceremonial' articulation, and ideological oscillation" (Raschke 1990, 678–679). Raschke may not condone Wilfred Cantwell Smith's "fideistic personalism," which he regards as "subjective atomism," but he does seek to explain what he argues Smith's otherwise commendable program fails to explain: how "the semantic discrepancies between 'traditional' formulations of the faith-encounter are resolved through 'imaginative' involvement in the lives of religious persons, whose habits of worship converge on a singular, yet ineffable, object of both *reference* and *reverence*" (Raschke 1982, 37–38). Enecstasis.

Analogous to the early thought of Heidegger, which aimed to destabilize metaphysics through an existential analytic of the ecstasis of *Dasein* in and toward Being, the move in this discourse is to destabilize the onto-theo-logic of phenomenology of religion and its aggressors through reflection on the singularity of subjective involvement. But for the reason that the early Heidegger privileged ontology over the ontic, and the later Heidegger replaced his earlier concern with the Beingness of *Dasein* with the Beingness of Being, the preoccupation with agential self-possession, exhibited through explicit ontic engagement, is post-Heideggerian in the sense outlined and, ergo, enecstatic. The "standing in" of this particular preoccupation is one grounded in a process of revealability that is ontically focused and whose proper referent is at once elusive, transcendent, and immanent. If these connections hold and enecstasis is indeed a feasible disposition for our times, it remains to fine-tune the reasons why and whether such a programmatic holds promise in managing concerns about the place of "religious" reflection in the academy. In the next chapter I develop this aspect further as I return to expand on the philosophical underpinnings of enecstasis in later chapters.

Chapter 2

The Enecstatic Jig

Personalizing Philosophy of Religion

Only in the dance do I know how to speak the parable of the highest things.

—Friedrich Nietzsche ([1883–1891] 1999)

The tragedy in recent years has been the almost total eclipse of the philosophy of religion within the study of religion.

—Carl A. Raschke (1999)

In this chapter I look to developments in and against phenomenology of religion as an opportunity to rethink the relationship of philosophy of religion to religious studies. A delicate balancing act is involved since the philosophical fault lines in religionist debates are not often clearly drawn or, in my opinion, self-critically reflexive. Further complicating my task are the philosophical horizons that roughly divide commitments typically identified as stylistically analytic or continental. My own bias becomes clear as I isolate the still pressing topic of experience in religious studies and in what ways the poststructuralist ethos mitigates the methodological gridlock surrounding the topic reached by religion scholars. I outline this in the

---

An earlier version of this chapter appeared originally in proceedings from a symposium, "Has Philosophy of Religion a Future?," held at McGill University in 2013 (Kanaris 2018, 173–188).

first part of the chapter. The upshot is that it boils down to an agonistic concerning the nature and extent to which personal involvement is seen as integral to or as a hindrance in religious studies. In subsequent parts of the chapter, I summon a certain reception history of Nietzsche and Heidegger whose visions of reflexivity I rework into a general philosophy of religious studies for the negotiation of standoffs as outlined in the first part of the chapter. In a nutshell, I argue for the philosophical integrity of a deracinating form of personal reflection, which is earlier described as enecstatic. While an explicitly philosophical stance, enecstatic reflection is pragmatically constituted and intends concrete dividends for the student of religion.

A Methodological Quandary as Bridge

Philosophy of religion occupies a nebulous space in religious studies. It is circumscribed by numerous different concerns and a complex history that predates its surrogate role for theology in *Religionswissenschaft*. In the introduction and first chapter I delineate aspects of this history and thinking style, which siphons off into a peculiar form of scholarly analysis in phenomenology of religion. This development is identified in chapter 1, which, as announced earlier, I wish to expand on more fully in this chapter.

Despite his now infamous reputation, I believe Mircea Eliade was basically correct about the philosopher's role in the field, although short-sighted when limiting the discernment of religious meanings and their application to the historian of religions. According to Eliade (1959, 90), the role of the philosopher in the context of religion is to engage in "'general theories' about religion," leaving the historical specificities of religions and the meaning of their varying symbologies to historians of religion (1959, 102–103). I should perhaps be upfront about my noncommittal use of Eliade and the specifics of his distinction. My purpose is strictly taxonomic.

Eliade serves my delineation of philosophy in a religion environment where the topical focus of analytic philosophy continues to have remote relevance. He also serves me in terms of how he represents that stream in religious studies that distinguishes itself from partisan forms of theology or as areas of study that are perhaps mutually exclusive. And yet it is the controversy over the nature of his program as crypto-theology that creates a fissure for my thinking. I am not partial to Eliade's view that philosophic engagement links with general theories about religion, whether he intends the humanist or social-scientific variety. Nor am I partial, a fortiori, to Eliade's idiosyncratic philosophy, his so-called 'creative hermeneutics," born of the wall he erects between the philosopher and symbolic expressions of faith. More appealing to me in this connection is Wilfred Cantwell Smith. His personalist subversion of Eliadean essentialism shows greater promise. And yet Cantwell Smith's personalism is also flawed for delineating what I imagine to be philosophy of religious studies.

For all their differences, and there are many, both Eliade and Cantwell Smith, represent "personalist" advances beyond the historicist appreciation of comparative religion. It is this single aspect that binds them to the tradition leading back to Friedrich Schleiermacher, Rudolf Otto, and William James. It is also what guides my project, albeit obliquely. While Eliade and Cantwell Smith are indifferent to phenomenology as a catchall, they nonetheless subscribe to the view that religious studies involves or ought to involve more than historical and seemingly impartial social-scientific analyses. Where Eliade takes this finally to antihistorical heights of eidetic vision (the structure of religious symbols), Cantwell Smith moves in the direction of privileging the irreducible form of material meanings (faith). Both scholars appear to be on opposite sides of the phenomenological spectrum, and in a certain sense that is true. But a deeper look reveals that their differences, while substantive, are nonetheless bound by a similar desire for engaged "religious" thinking, which is what interests me. Cantwell Smith, in what I call his negative essentialism, guards the agency of the insider with respect to faith. Eliade, for his part, forges a prescriptive essentialism in which he promotes, contrary to his claim to be founding an objective science of religion, a very personal formulation of his own faith. As a maker of religion, which Eliade's critics are quick to point out about him (Strenski 2006, 317, 327; McCutcheon 1997, 37–39), Eliade mitigates the potential broadside of Cantwell Smith that he (Eliade) merely indulges in reifying religion. If he does reify faith, it is primarily his own faith vis-à-vis the cumulative tradition of insiders, a point his critics put to an entirely different use (Segal 1983; Strenski 2006, 309–336). Eliade is as religiously invested as the person of faith whose right to renew her faith every morning Cantwell Smith (1959, 34) campaigns passionately for.

None of this is news to critics of phenomenology. In fact, it is for their "personalism," mobilized here for my argument, that critics essentially lump together Eliade and Cantwell Smith as equally problematic for religious studies. Russell McCutcheon (1997, 14), for instance, notes how Cantwell Smith is virtually in partnership with Eliade in a protectionist ideological strategy prioritizing "internal, intuitive, and essentially ahistorical categories over interpersonally available and historical categories." Eliade is a more obvious target on account of his creative hermeneutics and his zany indictment against "the audacious and irrelevant interpretation of religious realities made by psychologists, sociologists, or devotees of various reductionist ideologies" (Eliade as quoted in Strenski 2006, 326). Talal Asad's critique of Cantwell Smith is more telling. Asad (2001, 206) sees Smith as excluding the "materialities of religion" as constitutive of faith. The oversight is attributed to Cantwell Smith's cognitive approach, which privileges a Protestant (pietistic) conception of religion as faith (Asad 2001, 220). Asad makes the connection almost two decades earlier with respect to Clifford Geertz who proposes an essentialist definition of religion for anthropology that overlaps with the cognitive propensity in Cantwell Smith's definition for religion scholars. "This effort of defining religion," Asad (1993, 28) writes of Geertz, "converges with the liberal demand in our time that [religion] be kept separate from politics, law, and science." To the extent that anyone thinks religion in the space provided by the discursive formation of religious studies, the same may be said of Cantwell Smith. The individual approaches of Geertz and Cantwell Smith, then, illustrate different protective strategies contoured by the infamy of the subject-object dichotomy: the "secular liberal" strategy of confining religion, adopted by Geertz and critics of phenomenology (with completely different aims), and the "liberal Christian" strategy of defending religion informing Cantwell Smith and Eliade (again, with different aims).[1]

The strategy of confining religion circumscribes academic study of religion, oftentimes exclusively, to the examination of publicly observable phenomena. It can also manufacture interpretations of the religious dimension intended for public consumption, that is, it reconstitutes the function of religious discourse primarily for the benefit of the outsider while coddling the progressive insider. Nonetheless, both strategies—the confining of religion and the defending of religion—assume the space of legitimacy provided by post-Enlightenment society, specifically "the right to individual belief" (Asad 1993, 45). In other words, the separation of church and state, private and public spheres, frames each tendency. The strategy of defending religion protracts the frame of confinement while subverting the public dimension of religion as the exclusively normative domain for religious studies. The relationship is dialectical. Important for us is how both strategies are ideologically invested, in the descriptive (not pejorative) sense of self-conscious meaning-construction (see Roberts

2005, 371–372). Allow me to illustrate using the less obvious case of the strategy of confinement.

I believe it is safe to assume that McCutcheon (1997, 49), in his exposé of the strategy of defending religion, advocates more than the now commonplace view that scholarly distillations of religion invariably legitimize or contest "present distributions of social, economic, and political privilege." Whether we are talking about the "socially repressive functions" of fertility symbolism (McCutcheon 1997, 40) or the ethnocentrism of cosmogonic myths (McCutcheon, 1997, 43)—two dimensions Eliade elides—we risk, McCutcheon (1997, 49) warns, "uncritically propagating the social patterns to which [such symbolisms] once contributed." What staves off the possibility, McCutcheon (1997, 49, 194) acknowledges, is some form of participation in the discourse. The problem with McCutcheon's answer is that it reflects a disposition that rarely becomes anything more than a token appreciation of the constitutive role of meaning-construction in theorists of confinement.

Ivan Strenski comes close to the kind of self-critical reflexivity that I imagine in philosophy of religious studies. But even Strenski protracts the otherwise insightful social-scientific preoccupation with religion as object, as an explanatory force of what goes on in the world. "We . . . need to reform our notion of religion into a more usable comparative concept reflecting the many ways people the world over live in ways analogous to one another that can be called 'religious' . . . 'religion' is an appropriate name for a factor explaining what happens in the so-called political world" (Strenski 2010, 60, 61). However, it is important to be clear that Strenski is not party to McCutcheon's (1997, 192–194) naturalistic foundationalism. In the conclusion to his important work *Thinking about Religion: An Historical Introduction to Theories of Religion*, Strenski is quite unequivocal that McCutcheon offers a "mirror image" of the "theologian's game": "Where the founders felt compelled to link their pursuit of knowledge about religion—their 'scientific' inquiry about religion—with their belief in the divine nature and purposes of human curiosity, McCutcheon feels he needs to link his naturalistic approach to religion with commitment to a naturalistic metaphysical ground" (Strenski 2006, 340). However, in his admirable desire to avoid the "dichotomizing pronouncements" in McCutcheon's reductionist metaphysics—that is, that religion can be thoroughly explained as human without remainder—Strenski seems unable to negotiate his own metaphysical desire to exclude "metaphysics" from theorizing religion.[2]

The impasse of strategies I have outlined here is, to my mind, premised on an analytic effective history of the concept of (religious) experience that weaves together romantic hermeneutics and phenomenology of religion (Otto, Eliade, and Cantwell Smith) with Cartesian dualism (see Proudfoot 1985; Sharf 1993, 1995, 1998; see also the introduction). A wall is thus erected that makes it virtually impossible for strategists of confinement to imagine reflexivity as something other than self-awareness of public or power knowledge. Strategists of confinement, whatever their differences, are faced with an aporia, according to which a consciousness-raising analysis is curtailed by spectral participation. We have seen indirect cases of this in McCutcheon and Strenski. It comes to a head, I believe, in the work of Robert Sharf.

Sharf, a Buddhist scholar by trade, throws the deliberations of McCutcheon and Strenski into sharp relief by addressing the thorny issue of conscious experience directly. In his now infamous argument about how the so-called reality of religious experience is beset by the same problems that attach to reports about alien abduction, Sharf (1998, 113) feels he must concede that he is "not trying to deny subjective experience." Indeed, he can't even imagine the possibility. But in the same breath Sharf (1998, 114, see also 110) toggles the words of Samuel Beckett to his conviction that references to religious experience are simply "well-meaning squirms that get us nowhere." This wall within the strategy of confinement is so dense that even a recent moderate critic of Sharf is unable to penetrate it. Stephen Bush (2012, 219–220) argues that Sharf's rhetoric of experience assumes that "experiences are universal across cultures and so predisposes us to miss the variety of effects experiences bring about." This assumption further "privileges the interior subjectivity of the practitioner and so directs our attention away from social structures such as class, gender, race, and ethnicity in which experiences occur" (Bush 2012, 219–220). Attending to the experiences themselves, on this score, means attending "carefully to the experiences people have" and placing "these experiences in the context of the power structures inherent in the religious practitioners' society." In other words, Bush himself perpetuates the view that reflexivity in religious studies is primarily, if not exclusively, preoccupation with objects of knowledge. This seems to be insurmountable if one abides strictly by the rules of knowledge that inform the social sciences, with notable exceptions who tether the insights of these sciences to explicit hermeneutical, philosophical, and theological reflection (e.g., Geertz, William James, and Eric L. Santner).

To borrow a characterization from the philosophy of mind, this entire project avoids the "hard problem" of self-reflexivity in religious studies. Accordingly, it is no great surprise that the term "new materialism" attaches to this post- and antiphenomenological development, if ironic given my indictment of Bush. Like Bush (2012, 207), I believe the strategy of confinement attests to "our deep entanglement in the Cartesian program." Unlike Bush, however, I believe his corrective merely replaces the Cartesian paradigm of consciousness, which emphasizes the epistemic, private subject, with the paradigm of language, which emphasizes "the public, signifying activities of a collection of subjects" (Bush, quoting Benhabib, 2012, 200). Cartesian dualism, in other words, is not overcome. It provides the mortar of a new and improved stockade. More analytic philosophy or philosophy of language may clarify issues. But my interest in affirming the personalist accent of the strategy of defense intends to bypass this effective-historical musing. Something valuable is lost in the otherwise necessary critique of phenomenology of religion for which the strategy of confinement fails to compensate. Whether hard or soft (McCutcheon, Sharf, and Bush respectively), the new materialism in religious studies is, as I hope to have shown, so preoccupied with the phenomenological protectionist strategy that the level of reflexivity it proposes not only elides an important dimension in the agenda of its nemesis, but it also feeds its own type of protectionism (see Roberts, 2004). It is for such reasons as this that I look to the continental tradition, classical forms of which birthed "comparative religion" and, more specifically, phenomenology of religion. Its inclination for the existential in thinking pushes past the stalemate reached by personalist phenomenology and impersonalist new materialism in the dash toward academic legitimacy.

Philosophy of Religion as Enecstatic

The function of philosophy of religion in religious studies is complicated by nomenclature and a history of concerns that predate comparative religion. Traditional topics of philosophical theology have broadened to include methodological issues pertinent to scholars of religion; I have discussed this element in the previous section in connection with the notion of experience, which I will develop even more fully in chapter 4 Distilled from German romanticism and transcendental idealism, the cradle of philosophy of religious studies, are the hermeneutical frameworks that continue to solicit interest in the field. Out of this tidal wave of different and overlapping concerns has also emerged species of philosophizing in religion that manage the affairs of the field in a way that is sometimes appreciative and sometimes scathingly critical of this history. In my analysis, I feature the topic of personal involvement because it has a time-honored place in comparative religion qua phenomenology of religion; this foothold is crucial methodologically: the topic is both intrinsic to and general and foundational enough to be of concern to students and scholars of religion. Key is that philosophy on this score is not limited to its traditional theoretical role of adjudicating religious beliefs and practices or the scholarly status of methods, their objectivity. Beyond the thorny issue of epistemic hegemony, this approach also has setbacks when it comes to negotiating disputes within the field; the previous section provides only one example.

Philosophy in the key that I am suggesting resembles, conveniently, the "spiritual practice" of Nietzsche. According to Tyler Roberts (1998, 17), it is a style of philosophizing that is "more than an academic discipline: it is a practice by which [one] cultivates, strengthens, and beautifies the self and its relationship to the world and cosmos; it is the spiritual exercise par excellence." Alexander Nehamas traces the practice back to Plato's Socratic dialogues, which he describes in terms of "the art of living": "The study of philosophy as the art of living discloses our own ethical preferences and compels us *to reveal part of ourselves*. This personal type of philosophy reflects on our own person, and it is personal in that additional sense as well. To study it is also to practice it" (Nehamas 1998, 6, italics added). It is a *gnothi seauton* (know thyself), as Foucault (2005) reminds us, whose holistic thrust predates and transcends the cognitive constraints of the *cogito* as *epimelea heautou* (care of self).

As regards religious studies, the indicated shift in focus is from understanding those who practice religion to understanding oneself as practicing this understanding. Just to be clear, my use of the term "understanding" is deliberate and impartial to the reduction of the practical or personal to the ethical or moral. At any rate, adjustments in the study of religion, from substantive to hermeneutically pliable delineations of religion and ritual (see Roberts 1998, 10), seem to invite this level of intellectual and/or ethical engagement—especially in a culture grappling with and somewhat framed by the weighty saying of a madman.

How does this translate into the terms of my discussion about personalist phenomenology and impersonalist new materialism? Where Eliade and Cantwell Smith neglect their role in imagining and reimagining religion in defense of the autonomy and legitimacy of studying the faith dimension academically; where McCutcheon and Sharf neglect a similar role but in the protection of descriptively political knowledge of religious behavior, the philosopher of the religious, as I imagine her, self-consciously participates in the reconstitution of religion[3] while negotiating these differences in a cultural matrix. (Asad's observation, noted earlier, about the space of legitimacy provided to religion by post-Enlightenment society has a favorable connotation in my thinking.) There are basically two parts to my proposal. The first pertains to the broad background issue of a horizontal shift in academic culture indicated in my reference to Nietzsche and the artistic thinking it precipitates. It relaxes self-serving descriptions of academic legitimacy that divide phenomenologists and new materialists. "Culturalizing" religion and the academy or narrowing the divide between academic practices and the cultural practices scholars seek to study are apposite descriptions that have been proposed (see Davaney 2002, 147–148). The second part of my proposal pertains to enecstasis, the specific form of artistry that I find germane in this setting, which involves a different set of philosophical problems—while some of these are mentioned in the preceding chapter, a lengthier and more pointed discussion can be found in chapters 6–8 and the postscript.

As regards the first part, allow me to differentiate my perspective from that of Paula Cooey, whose proposal concerning theology as "a species of cultural studies" I find pedagogically compelling. Cooey's (2002, 182) designation "co-makers of culture" captures the current climate well, especially if we take religion to be a creative force that anticipates new values and meanings for the transformation of individuals and not simply reinforcing old ones (see Roberts 1998, 10). Cooey manages this challenge by what she calls, somewhat misleadingly, "academic theology," which reconfigures Kant's philosophical theology for today's broader audience of liberal education.

I share with Cooey (2002), and incidentally with Cocey's Kant, the view that philosophical engagement in religion is "devoted to questioning the presuppositions of religious life and thought for purposes of both critique and intentional construction" (178). But I part with Cooey methodologically in her laudable theological task of reconstructing specific religious symbol systems centered on "conceptual limit setters." She itemizes these in terms of "God, Goddess, Brahman, Nirvana, Sunyata, and Tao" (2002, 178). Philosophy of religious studies, as I imagine it, is more general and philosophical in its contribution to the negotiation of one's foundations with respect to critique and intentional construction.

The second part of my proposal conveniently spins off the first and marks my philosophical departure from Kant. Actually, it pertains to any endeavor that regulates foundational concerns via some explicit foundationalist method. My attitude at this level of the discussion is basically that of Michel Foucault (1999, 95): "I do not deny the cogito, I confine myself to observing that its methodological potential is ultimately not as great as one might have believed and that, in any case, we can nowadays make descriptions which seem . . . objective and positive, by dispensing with the cogito entirely . . . even though people were for several centuries convinced of the impossibility of analyzing knowledge without starting from the cogito." This echoes the sentiment of Nietzsche, who, despite himself, could see the value of what he would alternatively dub "methods of the spirit" (see Kaufmann 1974, 80). But congenital to foundational methods, it seems, is how they suppress the act of self-fashioning by robust directives occasionally intended for self-fashioning. The subtle nature and entanglement of our desire in this process doubtless explains why conceptions of philosophy as an art are de rigueur these days. However, as much as I embrace this trend, I am not of the opinion that foundational concern implies foundationalism, which is the difficult philosophical problem I alluded to earlier.

My negotiating term for this is, again, "enecstasis." As outlined in chapter 1, it positions the Heideggerian call for engaged thinking but in a hypertranscendental regard for singularity. The compound prepositional prefix (*en* + *ek*) points to a tension that Heidegger himself underlines in the ontological difference of ecstatic relation: *Dasein*'s standing (stasis) in care as, simultaneously, equiprimordially, *Dasein*'s standing out for (i.e., in the openness of) Being. The *ek* of ecstasis here is always already *en* and not fundamentally *ek* in the sense of "beyond" (*hinaus*) or "away from" (*weg von*) the primordial relationality suggested by the *en* of ecstasis. Moreover, the *ek* pertains to the objective genitive of Being's openness presupposed in the horizonal vista of *Dasein*.

This refiguration of ecstasis is one of the many ways Heidegger manages the disengaged perspective (*vorstellendes Denken*) intrinsic to Western metaphysics. Enecstasis commemorates this foundational concern but distills it, as a neologism, from Heidegger's primary difficult task of fundamental ontology (*andenkendes Denken*). As such, the compound prefix points to another tension, a philosophical one, concerning the possibility of a "transcendental interrogation of thinking" resigned to the "phenomenality of experience" as a singularity. The terminology is

Charles Winquist's (1995, 21). Winquist, whose name I drop here as a cipher, stands out as one of the few postmoderns unencumbered by what he called the "sham solution" of postmodern theory "to an unresolved set of experiential problems." That is why I turn to Winquist in chapter 6 as a crucial figure in the development of an enecstatic philosophy of religion. In any case, we may not like that foundationalism ghoulishly attaches to transcendental and/or phenomenological reflection, but it boots nothing to deny the revelatory potential of the latter on account of the totalizing ossifications of the former. If Heidegger and his quarreling disciple, Jacques Derrida, have taught us anything, an escape route is best left to dreamcatchers who insist on filtering out the bad tout court.

This enecstatic form of artistry joins the convoy of contemporary theorizing that disrupts rather than stabilizes. As a postphenomenological appreciation of the personalist concern, it takes the edge off such quibbles as McCutcheon's and others' that phenomenology of religion—and more obviously, of course, theology!—is incurably self-authorizing. Enecstatic artistry at the same time resists McCutcheon's antidote that theorizing become exclusively crane-like, eliminating the need for skyhooks. The story has been told time and again to which I offer the brief retort that it leads down a rabbit hole where cranes become skyhooks. As such, enecstasis waves in subjectivity through the gateway of ontological difference in its essence as singularity and not as ὑποκείμενον. And so, if "the whole point of singularity is that there is something about the self that is uniquely irreducible to the totality of a person's political relations" (Simmons 2011, 56), its thinking is necessarily allusive in its constructive modality of destabilizing discourse. I embrace Roberts's (2004) description in terms of a task, not of explaining or deciphering singularities but of opening discourse to them, "to interrupt or disturb ordinary ways of communicating and interaction with others and ways of 'being ourselves' in order to attend to disturbances caused by that which is ordinarily, and necessarily, excluded from consciousness or occluded by various discursive strategies" (162). Carl A. Raschke (2012, 84) is more definitive, in words that commemorate Jean-François Lyotard's differend: "a 'theory' of the singular is *ipso facto* impossible. We have only the 'event horizon' beyond which we cannot peer and where nothing is 'presentable' or 'representable.'"

Enecstasis, then, is Janus-faced. Its allusive function looks forward to the semantic content of discourse as it fissures for singularities and backward to the self-reflexivity in the task itself. When the disruptive logic plays up the singularities in discourse, when the carnival of terminology, in other words, is "God," "Sunyata," "self," or what have you, we get something like Raschke's (2012, 84) "epicalic" semiotics of representation, or John D. Caputo's (2018) refiguring poetics of radical theology. To my mind, the artistic intent of self-fashioning, while indirect, is nonetheless present. I basically endorse these discourses while wishing to highlight my own interest in enecstasis as first and foremost pedagogically construed. It marks a shift in emphasis from the notion as semiotic and hermeneutical vis-à-vis disrupting content to enecstasis as personal engagement in the "excess," the self, being disrupted. This provides a platform in religious studies where individuals concretize for themselves "the self-deconstructive imperative" (Roberts 2004, 167). This imperative is nascent in the discourse itself but the decision to appropriate or participate in a specific construal is left up to the individual.

Here my task hooks up again with Cooey's, specifically her pedagogical aims. However, I wish to continue to maintain the philosophical generality of my proposal.[5] In adopting the posture of self-critical reflexivity via academic theology, Cooey (2002) provides her upper-level undergraduates with diverse literature dealing plainly with religious and existential themes. The goal is to get students to "think critically and constructively about religious meaning and value in ways that consider explicitly their own possible responsibilities and choices as 'co-makers of culture,' in relation to the culture in which they live" (Cooey 2002, 182). In this way, Cooey facilitates discussion in a climate that is theologically nonpartisan and whose principal rules of engagement presuppose the values and commitments of liberal education. Sheila Greeve Davaney (2002) provides a useful enumeration of these liberal values and commitments in terms of "open inquiry, critical reflection, and public argumentation" (149–150). Enecstatic philosophy of religion has a similar aim but differs in form. For example, I provide students with select literature that exemplifies philosophy as the art of living, linking foundational concern with self-critical reflexivity in method and religion. In one context students navigate through writings of Nietzsche and Heidegger, Derrida and Foucault, Spivak and Irigaray, among others, to engage personally and directly in the problematics of an ethos that has provided for the current understanding of religion as "part of wider cultural interactions and mechanisms" (Davaney 2002, 148).[6] This translates into the relevance of the art of living in enecstatic appreciation of religion with respect to the fundamental concerns of the thinkers. Derrida's (2002, 71) general description of it is: analysis concerned above all with pragmatic and structural and political functional effects, a proposal that really only provides surface support for the "postmodernism" of McCutcheon, Bruce Lincoln, Willi Braun, and others. For impersonal logocentrism, to sally a paraphrase of deconstruction, does not escape, nor should it think it overcomes, the aporia of personalism through negation.

In another context, I provide students with literature that interlaces the possibility of enecstatic discovery with the concept of religious studies, its history.[7] It opens a space for personal negotiation of the celebrated insight of Jonathan Z. Smith (1978, xi) that "religion is solely the creation of the scholar's study." The benefits are many and more direct than one might suspect at first. Antipathy, should it exist, is often owed to students' practical concerns about the pretense of philosophy or the fear of performing poorly outside their chosen discipline. But specialized knowledge of philosophy, while beneficial, is not requisite for its enecstatic embodiment nor is it its principal aim; such things usually emerge through protracted study. The advantage of enecstatic philosophy of religious studies, considered from a pedagogical point of view, is that students are invited to negotiate their complicity in this history, making up their own minds about the "cumulative tradition."[8] A desideratum of the practice is to forge a philosophy of religion, according to which philosophical artistry converges with spiritual practice. And should the adjective "spiritual" incite alarm, perhaps its evidence in so unlikely a cloud of witnesses such as Nietzsche, Foucault, and Derrida can serve to mitigate it (Caputo 1997b; Carrette 2000; Roberts 1998). Another desideratum endorsed by the enecstatic gesture is to keep intact the integrity of scholarly research. Students of religion are rightly wary of the imposition of categories potentially compromising the goals and techniques of their specific areas, which, somewhat needless to say, presupposes they even give the philosophical inclination the time of day. Enecstatic philosophy of religious studies accommodates this concern in theory as a practice whose task of application, when relevant, is left to the informed and developing perspective of the individual.[9] It relaxes the ever-present temptation, too often ceded in past and present philosophy of religion, to march on the religious studies capital and assault its citadel.

Learning to Dance

The enecstatic gesture of philosophy of religion replaces the protective strategy implied in sui generis religion and its negation by a topology within which individuals philosophize variant cultural forms, nurturing their own appreciation of and for "transcendence." In the context of the debate outlined in the first section of this chapter, the understanding supported in the second part is the following. In the experience that Eliade and Smith rally in support of personal involvement in religious studies, as well as in the blockade that McCutcheon and others aver in support of a naturalistic frame, is an interstice for thinking religion and power together in the context of "care," self-care. The binary of religion and power in this enecstatic space is kept in productive tension. It is wary of the tendency to downplay the techniques of domination in constituting the personal and irreducible, as is sometimes done in phenomenological strategies of defense. But it is also wary of the tendency to overstate these techniques in excluding the same, which strategists of confinement in new materialism tend to do. The later Foucault managed this tension by coping techniques of domination with what he called techniques of the self. Jeremy Carrette (2000, 129–141) sees the potential of Foucault's academic negotiation in terms of "political spirituality." But my point is not simply to endorse Carrette's thesis or whether the semiotic product of Foucault's thought is to be emulated. Rather, it is the banal observation that someone as committed to the political as Foucault—and as dubious about the faith dimension as he—nonetheless made it his lifework to be in enecstatic relation to his object. Not only was he after a diagnostic of culture "out there," as it were, he was also concerned preeminently with the reconstitution of the self. Whatever the peculiar form, *Jemeinigkeit*, *souci de soi*, or whatever, enecstasis is the personal expression in the service of meaningful pedagogical outcomes.

Despite the whimsical reference of my chapter title, I really do mean the dance of enecstasis seriously. Like that to which one aspires in a skillful gyration, the proposal means to combine the grace of movement with the individuality of the interpreter. As disruptive agential self-possession, enecstasis speaks to both the artistic nature of the venture and the challenge in its execution. This is not a simple two-step. It is at once primal and passionate, spiritual even, if we follow Nietzsche. The terms Nietzsche conjures are a lexical train typical of the religious sphere. As he famously states in *The Gay Science* (1882), the philosopher's dance is not only his "ideal" and "art" but also his "sole piety, his 'divine service'" (¶381), a peculiar dance of "faith" (¶347). Roberts (1998, 12, 110) even describes it as a "worshipful" and "ecstatic" dance. For it is only in the dance that thought meets grace and skill meets concern.

Part II

Contouring Enecstatic Philosophy of Religious Studies

Chapter 3

Philosophy of Religious Studies
The Changing Face of Philosophy of Religion

> We must bring to an end theology and sociology. We must begin to speak.
>
> —Carl Raschke (2001)

> The semiotic imperative can, and must, gain new life with the opening of the new "territory" of religious theory. Religious theory in the future will be viewed in deference to "religious studies" and "religious thought" as what psychoanalysis in the twentieth century was to philosophical psychology and earlier genres of empirical psychology.
>
> —Carl Raschke (2005)

In the context of postphenomenological religious studies, philosophizing, as I imagine it, is about religious studies, not religion as the term "philosophy of religion" suggests. I hope to show this by offsetting philosophy of religious studies from extant types of philosophy of religion—the point, in other words, is not to capture the *status quaestionis* of current philosophy of religion, analytic and/or continental, or even to develop it, but rather to articulate the broad contours of the two main currents of traditional philosophy of religion with an eye to extending the philosophical con-

---

This chapter is based on a public lecture presented at the Faculty of Religious Studies, McGill University, Montreal, Quebec, March 22, 2011.

versation about religion beyond these foci. It is the first important step in what I conceive philosophy of religious studies to be, which is more inclusive programmatically than, for example, Carl Raschke's otherwise constructive alternative, hailing the end of religious studies and theology. The second important step, which I will develop in later chapters, consists in the more strictly technical preoccupation of engaging the philosophic foundations of religion scholars.

In the first two sections I develop aspects pertaining to the topology of philosophy of religion, the loci of philosophy of religion, and the various shapes that it has assumed on account of different styles of thinking. This provides the necessary background to a research and pedagogical interest of mine that aims to formalize philosophy of religion in a religious studies sense. The remaining sections facilitate this interest by tracing the contours of postphenomenological philosophy of religion. I do this in connection with two contemporary forms that advocate, in their own unique ways, a demeanor of self-critical reflexivity I call *enecstasis*. I conclude the chapter with some remarks about the practical benefits of conceiving the relationship between philosophy and religion in this way, a feature that will remain constant throughout this volume.

From Philosophical Theology to Philosophy of Religion: Classical

I am fond of Stephen Crites's analogy of philosophy of religion as a zoo, both for what it intends and what it implies. The field is very much like a zoo that contains many separate enclosures containing a wide variety of species. It also contains enclosures where one can hear a cacophony of different onomatopoeia (Crites 1996, 39). The conjured image is of an organized disorganization, which contains elements of a jungle whose ecosystem is not completely unruly.

Philosophy of religion is one of those hard-to-define areas complicated by a very long history and cross-disciplinary interests. One may pursue it in a theological context where the aim is to formulate a consistent set of normative religious beliefs, or in a philosophical context where these beliefs are put to the test. The dichotomy is admittedly simplistic. Clearly, there is a sense in which these operations are equally shouldered in both contexts. My distinction is qualitative, not technical. The distinction points to a general modus operandi that assumes different forms in the guise of what is known as "philosophical theology." In its earliest incarnation, philosophical theology consisted in an open inquiry about the nature of nature and the precarious involvement of the divine with respect to nature. Think the pre-Socratics here. Graham Harman may object, arguing that *philosophia*, the *love* of wisdom, is not *sophia*, wisdom, knowledge—in a word, science. This, he would insist, confuses the species of reflection inaugurated by the figure of Socrates with the 'undermining" endeavors of Thales, Anaximander, Anaximenes, Democritus, and others. Pre-Socratic "philosophy" shares more in common with the paradigm of knowledge celebrated by modern, reductionist science than Socrates's *docta ignorantia*. Socrates, unlike his predecessors, knew that the only wisdom philosophy delivers is one invested in questioning boundaries, not fixing them.[1]

Harman's point should not be lost on us. He's right! However, he's right for similar, if contrary, taxonomical reasons to Alain Badiou who settles on Parmenides, the pre-Socratic, as the first philosopher. For Badiou, Parmenides earns the title because he is the first to narrate, from even older, non-Western attempts, the conceptual suture linking thinking, being, and nonbeing (Badiou 2015a). Parmenides serves Badiou's aim of releasing philosophy from theological presuppositions, represented in its most radical form in Malebranche, and connecting it to ontology as mathematics. This reconnects with Heidegger's desire for original thinking that stretches back to the pre-Socratics, whose inkling was masked in and hence forgotten by subsequent ontotheological gestures. And yet Badiou (2015b) dissociates the task from fundamental ontology since it purportedly conflates knowledge of being and event, not inconspicuously containing vestiges of transcendent configurations of truth.[2] Socrates, on the other hand, serves Harman's aim of releasing philosophy from the grip of science and mathematics, that is, from individuals such as Badiou, who, incidentally, yearns for an immanentist schema of the absolute, the in-itself. In other words, Harman's object-oriented ontology participates in the same "post-finitude" model of knowledge as Badiou and Quentin Meillassoux, Badiou's student. However, Harman (2018, 12) refuses to ride shotgun with them, invoking Kant's "things-in-themselves" sans Kant's tragic assumption of finitude: "objects never make full contact with each other anymore than they do with the human mind."[3]

Whether pre-Socratic or Socratic, whether scientistic or mathematical, speculative realist or ontologically object oriented, thinking that has been dubbed philosophical has been shaped by considerations of a relationship to some "absolute," however conceived (ἄπειρον, ἡ τοῦ ἀγαθοῦ ἰδέα, ὕλη, θεῖος, *an sich*, etc.). What this also means (importantly for us) is that religion and theology have shared in and contributed to that relationship, thanks to trafficking in understandings of ultimacy. However, as much as philosophers want to emancipate philosophy from religion or theological reflection,[4] historically they are inextricably related. Understanding Parmenides or Socrates as embodiments of true, even if rudimentary, philosophical speculation does little to change this, whether religious themes and thinking correlated precisely as we imagine today.

Later philosophical theology morphed into an inquiry about the nature of the divine and the created order beset by thorny issues of knowledge and revelation, their relationship.[5] As developments in the natural sciences took hold, disciplinary boundaries became more rigid. Philosophical theology summoned a different climate of rational demonstration, dividing the pure and autonomous from the emotive and clerical. The face of philosophical theology begins to change in a major way at this point, as exuberance about the possibility of demonstrating fundamental truths about the divine life comes under rapid fire. The mere mention of "David Hume" suffices as a symbolic marker of this watershed. I should probably mention a few more names since we are approaching an upheaval in the historic record where nameless allusions will not suffice.

As is well known, Hume's skepticism about "objective" knowledge, whether of the world or God, roused the otherwise punctilious Kant from his dogmatic slumbers. It became necessary to elide the Humean quagmire through an elaborate epistemology, an epistemology that saw Kant quite literally put the divine in its place—its transcendent, noumenal place. As a result, God becomes an important postulate of practical, moral reason but is virtually inconsequential to the objective, phenomenal realm. Kant believes he has solved the problems at which Hume hints, although significant contemporaries would hesitate to say that he did so without remainder. Enter Friedrich Schleiermacher and G. W. F. Hegel. Enter also, by the way, "philosophy of religion" proper.

Schleiermacher, the great Protestant hermeneut of liberal theology, exploits this room made for faith by exorcizing the Pietistic ghost of Kant. Summoned in its stead is what some might consider the wraith of religious psychology: feeling (*Gefühl*). As discussed in the introduction, this incantation would prove fortuitous to the emerging field of religious studies. Basic to religion, then, for Schleiermacher, is our "sense of the infinite," our "feeling and intuition of the universe," which he chides Kant for reducing to mere corroboration of autonomous moral reason. The move from God to religion is relevant here as it incites Hegel to reformulate matters, dissatisfied as he was by Kant's revalorization of reason and faith and what he considers Schleiermacher's confused thinking about religion.[6] Their failure, in a word, and according to Hegel, consists in elevating faith and religion by expunging true knowledge of God, the Absolute. And so, ironically, Hegel would forge a philosophy of *religion* that elevates faith into reason and knowledge of *God*.[7] Of course, knowledge of God for Hegel includes knowledge of religion since religion is about the real (however inadequate for Hegel) and the real is rational; knowledge of the real is knowledge of the Absolute and knowledge of the Absolute is all-encompassing. Even if Hegel's philosophy of God trumps philosophy of religion à la Kant and Schleiermacher, his thinking style, among that of others—I'm thinking principally of Nietzsche here—marks a division in the field that leaves the topical preoccupations of philosophical theology to analytic thinkers and the more hermeneutical preoccupations of philosophy of religion to the continental stream.

Not only was this fateful move the sine qua non of social-scientific study of religion (think Ludwig Feuerbach, for example), but it also managed the disciplinary boundaries that would come to define philosophy of religion, one's philosophical allegiance, and where to practice it. Nicholas Wolterstorff captures this nicely when, speaking on behalf of analytic philosophers, he writes: "We all know Kant; we just don't accept his point of view" (Westphal 1996, 27n1). Kant, and as I argue Hegel, marks something of a cut-off point, distinguishing one line of philosophy from another. As Wolterstorff continues, being post-Kantian—as he insists contemporary analytic philosophers of religion are—is not to be pro-Kantian or to subscribe to some conceptuality indebted to Kant. Merold Westphal, a philosopher of religion of continental leanings, agrees with Wolterstorff but quips that while contemporary analytic philosophy is not *naively* pre-Kantian, it is nonetheless *stubbornly* pre-Kantian.[8]

This exchange captures a mood in philosophy that hinges on distinct thinking styles represented by figures as different from one another as John Locke and Hegel. Lines of commitment typically divide between those who have definite views about the role of philosophy and logic in evaluating "propositions," and those who would rather contextualize logic largely indifferent to the language game of propositional knowledge. The analytic tendency weds topics such as the nature and existence of God to the former mien. Continentals, as they are affectionately called, focus the latter mien on proposals based on realities fundamentally non- or transrational, translogical, in nature. Think, for example, of the economy and class struggle in Marx, the personal unconscious in Freud, and the will to power in Nietzsche.

Contemporary Analytic Philosophy of Religion

Irrespective of whether it "stubbornly" bypasses developments in post-Kantian philosophy, the analytic approach tends to dominate. This is the case whether considering realist or nonrealist forms, although at first blush one may hesitate to include nonrealists in this stream. Realists are of the opinion that "propositional claims are either true or false, independent of human conceptual frameworks or whether any human being knows or believes whether they are true" (Taliaferro 1998, 38–39). The realist argues, "If there is a God then it is true that God exists regardless of whether any human beings think God exists or practice forms of life in which God is recognized." Nonrealists obviously hold the obverse: "All propositional claims about the world are neither objectively true nor false, where 'objective' means independent of all language, social forms of life, and conceptual frameworks." As Charles Taliaferro (1998, 39) notes, "If nonrealism is adopted, it makes no sense to claim 'God exists' in the abstract as a claim about *how things are* without this being understood in terms of the context in which such a claim is made." However, insofar as nonrealism is the negation of realism, propositionally rejecting the view that religion consists in propositions about how things are, its difference from realism is one of degree and not of kind. The very form in which the debate between realists and nonrealists takes place—the aim to settle whether it is appropriate to imagine religious expressions as propositional—assumes the centrality of logic that continental philosophers of religion are wont to dismiss or simply contextualize. To put it more explicitly, nonrealism, in such dialectical partnership with realism, is just another form of analytic philosophizing, albeit one that subverts realist claims. One will struggle to find this form in continental philosophizing, although it shares an affinity with it. That is why I say that the difference between realism and nonrealism, when placed in the context of philosophic style, is really only one of degree and not kind.

I believe this applies as well when narrowing the spectrum to specific religious epistemologies such as the Catholic or Reformed variety or Wittgensteinian fideism or comparative philosophy of religion.⁹ The point is made even stronger when scouting companions or handbooks or anthologies of philosophy of religion. Topical treatments abound: theism and divine attributes, proofs for God's existence, nontheism and nonduality, good and evil, religion and science, and so on. A sardonic cultural anthropology of philosophy of religion reveals that members of this tribal society live in villages called "departments of philosophy." Members of the philosophy tribe practice many crafts, according to this study's author, Philip Quinn (1996). One of them is to gather from all over the United States to perform rituals. "These ritual gatherings," Quinn writes (1996), "are the annual meetings of the Eastern, Central and Pacific Divisions of the APA," the American Philosophical Association, where "practitioners of various philosophical crafts display the products of their crafts" (47). Quinn, himself a tribal practitioner, offers the interesting historical explanation that the neglect of the continental tradition in the contemporary village is due in large part to a "complacent atheism . . . so deeply ensconced in the culture of American academics that even passionate atheists . . . find it easier to dismiss theism as an outdated superstition than to argue against it" (Quinn 1996, 51). This has fueled a renaissance of philosophical theology, spearheaded largely by theists (Christians for the most part) who are motivated to defend the philosophical credentials of theism in conversation with medieval and pre-Kantian traditions, traditions valued for their clarity and logic (Quinn 1996, 51). Not surprisingly, the continental traditions are "almost entirely ignored," from Hegel through Feuerbach and Marx to Nietzsche, Schleiermacher to Ritschl, and twentieth-century continuations of such traditions. Why? Because they "depart, more or less radically, from the theistic doctrines most analytic philosophical theologians are trying to defend" (Quinn 1996, 51).

If practitioners of the continental style value the philosophic techniques of neighboring analytic villagers, it is usually as a corollary of the noncognitive, call it what you will: the unconscious, history, society, Being, differance, or whatever. The domicile of this élan is "departments of religious studies," their mainstay of ritual practices, according to Quinn, being the AAR. Having dealt with these chronologies of style and topological differences, it is time to delve more deeply into the specific contours of "the religious studies tribe," which is the primary interest of this volume.

Contemporary Continental Philosophy of Religion: Mapping the Terrain

Quinn observes that philosophers in the village of religious studies focus on religious theory and practice burdened by the need to "support their discipline's claim to objectivity" (Quinn 1996, 53). He is right, of course, albeit partially. At least two tribes exist in this village claiming objectivity for their individual rituals: the social-scientific tribe, now conveniently described as new materialists, and the phenomenological one, with character traits distinguishing European and North American offerings. Both advocate what Quinn (1996, 52) calls "the external point of view," according to which practitioners exclude personal religious beliefs from academic analysis. However, Quinn conflates issues by settling on the exclusion of the personal as somehow decisive in the tribal determination of objectivity. It is and it isn't.

Social scientists in religion with a soft spot for philosophy focus on the "outer" phenomena of religion in their external point of view (i.e., beliefs and practices and how they manifest in culture to form pockets of culture). Here you have a case of the external meeting the external: the scholarly disposition explaining religious behavior. Theorizing religion in this context amounts to submitting religion to a naturalistic frame: the historical, psychological, anthropological, sociological, and so on.

Phenomenology of religion, that fugitive practice of philosophical phenomenology, grew out of this ethos. In fact, it defined itself in opposition to it. The general thought is that one understands religion only in part when focusing on the external. Moreover, a heightened alienation is said to occur when one is completely shut off from the *sensus numinous*. Here the die is cast in favor of the internal or the experiential over against mere phenomena; it defends a version of objectivity that walks the tightrope between the objectivism (tendentiously reductionistic) of the social sciences and the normative reflection of partisan forms of theology. This is where Quinn gets it only half right. This particular religious studies tribe also aims at being objective but underlines the personal, which is the primary difficult task of its unique contribution to the village. What is more, interestingly, is that while phenomenologists may refrain from introducing their personal religious beliefs into serious academic conversation, as Quinn rightly notes, phenomenologists' own village critics have no qualms describing phenomenologists' conversation as quasi-theological. Rudolf Otto and Mircea Eliade, examples of the classical form, are often harangued for their theologically essentialist comparativism; Wilfred Cantwell Smith's more contemporary—and Kantian—move of stonewalling faith, although less harangued, manages to raise a few eyebrows of its own.[10]

What all this amounts to is a struggle for academic legitimacy in the public square. The aspect of religion as ideology is what marks off the area as controversial. By religion as ideology, I mean not only that religions involve beliefs, concepts, attitudes, and dispositions, but also that the interiority of such phenomena cannot be easily removed from their study. The existence of both tribal philosophies in the religious studies village exemplifies this. But the context has widened. Ideology is no longer limited to the religious and its expert classes packaging so-called false consciousness for the masses. We have made many strides since the early translators of Marx and the view that ideology marks a stark contrast between illusory and true discourse. Thanks to Marxists such as Louis Althusser most nowadays recognize ideology in broader terms as an inevitable part of all human discourse (see Roberts 2005, 371). And yet traces of the pejorative meaning of the term (ideology) persist despite the more inclusive setting. It is an issue that forms the contours of continental philosophies of religion in our times.

An example is in order. Scholars of religion, writes religion scholar Russell McCutcheon (2001), should be "critics' not "caretakers" of religion. Caretakers, McCutcheon's term for phenomenological types, are too invested in the production of meaning. In the appeal to concepts such as the *sensus numinous*, they mimic religious discourse, simultaneously authorizing their practice and halting critical examination. McCutcheon's pet discourse, which is a combination of historicism and sociologism, is by contrast presumably more transparent—less "religious," if you will—acknowledging its historical and social particularity and fallibility. It redescribes religious discourse by explaining religious ideas and practices in terms of naturalistic, empirically accessible causes and effects (Roberts 2005, 376). It is curious how McCutcheon fails to see his preference as any less invested in the production of meaning, especially since he advocates the views of Foucault, whom I believe would share my bewilderment. In any case, I side with those who see in McCutcheon a form of protectionism that McCutcheon and others are too quick to attribute to his methodological foes. That his discourse embodies the alter ego of his adversaries does not elide the fact that his practice, too, is self-authorizing. We may not see it in these terms or react to it as violently as we perhaps would to phenomenology, but I suspect our reaction is due to a value system we would be foolhardy to completely reject, rather than anything inherently valid in McCutcheon's logic. His rhetoric is effective but stifling in parading an ideology that monopolizes critical thinking.

So, we see that Quinn is not entirely wrong about an externalism in religious studies' philosophy of religion. McCutcheon is only one among several who secure objectivity in the field by being highly selective about the personal equation.[11] What does the postphenomenological context look like? The negative moment that McCutcheon represents has generated at least three currents of thought. The first, more scholarly in orientation than philosophical, cautiously advocates the insights of phenomenology with something of a sidelong bow to McCutcheon, namely, problems with the phenomenology of religion. One may attach to it the names of Daniel Pals (1987), Ninian Smart (1996), and possibly Martin Jay (2005). The other two currents represent something of a united front against antiphenomenologists such as McCutcheon. Although cognizant of the limitations of phenomenology of religion, they are unaffected by the bugaboo over subjectivity. Their response, unlike that of the first group, is more overtly philosophical, theological even, and yet wary of the thesis that "everything is really theology in disguise, so theology should be included in the academy" (Davaney 2002, 149; Cady 2002, 117). I see these two latter groups as new players on the scene, which I mark out as enecstatically inclined.

Enecstasis, as already noted, is a term I have coined that heralds a discourse emergent in the wake of Heideggerian ontology, a discourse that embraces a notion of engaged agency or personal involvement.[12] It earmarks, in other words, a disposition that takes a stand with respect to the content of a given discourse, in the context of a given discourse. This covers the *en* and *stasis* parts of the term, the standing-in aspect of *enecstasis*. The standing-out aspect, the *ek* and *stasis* parts of the term, consists in cultivating an openness toward the "other" *of* a given discourse—I hesitate to say an "other" inside or outside discourse, in deference to Jacques Derrida. When I invoke the term, it usually assumes the ethos or tribal particularities of the continental wing of religious studies, hence the Heideggerian form of the term. It is not restricted to that context, but it grows out of and responds to its particular problematic. As a general marker, it pertains to what both tribes see as a needed exigency to be critically self-reflexive.

Academic Theology qua Philosophical Theology

One of the two currents I mentioned in passing adopts the enecstatic posture in an explicitly theological vein. It advocates an "academic theology" that Paula Cooey models, at least structurally, after Kant's philosophical theology. Kant, she writes, "proposed nothing less than an area of study devoted to questioning the presuppositions of religious life and thought for purposes of both critique *and intentional construction*" (Cooey 2002, 178, emphasis added). Culture studies has provided for such reenactments by stressing the porous nature of our ideological commitments in a context where culture no longer signifies a sphere of ideas and symbols separate from the material aspects of human history. This problematizes any self-legitimating discourse that—to put it in the enecstatic terms of Sheila Davaney—sees itself as "standing above or outside the cultural fray" (Davaney 2002, 148). The indictment applies to "the academy's pretensions of objectivity, neutrality, and impartiality" (Davaney 2002, 149), whether in the guise of historicism or phenomenology. As Davaney advances it, "According to this position, the university is not a neutral site but one that does embody all sorts of values and commitments, including commitments to open inquiry, critical reflection, and public argumentation. These are indeed not impartial values. They have emerged within human history . . . and represent certain cultural values and options over others" (Davaney 2002, 149–150).

Cooey weds this inclusive value system of public argumentation to an explicit program of intervening in the systems of thought we study, as poets and fiction writers who teach English, as composers who teach music, as clinicians who teach psychology. It follows the call of Kant to become "critics and construers of culture," to develop theological anthropologies, cosmologies, and ethics, just "as philosophers intentionally construct theories of human moral life and practice, of justice, of aesthetics, of nature, and of language" (Cooey 2002, 179–180). The point is to enter the study of religion cognizant of the multicultural and pluralistic interactive contexts as philosophers of religion make and unmake the central symbols of religion such as God, Goddess, Brahman, Nirvana, Sunyata, and the Tao. What this means is that contemporary philosophical theology in the religious studies village engages students and greater society concerning the norms and symbols that inform university patronage.

Philosophy of Religion as Disruptive

The other current of philosophy of religion is less about intentional construction and more about intentional disruption. Derridean deconstruction is the inner lining of this discourse or its presupposition. The preoccupation is with singularity, the wholly other in each experience, unique event, or specific discourse that finally eludes these singularities, specific discourses. Tyler Roberts, an important representative, uses the notion to destabilize discourse to encourage the peculiar nature of engaged religious reflection. Where McCutcheon considers religious discourse to be self-assuring and self-authorizing, Roberts, after deconstructing the protective strategy of McCutcheon and others, argues that singularity in academic religious thinking encourages the disruption of its own discourse.[13] Obvious examples include monotheistic negative theologies and, a fortiori, the middle-way philosophies of Buddhism, Madhyamaka, and Yogacara. But the preoccupation with religious signs in Roberts's theorizing and in that of like-minded individuals is, I believe, about the impact of signs on the theorizer rather than a focus on the signs themselves, a distinguishing factor for me that marks philosophy of religion (qua religious studies) off from comparative phenomenology. And so, while the discourse is centered on signs such as God and Sunyata, the search, fraught with logical conundrums, is for "the 'other' and the 'other of language'" (Charles Winquist as quoted in Roberts 2004, 161).[14] Granted, this "other" may not be the self as other, as I am suggesting. However, the primary focus or function of this peculiar search is almost wholly fixed on the self and personal development. The point, as Roberts writes, following Eric Santner, is "to open ourselves up to [the] excess" of language (Roberts 2004, 163), to allow a disruption in us, persons unexhausted by the predicates forming their identity (162). Roberts continues in this vein by discussing the aim of this process, which consists in identity formation, further demonstrating my enecstatic point. Religious signs, he writes, "unplug" us: "*not* by substituting a new identity for an old one but, rather, by disrupting identity, disorienting us in a way that productively unloosens the bonds of identification and ideology, opening us to the world and others in a way that is not constrained by our own fantasies, needs, and neuroses" (Roberts 2004, 164).

Carl Raschke of the University of Denver also follows this enecstatic gesture of the impact of religious signs on their users. His aim is to make a connection with religious representations in "the 'carnival' of popular culture," which he contrasts with the aim (perhaps Roberts's and Santner's) preoccupied with "highly formalized" thought-forms (Raschke 1990, 672). Still, one detects in Raschke an MO similar to Roberts's. To put it in the terms of Raschke's earlier work, "it is the semantic displacement of the signified by the act of signification. Signification is disruption, a violation of context, a transgression" (Raschke 1990, 672). He means to dislocate this signifying activity from the high-minded objects examined by what David Levin catalogues as "analytic postmodernism"—hypermodernism, if you will—tying it to the concrete sign-performances of popular culture presumably examined more authentically by Raschke's own preference of "metaphoric postmodernism."[15] But however you slice it, Raschke is after the same experiential openness to excess that Roberts and Santner are, although he deflects the thinking that informs their enecstatic burden. Whatever the case, his focus—representations of culture (events, songs, films, novels, sonnets, sitcoms, etc.)—joins him with Jean-François Lyotard in the search for new presentations, "not in order to enjoy them but in order to impart a stronger sense of the unpresentable" (Lyotard as quoted in Raschke 1990, 674). Representation, in this sense, does not consist in the traditional idea of mimesis: re-presenting the real in one form or another. Rather, representation becomes an act of reference, signification, which paradoxically overcomes the referent. In this act of overcoming, exemplified in the asymmetry of religious semiosis, the object signified is neither visible nor recognizable, producing the mythical, the numinous (Raschke 1999, 8). And so Raschke wants to explain how "the semantic discrepancies between 'traditional' formulations of the faith-encounter are resolved through 'imaginative' involvement in the lives of religious persons, whose habits of worship converge on a singular, yet ineffable, object of both *reference* and *reverence*" (Raschke 1982, 37–38). My notion of philosophy of religious studies is sympathetic to Raschke's philosophy of religion but differs from it by making room for the highly formalized thinking Raschke, at least in his earlier work, seems to harbor antipathy toward.[16]

Diminishing the Tyranny of Omnicompetence

Philosophy of religion is truly a zoo, rich but also deceivingly simple in form, as I hope to have indicated here. Key points are that philosophy of religion basically divides between analytic and continental types, where "philosophical theology" and "philosophy of religion" (in the specific, not generic, sense) are defined by different histories, thinking styles, and objectives. The analytic form we can put aside for the moment, since it has really only served as a springboard for my discussion of the less dominant and hence less known type in religion and philosophy departments.[17]

This taxonomy has grown out of my own teaching experience. It was forced on me by a sense of professional bewilderment analogous to the mythical business major who ventures out into the "real world" equipped with crucial generic skills for the specific needs of companies. Moreover, the real world into which I ventured lacked a well-defined structure; it condoned only the innocuous rule that philosophy of religion should be wide-ranging and comparative. In such a context traditional analytic philosophical theology obviously will not do, especially if exclusively theistic. Were it not for the very topical nature of the approach, which is necessarily constrained to engage reified religious beliefs, it might hold some promise.[18] Such an approach tends to work in the village of philosophy departments but tends to fall flat in religious studies villages where specialized scholarly concerns tend to capture the imagination of a bewildering student demographic.

What one will find in religious studies villages is a nebulous form of analytic "comparative" philosophy of religion occasioned by debates between phenomenologists and new materialists. The currents mentioned earlier, "academic theology" and the disruptive philosophic form, are relatively new players on the scene. They hold great promise, in my opinion, for the religious studies village for various reasons. First, they operate under the assumption that engaging reified forms of religion, while intoxicating to the freshman, manages to alienate both the believer and the specialist. Second, their enecstatic treatment of religious symbols as objects of critique and intentional construction is particularist, that is, it abstains as much as possible from a generalized reification of religious traditions. Cooey, for example, has students reading a mix of Jewish, Christian, and secular works, "among them the book of *Job*, Elie Wiesel's *Night*, [Albert] Camus' *The Plague*, [Harold] Kushner's *When Bad Things Happen to Good People*, the gospel according to *Mark*, and [Kathleen] Sand's *Escape from Paradise*" (Cooey 2002, 183). The objective is not specialized knowledge, but reflection on religious legacies that "forces questions of meaning and value" (Cooey 2002, 182). When treating religious symbols as vehicles of self-reflection, as in the case of a disruptive form of philosophy of religion, the demand for specialization is further obviated. What is welcoming about this development is that it creates a space for open philosophical dialogue without the pretense of omnicompetence on the part of philosophers and theologians. Finally, these two currents of philosophy of religion take seriously that many embark on a study or career in religion for personal "philosophic" reasons that may or may not be "religious." Whether they are religious, areligious, or antireligious is irrelevant to the study of religion; that they are human, however, is not irrelevant. Philosophy of religion in this key (qua religious studies) provides an opportunity to cultivate this interest in conversation with traditions that form our horizons directly and indirectly. It challenges the move to reduce "all humanistic and social scientific studies to some form of historical studies" based on "the erroneous assumption that because . . . scholars . . . do not *intend* to intervene in the systems they study, they are not actually intervening through their study of them" (Cooey 2002, 179).[19] As Cooey (2002) rightly proffers, this assumption is "simply methodologically and epistemologically self-deceptive" (179).

Enecstatic philosophy of religion includes this dimension but is concerned fundamentally with mapping the terrain for students and scholars to engage personally in the issues themselves, a possible manner for doing so. It is a mode of philosophizing that, based on my experience, seems to work in this particular village. Space is provided for students who do not specialize in philosophy to discover and form their own rationale about issues that are fundamentally philosophical in nature. Once their sense of inadequacy about venturing into the philosophical is overcome, students begin to feel as though they are participants in a discourse that relaxes their learned and tutored demand for scholarly objectivity. The process could be dubbed, ironically: the diminution of *epochē*. Teaching philosophy of religion along these lines diminishes the tyranny of omnicompetence on the part of student and instructor alike.

Philosophy of religious studies treats the theorizers of religion, not religion per se. We can loosely refer to it as a "practice" in the Greek sense of the application and exercise (*praktikē*) of something that intends meaningful personal and pedagogical results. In studying the theorizers of religion, we learn something about ourselves proximate to some object of study. Nor do we simply acquire a skill in studying that object. We learn about what we value and loathe in our/their theorizing about objects. In effect, we learn about ourselves. Pierre Hadot beautifully captures my sentiment when he writes about the Stoics that

> philosophy, for them, was an "exercise." In their view, philosophy did not consist in teaching an abstract theory—much less in the exegesis of texts—but rather in the art of living. It is a concrete attitude and determinate life-style, which engages the whole of existence. The philosophical act is not situated merely on the cognitive level, but on that of the self and of being. It is a progress which causes us to *be* more fully, and makes us better. It is a person who goes through it. It raises the

> individual from an inauthentic condition of life, darkened by unconsciousness and harassed by worry, to an authentic state of life, in which he attains self-consciousness, an exact vision of the world, inner peace, and freedom. (Hadot 1995, 83)

Enecstasis, as described in part 1, is my term for signaling this sensibility as a programmatic for our times. We will now need to look to general issues surrounding the practice of philosophy of religion, which enecstasis aims to reconfigure for religious studies and theology.

Chapter 4

Philosophy of Religion Religious Studies Style

Philosophy of religion, at least as a university exercise, comes in different sizes and shapes. As a practice that evolved from ancient Greece through medieval Europe to modern and contemporary empiricisms and rationalisms, the preoccupation has tended to be with fundamental "religious" topics such as proofs for God's existence and theodicy brought to bear through issues of logic, language theory, and cosmology. This analytic approach continues to be the dominant form of "philosophy of religion." One finds it commonly in philosophy departments, and also embodied in the more normative discourse of philosophical theology practiced in professional schools of theology.[1] A younger development stems largely from German schools of thought in the nineteenth century, to which contemporary French forms are indebted in their significantly less topical, political-hermeneutical restructuring of the field. Conveniently dubbed continental, one finds this approach in philosophy departments in both Europe and North America, although in Europe one senses an indifference to identifying with a subfield of philosophy of religion as such. It is also the more dominant form of philosophizing found in religion departments, a fact that is hardly surprising when one considers that continental reflection birthed comparative religion.

What philosophy of religion offers the modern university is an arresting question. How one answers it will depend on the type of philosophy

---

An earlier version of this chapter appeared on philosophyofreligion.org (see Kanaris 2016), which asked numerous philosophers of religion to answer the question "What does philosophy of religion offer to the modern university?"

of religion one practices, which is usually shaped by the environment one teaches philosophy of religion in, and the professional communities with which one associates. Philosophy of religion in a philosophy department, for example, will have an aim different from "philosophy of religion" in a theology department or religious studies program. In one context the aim is to introduce students to epistemological issues such as, for example, whether religious language is properly understood in, say, realist or nonrealist terms. In another context the aim will differ slightly, developing the normative claims of a specific tradition philosophically, either in terms exclusive to that tradition or in comparison to other traditions. In still other contexts the aim may be to critically assess religious beliefs and practices as one siphons off issues surrounding humanity's existential plight or as one connects them to some social-political reality. In my estimation, all the positions in this broad taxonomy possess a legitimacy, especially if the aim is to avoid parochialism. Be that as it may, philosophers of religion have their preferences, with the more responsible among them interfacing these preferences to mitigate issues dividing the field.

In line with our theme of philosophizing in a religious studies manner, I will bracket these broader boundary questions and focus instead on my own teaching environment, which happens to be religious studies. This forces me to think differently about philosophy of religion than colleagues practicing more traditional approaches. The irony does not escape me. In my desire to avoid parochialism, my contribution does seem dangerously close to being parochial. Nevertheless, its application is, I believe, transdisciplinary.

Allow me this one assumption. A deep wedge exists between the student demographic in religious studies and the concerns and procedures of the card-carrying philosopher of religion, the individual noted earlier who manages traditional topics in the field. Couple this now with another assumption. The specificities of the intellectual climate and history surrounding these procedures are no longer privileged in glocal consciousness. The inclusion of diverse perspectives, whose religious worldviews are assessed in terms of their propositional weight, continues to have remedial value. But the extension of this analytic procedure, the traditional approach, is simultaneously too specific and too general to be wholly effective in religious studies. It is too specific because it is bound to a tradition of philosophy whose aims have been quite apologetic and modeled on Western scientific ideals. It is too general because this approach tends to essentialize religious traditions, their handpicked beliefs and practices. Ever since the publication of modern classics such as Wilfred Cantwell Smith's *Meaning and End of Religion* (1962) and Edward Said's *Orientalism* (1978), to mention only two renowned examples, students of religion, sensitive to cultural diversity, have become dyspeptic toward the analytic mien.[2] Issues of power, status, and identity tend to take precedence, displacing the traditional platform of knowledge while extending it to the problem of representation.[3]

In this environment, the role of philosophy can be both object- and subject-constitutive. In a revamped form of "epistemology,"[4] philosophy links up here with an issue-based attention to "socio-economic disparities, environmental degradation, and ongoing biases linked to race, sexual orientation, or colonial exploitation" (Rodrigues and Harding 2009, 104). This, what I take to be object-constitutive, replaces the systematic scholastic and analytic orientations of premodern and modern epistemologies with critical-cultural strategies of contemporary theorizing (about) religion. Philosophy holds much promise in this regard for critical scholarship attuned not so much to the cognitive dimension of religious beliefs as to the "historicality" (*Geschichtlichkeit*) of diverse religious phenomena.[5] Although not classified as philosophers of religion, noting the philosophical differences between celebrated anthropologists Clifford Geertz and Talal Asad may help to contextualize my concern with philosophy of religion religious studies style. The distinction between a "cognitive" emphasis and one attuned to "historicality" is not exactly taken from Asad's well-known critique of Geertz but rather is inspired by it. It behooves me to proceed slowly. In what follows, then, I provide an example of what philosophy of religion looks like in religious studies, transposing the particular concerns and issues of analytic and continental philosophy accordingly.

An Example from Anthropology

Asad (1993, 44) disapproves of Geertz's otherwise redoubtable anthropology of religion. A principal concern is how the configuration proposed by Geertz replaces one set of problems with another. When Geertz set out to rectify the "general stagnation" he perceived in the field, he intended to reclaim the jouissance of the tradition's "transcendent figures." The aims of these figures, Geertz bemoaned, were all but lost in the reigning anthropology that selectively modeled itself on these aims. "Virtually no one even thinks of looking . . . to philosophy, law, literature, or the 'harder' sciences . . . for analytical ideas," as Durkheim, Weber, Freud, or Malinowski had done (Geertz 1966, 1). It fell to Geertz to mine this ideational grotto, an activity that would result in his more comprehensive view rendering ailing social anthropology secondary to "an analysis of the system of meanings embodied in the symbols which make up [a] religion proper" (Geertz 1966, 42). Asad joins the fray inspired by developments in poststructuralism that collapse both social-psychological processes *and* systems of meaning into their "conditions of possibility," as the early Michel Foucault would say. As cognitive in emphasis, these earlier approaches neglect the role of power as constitutive in the process and analysis of meaning construction. Asad virtually argues that, in the case of Geertz, double-dealing seems to be at play, where a post-Enlightenment, secular tendenz adjudicates the religious perspective. Even more interesting is that Geertz comes to represent a position that is deemed to be both theological and Christian (Asad 1993, 45–48). This may have come as a surprise to some of Geertz's readers. Geertz himself snubbed the suggestion as Marxist turned "power-reductionist" (Micheelsen and Geertz 2002, 9–10). Whatever the case, the fact that such a reading has become typical bespeaks a shifting tide that Asad's historicality perspective represents.[6]

Asad mounts his case by an apt reference to the fourth-century Donatist controversy.[7] St. Augustine's arguments against the Donatists isolates an element of religious practice that is seriously at odds with Geertz's symbolic anthropology. Geertz comes dangerously close, for Asad, to excluding what the anthropologist tries to establish or should establish: a description or explanation of the believer's perspective. Imagine St. Augustine confronted by the view that the meaning and effectiveness of the Eucharist consists in certain "powerful, pervasive, and long-lasting moods and motivations" whose "aura of factuality" inspires these "uniquely realistic" states (Geertz 1966, 4). This "aura of factuality" surrounding the Eucharist is, Asad would want to argue, neither spontaneous nor uncoerced. Obviously, the phrase "moods and motivations," which suggests a placid state of affairs, needs some nuancing.

Religious acclimatization is a long and elaborate process compelled by learned psychological dispositions parasitic on a host of horizonal assumptions. For a believer like St. Augustine, the process is one grounded in God who, through the mechanism of the church, coerces the proper disposition and the real motivation for consuming the body and blood of Christ, "ranging all the way from laws (imperial and ecclesiastical) and other sanctions (hellfire, death, salvation, good repute, peace) to the disciplinary activities of social institutions (family, school, city, church) and of human bodies (fasting, prayer, obedience, penance). . . . It was not the mind that moved spontaneously to religious truth [contra Geertz], but power that created the conditions for experiencing that truth" (Asad 1993, 35). St. Augustine describes the process by the term *disciplina*, "essentially [an] active process of corrective punishment, 'a softening-up process,' a 'teaching by inconveniences'—*a per molestias eruditio*" (Peter Brown as quoted in Asad 1993, 34).

Because Geertz is after an understanding of religious moods and motivations on a cognitive level, this social element of power is elided by an ideational procedure that aligns more with the theological inclination than it does with the anthropological. Moreover, because the space within which Geertz formulates symbolic anthropology is afforded by post-Enlightenment liberalism, Asad calls it "Christian." The scare quotes indicate that caution is required. Geertz's anthropology is Christian in the broad sense: a contemporary, secular production supported directly and indirectly by the Christian heritage.

Caution needs to be exercised in another sense as well. Asad is not attacking theological discourse per se. Theology is a prerogative of religious communities. It serves as the anthropologist's data. Asad is critiquing instead an interpretive framework, Geertz's, which aims to adopt a relatively neutral posture in adjudicating cultural systems. The implication is that a theological agenda, which has fueled Western liberalism historically, along with its accompanying ideals of secularism, skews the data as it promotes an ideology reworked in tandem with—and hence modifying—the data itself. Asad may have his own theological reasons for arguing this. However, I am going to mute discussion of this to identify the contours of his poststructuralistly attuned historicality perspective, what it looks like in the context of religious studies, and how it parallels a characteristic trait that separates analytic philosophers of religion from continental types.

The cognitive emphasis in Geertz, about which Asad complains, is analogous to a sticking point in philosophy responsible for making a regional adjective (continental) synonymous with a thinking style (nonanalytic). The complaint of continental philosophers, like Asad's with respect to Geertz (see Asad 1993, 44), is not that the specificities surrounding social-political practice, the historicality frame, go unnoticed in analytic philosophy. It is that these specificities are bracketed *in actu*; they are not regarded, in other words, as constitutive. This touches on the theological/ideological concerns of Asad when assessing religious phenomena anthropologically. Let us turn now to philosophy of religion for a more direct application in religious studies.

Asad's charge exemplifies a manner of philosophizing about religion that scholars of religion appreciate. The tendency may be to view such a procedure as methodological and not, strictly speaking, philosophical. However, this is presumption. Philosophers themselves are often harangued by disputes surrounding the nature and scope of their field. Analytic characterizations aside, the question remains an open one. What I consider to be Asad's object-constitutive orientation philosophizes about matters that pertain to identity formation in religion, a preoccupation that sits comfortably with Carrette's "problem of representation" mentioned earlier. It transposes the phenomenological appreciation of religious symbols and the "true" dispositions they are said to instill concerning the religious institution and how it creates religious dispositions. The question, as—interestingly, Asad (1993, 33) interjects—the *nonbeliever* would put it, is: "How does (religious) power create (religious) truth." In addition to power, issues of status and identity take precedence as they displace the traditional platform of knowledge, which Geertz symbolizes, within a frame suffused by the problem of representation. With the now tired orthodoxy of symbolic anthropology behind us—thanks to denuding the post-Enlightenment, Christian-influenced secularism that informs it—the benefit, it is suggested, is that an understanding of first-order religious traditions will more accurately reflect the data.[8]

In this respect, then, Asad embodies the sensibility of continental thinking that takes historicality—again, in the context of poststructuralist developments—to be properly basic. However, his critique of Geertz's "theology" suggests a strain in his own appropriation that runs parallel with the concerns of social science crosscutting those of the humanities and phenomenology. Asad thus unwittingly reconnects with the celebrated scientific orientation of analytic philosophy that summons the ire of continental philosophers. Paradoxically, that which connects is also that which separates. This causes us to ask whether Asad's critique of the cognitive emphasis in symbolic anthropology is an embodiment of the historicality perspective. It is and it is not.

Let me be clear about some things before nuancing a response. The first concerns Geertz and fairness to him. The cognitive emphasis that Asad sees in Geertz is not altogether the same as it appears in the analytic emphasis on propositional truths. Asad would doubtless agree. The import of translating "the aura of factuality" attached to religious symbols is different from a procedure that essentializes religious experiences in terms of their propositional content. Geertz's arguably phenomenological comportment is sensitive to the particularity of cultural systems. Geertz does not a fortiori manage religious truths propositionally as analytic philosophers typically do. This dimension is quite simply not a pressing concern in symbolic anthropology, if even taken seriously. Even so, the significance of symbolic statements and behavior pivot, in Geertz, as Asad insists, on their cognitive function. That is, the focus is on and is sourced from the intellective plane facilitated by modern, secular sensibilities. Asad's complaint—to nuance Asad now—echoes an aspect of the historicality perspective discoverable in continental philosophy. One notices it in Geertz as well. But Asad's point is that, despite Geertz's recognition of the nonpropositional, the token appreciation of social practice in analytic philosophy is operative in Geertz in another form. Indeed, Geertz's "power reductionist" quip invites the suggestion. This marks the limit of most, if not all, cognitive approaches.

The story is relatively old, narrated by the so-called masters of suspicion and given currency in the work of contemporaries such as Foucault and Said. To reiterate, it fixes the guiding questions of this discourse for religious studies. As Asad (1993, 33) nicely puts it: "What are the conditions in which religious symbols can actually produce religious dispositions? Or, as a nonbeliever would put it: How does (religious) power create (religious) truth?" Asad thus connects matters with the philosophical tradition in a way that harks back to German idealism, its critics (Nietzsche, Marx, and, to a certain extent, Freud), and their contemporary reformulators (Foucault, in the main). And just to avoid confusion, it is important to note that the cognitive dimension is not altogether absent from this tradition. It is displaced, following Carrette, by the problem of representation.

This is my "yes" to the question of whether Asad embodies the historicality perspective.[9] My "no" centers on what I consider to be problematic with Asad's object-constitutive approach, which is important to negotiate in the context of religious studies.[10] One can detect it in numerous contributions to what is commonly being described as the new materialism in the field. If the aim were solely to identify a blind spot, the critique of the cognitive emphasis would be more than welcome. The problem goes deeper, however, deeper perhaps than Asad himself might care to admit. In my estimation, the problem consists in protracting a bias that rightly forces the hand of phenomenologists and theologians. Without conflating their discourses,[11] I would like to press matters further. It is precisely this tendency in object-constitutive discourse, which I understand Asad to represent, that renders reasonable and perhaps necessary the explicit normative inquiry that theologians and phenomenologists spearhead.

The Category of Experience

For the sake of convenience, I will oversimplify by centralizing what I consider to be the fundamental issue in debates apropos to philosophy of religious studies surrounding the term "experience." Experience, as a desideratum to be understood, usually divides academic ideological commitments in religionist scholarship. While wildly elusive categorically, it has configured debates, pivoting on issues of normativity, since at least Friedrich Schleiermacher penned his famous *Speeches*. It turns out that *Gefühl* (feeling), a cognate in Schleiermacher for the experiential dimension, divides not only different religious camps, so-called traditionalists from so-called liberals, but also camps in religious studies, social scientific from humanist and phenomenological. The issues are undeniably complex and center around normative questions of authority—in theology, for example: whether answers to questions of ultimate concern should be negotiated by scripture and/or tradition or by the guiding role of personal experience. This question will not concern us. Nor will ascertaining the "true" significance of the category in Schleiermacher.[12] That exegetical preoccupation, while helpful for resolving historical-critical issues, does little to elucidate the problem that I consider to be a task of my proposal for philosophy of religious studies.

In his important study, which inspired a great deal of controversy over the notion and its categorical determinates in religious studies, Wayne Proudfoot (1985) demonstrates how experience functions as a "formal operator, or placeholder" in religious discourse (127). References to experience guarantee the ineffability believers describe as irreducible, that is, as something to be experienced, not understood. Confusion arises when this function translates the prescriptive and evocative rules of religious language into categories whose grammatical rules follow the dictates of descriptive and analytical language—these are Proudfoot's distinctions. Proudfoot's point is that a categorical faux pas takes place in the tradition that harks back to Schleiermacher. The error is, we might say, hermeneutical. It consists of melding the prescriptive and evocative rules guiding religious discourse with the descriptive and analytical rules considered proper for guiding scholarly discourse. When Schleiermacher asks us to consider *Gefühl* (religious "feeling") as a properly basic faculty of human consciousness, suffusing thinking and doing but reducible to neither, he effectively conflates the grammatical rules that govern these two different types of discourses: the prescriptive/mystical and the descriptive/analytical. Schleiermacher's incantation, if you will, is practically on a par with acclamations about, say, Brahman in the Upanishads as *neti-neti*, or *śunyātā* in Nagarjuna as emptiness itself; it is a subjectivation of them. These mystical statements—readily available in most religious traditions—guarantee the ineffability that analytical discourse aims to describe as its primary function and purpose, not prescribe or evoke. Proudfoot groups together William James and Rudolf Otto, among other, more contemporary thinkers of religious experience, in this scholarly tradition. They bridge the theological developments spearheaded by Schleiermacher and what comes to be known as the phenomenology of religion proper. Thankfully, though, Proudfoot's treatment, of James in particular, is what makes his contribution sober when compared to others' who rely on his finds.[13]

Proudfoot agrees with critics of this tradition, most notably Steven Katz, who argue against (without wanting to oversimplify here) the European, phenomenological narrative that a raw or core mystical experience underlies all religions. Contrary to liberal Christian perspectives, rooted in Schleiermacher, Katz finds mystical traditions to be characteristically conservative by contrast. Looking at the discourses themselves, one sees that religious beliefs not only (in)form the experience, but they also validate it; they constitute the experience as such. Experience, in other words, is, argues Proudfoot, not some vague, elusive universal said to trump beliefs; religious beliefs fortify the experience against categorizations whose "placeholders" annul the specificity of the beliefs in question. Thus, Katz concludes,

> all experience is processed through, organized by, and makes itself available to us in extremely complex epistemological ways. The notion of unmediated experience seems, if not self-contradictory, empty at best. This seems to me to be true even with regard to the experiences of those ultimate objects of concern with which mystics have intercourse, e.g., God, Being, nirvāṇa, etc., and this "mediated" aspect of all our experience seems an inescapable feature of any epistemological inquiry, including the inquiry into mysticism. (Katz 1983, 4)

Proudfoot echoes Katz's observations but is categorical that *phenomenological* placeholders, let us call them, such as "ineffability," should not be relegated to the ash heap of history. It turns out, on his reading, that categories such as ineffability and noetic quality—privileged marks of mysticism in James—surface an important structure in mystical discourse itself. Once we disentangle the function of phenomenological description from the prescriptive and the evocative, tethering it to the analytical, we can see clearly in what the experience consists, namely, its logic and function. This, Proudfoot argues (contra Katz), is quite meaningful to practitioners and for that reason should be to analysts as well. In fairness, it may be prudent to note that Katz does not seem to venture down the same eliminativist rabbit hole of religion scholars as Robert Sharf (1995, 1998), who would see the category disappear altogether.[14] But Proudfoot sees no reason to trail in Katz's dismissal of properly managed categorical descriptions, be they broad. Such categories are useful for comprehending the rule-governed discourse of mystical experience. Even if slippage exists in James's language, confusing the evocative with the analytical, his methodological directives for analyzing mystical claims indicate that he (James) was careful not to confuse the prescriptive with the descriptive, a principal goad stirring critics of the notion of experience (see Proudfoot 1985, 151–153).[15]

While I would not enlist Proudfoot as an object-constitutive analyst in an enecstatic sense, he (and I would include Asad) embodies what I consider to be a moderate perspective in the critique or contextualization of normative categories in the phenomenological tradition. Proudfoot is more overtly analytic than Asad, whose approach mirrors procedurally the dividing practices of the social-scientific stream in the continental tradition. But the procedure of both, to put it in the terms of Imre Lakatos (1970), tends to surround the "hard core" of knowledge, what it means to acquire it, with the "protective belt" of their respective theories. Proudfoot does this by keeping the descriptive and prescriptive, the analytic and evocative, separate in scholarly analysis (reflected in James's advice regarding the limit of authority religious claims can have over the analyst). Asad does it by advocating for the role of religious practice constituted by power relations as the *terminus ad quem* of a scholarly appreciation of religious meaning (thanks, in certain respects, to Foucault). Before turning to the issue at hand—whether experience as a category serves description, explanation, and normative reflection—we need to consider a little more closely what this hard core is.

The hard core, methodologically speaking, is what has constituted religious studies since its inception: the study of religion as *the examination of* religious experiences (in the broad sense of the term), not the inclusion of experience as an ingredient of the study. *When this inclusion is imported into religious studies*, the fear seems to be that a phenomenological appreciation of experience flirts with—and is perhaps already in alliance with—a potentially degenerative theological modus operandi, to continue with Lakatos's characterizations. Despite painstaking efforts to show that phenomenology of religion is not theology in different garb,[16] advocates of the hard core are less than convinced.[17] Even what I consider to be the temperate position of Hillary Rodrigues and John S. Harding (2009) contains vestiges of this latter sentiment. They distinguish *religious education* (education by believers for believers) and *religious studies* (examination of all aspects of religion with a "value-free" orientation), which is, on the surface, a very fair way of looking at things. But polarization creeps in when they discuss differences between religious studies and neighboring disciplines such as theology and metaphysics, the former, religious studies, being illustrative of the hard core. Understandably, nuance is missing. Their outline is, after all, from an introductory textbook on the study of religion. And yet it shows how deep-seated the sentiment is in this tradition of scholarship.

Briefly, Rodrigues and Harding state that religious studies is a field that aims to be neutral and objective. Theology and metaphysics, by contrast, are "speculative" and "apologetic," theology being a special "exercise" in the latter.[18] The train of thought is as follows. Religious studies, as an examination of culture, does not enjoy the status of empirical knowledge vouched for by the physical and life sciences. However, religious studies, unlike theology and metaphysics, mirrors these sciences by not being meta-physics (beyond physics) and apologetic (personal, subjective). As a social *science*, religious studies endorses the desiderata of its "harder" scientific siblings: neutrality and objectivity. How it limits its venture into subjectivity as a *social* science can be compared to what some call imaginative projection.[19] Such an approach stipulates that students of religion preoccupy themselves with what it would be *like* to hold a religious belief without believing or advocating such a belief. Rodrigues and Harding refer to this as "subjective involvement," which is misleading; the procedure is more clinical than the phrase suggests. That is why the undertaking is said to involve degrees of participation. "Ideally, one needs to be able to explore the unknown religious territory with a great degree of subjective involvement and report back on what one has discovered with a high measure of objectivity" (Rodrigues and Harding 2009, 9). While oddly not considered speculative, this level of involvement is shielded from the subjectivity of extraneous experimental ventures (metaphysics and theology); it is weighted toward the objective rather than subjective pole in the task.[20]

It seems clear that positions ranging from Asad's critique of Geertz and Proudfoot's qualifications regarding mystical discourse, to Rodrigues and Harding's depiction of study constraints in examining religious phenomena, are principally concerned to guard academic inquiry from *certain kinds* of normativity. Proudfoot's reliance on James's methodological directives, specifically against the imposition of religious truth claims on analysts, is, it seems to me, level-headed. We could couple this with Rodrigues and Harding's sentiment to keep "religious studies" and "religious education" separate, and with Asad's social determinants, historic and otherwise, of religious beliefs. But things go awry when assuming normative engagement dubbed "theological" is mere speculation and apologetically at cross-purposes with academic inquiry.

Before launching into an alternative reading, pausing to connect the dots is prudent. Asad's critique of Geertz, which represents a historicality perspective of the social-scientific variety, is wary of analysis aimed at engaging directly with what it takes to be the normative element in religious worldviews. To put it in Proudfoot's terms, to do this confuses description with prescription; it evokes an experience rather than analyzes it. Proudfoot thinks that such distinctions illuminate the function of mystical discourse, the roles surrounding which should not be confused. Doing otherwise reels into our analysis the truth claims of the mystical discourse we simply wish to describe. Robert A. Segal is famous for disavowing such activity, not only because it equivocates prescription and description but also because it conflates religious experience/belief and explanation. It requires analysts to temper explanation by the claims and practices that analysts seek to unveil rather than condone. Such a stance also disqualifies contravening religious sentiments, which is odd to impose on nonbelieving analysts (see Segal 1983, 115–116).

Donald Wiebe, who overall condones the importance of maintaining these distinctions, pinpoints a problem with the type of assumptions we find in Segal. Even if the assumptions in explaining or phenomenologically describing religion (à la Schleiermacher, Otto, Eliade, et al.) are incommensurate, an exclusivist argument for exchanging one set of assumptions with another, what we are left with are unresolved and quite possibly unresolvable metaphysical and philosophical arguments dictating methodological procedure (see Wiebe 1984, 162, 164). This is as unnecessary as it is categorically and methodologically problematic. Ivan Strenski argues similarly in the conclusion to the first edition of his book *Thinking about Religion: An Historical Introduction to Theories of Religion* (2006), which he expands upon in the second edition (2015). In the first edition, Strenski is vehement that appeals to "a naturalist foundation to the study of religion"—Russell T. McCutcheon's variant receives special attention—is "to engage in a deviant 'theology' of its own" (2006, 340). The ontology is naturalist and as such traffics in "metaphysics" (Strenski 2006, 340).[21] In the second edition, Strenski (2015, 243-244) tones down the metaphysics charge but is equally vehement in targeting "post-modern eliminationists" (i.e., McCutcheon, Timothy Fitzgerald, Bruce Lincoln) for making "criticism" of the concept of religion "an end in itself." That is, these "post-colonial theorists" have no intention of ever putting the concept of religion to use in the world of anything conceivably called "religion" because, for them, "no such thing exists" (Strenski 2015, 243-244). Strenski's corrective—"being smart about bringing religion back in[to]" religious studies (2015, 241)—breathes new life into the phenomenological program, modeled as it is after the work of the late Ninian Smart (1927-2001), contemporary phenomenologist extraordinaire. But Strenski stops short of the proposal for a hardy enecstatic philosophy of religious studies—a move typical in most traditions of scholarship that see an impenetrable wall between a dialectical treatment of data and its potential for explicit foundational, horizonal expansion.[22]

Tradition

A specter that has been haunting the current exposition is "tradition." It carries a serviceable connotation to the discussion in hand. The term commonly inspires associations to a religious sect or community. In the mouths of those using it in this way, tradition becomes shorthand for something disparaging and backward. A scornful view or practice for a deserving community. Such a federation, however, is unnecessary. Tradition more properly denotes a general process of documenting, gathering, preserving, and disseminating beliefs and practices in a wide variety of ways and in groups from generation to generation. In his classic study

Religious Studies: The Making of a Discipline (1995), Walter Capps describes the "intellectual discipline" of religious studies in a way that bolsters the concerns we have encountered about a scholarly "hard core" without capitulating to the general bias against subjective engagement, commonly, derogatorily, identified as metaphysical or theological.[23]

For reasons unclear to me, Capps speaks only of one order of tradition: the second-order tradition of religious studies. What we might presume is the first-order tradition of religion, Capps appears content to describe less committedly as "the subject" of the second-order tradition. Whereas the task of religious studies is "to discover as well as to elicit its subject's intelligibility" (Capps 1995, xiv),

> traditions are composed: they are not simply discovered. They are always in process, perennially susceptible to innovation and transformation. They stand as *givens* only after they have been designed and constructed, and their design and construction are always at least partially idiosyncratic and of pragmatic origin. Traditions are used for parameter-setting. They offer working environments within which inquiries can occur and by means of which they are framed. They are not committed to definitional exactness, except the exactness that is internal and contextual. Such traditions are formative but not causal. They are composed; they can hardly be deduced. They are subtle and flexible but not forced. They are like designs that depend on aesthetic nurture rather than like conclusions that can be deduced with precision from logical, discursive, and tightly sequential reasoning process. And traditions involve narratives—stories that can be traced, stories that get retold, stories in whose retelling the traditions find ongoing shape, design, and purposes that may not have been recognized or anticipated by the founders. (Capps 1995, xxi–xxii)

This is a serviceable outline of what tradition is. And yet it is equally applicable to "the subject" of religious studies itself. Religions, like religious studies, are composed and not simply discovered, even as Capps (1995, xxii) goes on to qualify religious studies, the second-order tradition, as "also a matter of discovery." We are confronted by spectra of engagement with proximate levels of commitment to preserve, shape, and (re)design an activity held dear, even if one remains passionately indifferent to the subject matter.

My thesis is multilayered. Religious studies is a second-order tradition that distills elements of first-order religious traditions and is shaped by a normativity that works either in tandem with or contrary to the elements in question. Religious studies, historically Western European, embodies elements of a multifaceted tradition for examining first-order religious traditions. In such an examination, elements of first-order traditions are distilled by a comparative venture in search of similarities and/or differences that fashion an object or collection of objects commensurate with (and here is the clincher) the normativity informing the second-order tradition. Some might provocatively describe this object and activity as religious. I am not as committed to the provocation as I am to what it implies, that a second-order *tradition*, ascetically intellectual, contains and is guided by a "structure" of normativity affected by first-order traditions while being formed by its assessment of them. Whether that interaction is imagined as seamless or discontinuous is secondary. It begs the larger question of tradition itself, preserving, shaping, (re)configuring patterns of normativity that reflexively nominate themselves as other from its other, normative objects of study. This comes in many forms, from selective variants to denials of the reflex altogether. In considering the normativity of first-order traditions as object, second-order inquiry is guided by its own scale of beliefs, values, enunciative fields, boundary questions, and so on (call them what you will). Its register is configured differently, to be sure, objectively considered, but it does offer a scale liquidated from the second-order *tradition*. The point here is not simply Henri Poincaré's that "it is the scale that makes the phenomenon." Rather, it is to push the insight further. The scale is produced by a tradition with a normative function congeneric with its proper object.[24]

I say this not to endorse social constructivism disparaging the second-order tradition. It is to lasso the object-constitutive disposition of the tradition as essentially subject-constitutive or at least requiring such reflection because it is so implicated. The normative impetus is already operative, in other words, in the object-constitutive venture, whether framed according to the Enlightenment ideals of epistemology or extended to the concern with representation. A subject-constitutive approach surfaces this more, conflating the preoccupation with consciousness-raising concerning the stakes at play in agential self-possession and the responsible mediation of whatever the object happens to be.

Religion, first order, is changed according to the strictures of analysis, second order. The distilled element that results becomes the tipping point when object summons subject and the norms matricizing the relationship.

We can compare this to the genre of study that tracks Jesus through the ages. More is learned about the ages than Jesus. Even if historical Jesus research corrects or complements the genre, another layer of normativity surfaces that resonates specifically with sensibilities regarding "what really happened" (*wie es eigentlich gewesen*). To borrow imagery from sports—the high jump—we can say that "what really happens" never clears the reality bar sans judgment, sans the normativity of a tradition thinking about traditions.

I will return to the issue of normativity in the last chapter. It remains to say how the elements covered in this chapter exemplify philosophy of religion under the suggested burden. An analytic overview of topics comparing different religious claims can be included, but that is not the primary difficult task of enecstatic awareness. Also, the conceptual limit setting of continental reflection is incorporable. However, enecstatic philosophy of religious studies offers analysis at a remove from such an emphasis as well. When discussing Asad and Geertz, we noted that each individual proffers a protective belt of hypotheses surrounding the hard core of their respective normative preferences. Geertz (let us say for convenience) essentializes the religious disposition to create an *Anknüpfungspunkt* (point of contact) for a modern audience to appreciate anthropologically the significance of religious carriers of meaning, symbols. Asad counters that such a move services theology, provided by secular, post-Enlightenment "Christian" concerns, more than anthropology, the proper methodological constraints of which, incidentally, can service historical religious communities more adequately than Geertz's (secular) theology. Enecstatic philosophy of religious studies recognizes both dispositions. Asad's anthropology "protects" the study of first-order traditions by redefining the space of religions' intelligibility. It is a cultural production of the second-order tradition interruptive of the sibling task of intentional meaning construction. Geertz, manning that sibling task, is not content to let the chips fall where they may, modern secular sensibilities be damned. He is more intentional in framing the intelligibility of religions in terms of the inheritance of wisdom (in David Ford's sense below), shaped by the tradition of the study of religion in which both he and Asad are celebrated fixtures. We can include Proudfoot, who interrupts the apologetic and evocative norms of the tradition of the phenomenological study of religion, insisting, apologetically, on the limit-setting norms of description and analysis of rule-governed religious discourse, also part of the tradition. Enecstatic philosophy of religion differentiates these pursuits, hypervigilantly aware of the difference between the normativity guiding their respective inquiries, their specific scale configuring the phenomenon.

The problem with critique that excludes this type of hypervigilance is in conflating issues unnecessarily at odds with one's methodological objectives. It boots nothing to call Geertz a theologian as one advocates for an anthropology conducive to a community inimical to theology or that happens to view theology as inherently Christian. This merely inverts the theological inclination, a special kind of negative theology, a hyper-theology disavowing itself as theology. David Ford (2010) attempts to heal this rift between theology and religious studies by redefining reflection specific to first-order traditions. Like others aiming to define theology more generally as normative discourse in the university, he offers the following as a working definition: academic theology *"seeks wisdom in relation to questions, such as those of meaning, truth, beauty and practice, which are raised by, about and between the religions and are pursued through engagement with a range of academic disciplines"* (94, his italics). I extend this to include reflection specific to the object (distilled religion) and subject (scholar, theologian, etc.) of the second-order tradition. In other words, in a concentrated enecstatic philoscphy of religious studies, discussion of first-order traditions is secondary, its proper object being the cultural production of the second-order "religion," for good or ill. The object, put still otherwise, is not dismissed because of penetrating diagnostic analyses about the Western colonizing mind, with its laundry list of pathologies, sexist, racist, and what have you. It becomes the object of a peculiar experience siphoned from methodological boundary questions. This provides as viable a canvas for reflection as extant analyses purporting to reinvent a "respectable" relationality toward first-order traditions. Other names for the latter are scholarship and religious studies.

Wisdom seeking meaning, truth, beauty, and practice is also part and parcel of the object in the second-order tradition. It is distinct from the form acquired through engagement with the range of academic disciplines, as in David Ford's academic theology. The "subject-constitutive" accent in enecstasis (1) elevates reflection concerning the subjectivities involved in that range, the normative horizon furnished by select methods, how they extend to their proper object, and (2) encourages self-reflection in the encounter, self-assessment concerning a course of action. The subjectivities involved may not be of the immediate order condoned by religious adherents or the mediate order in which scholarship takes an interest. And yet such reflection recognizes an immediacy of its own in the mediations of scholarship.[25] The object of the second-order tradition may not be that of the first or like it. Archaeological interest in Buddhist stupas may not be party to the beliefs and practices precipitating their erection. But such interest regarding the descriptive significance of stupas and what it reveals historically, or how such study merely proffers an interesting idea, is not passively incentivized either (see Schopen 1991). The normative stakes at play go far deeper, which enecstatic philosophy of religious studies prioritizes.

What all this also implies—to invoke the earlier discussion of experience—is that, while true that experience should not be appropriated wholesale from early phenomenology of religion, it would be rash to banish it tout court. Stephen S. Bush (2012) wrestled with the prospect over a decade ago, rebranding religious experience for religious studies but short of enecstatic intent. He leaves us with the "capacity to study and theorize the episodes that so many adherents report as awareness of gods, spirits, nirvana, or something else," leaving little to no room for agential self-possession, except in terms of that which is rejected: "absolutely private subjective episodes that serve as the basis for what is universal and most authentic in religiosity in general" (220).[26]

Proudfoot's advice against such a procedure is apropos only insofar as "the rhetoric of experience," to solicit Robert Sharf's rhetorical designation, is seen as the only game in town, which understandably fuels the normativity configuring prescription and description, evocation and analysis, as respectively incommensurate. Early phenomenology of religion was vulnerable in this regard, because it valorized the assumptions of this frame in pursuance of its own version of academic religious studies, one that precluded theology. The context has changed thanks to developments in culture studies and ideology critique, which provide for the rethinking that enecstatic programs represent. Subsequent chapters unpack this claim. In this chapter, I offer an example of enecstatic religious studies sparked by a context of philosophical concerns that have preoccupied scholars of religion specifically. An enecstatic appreciation of issues of fundamental methodological convictions (e.g., in anthropology) and topics of cultural significance (i.e., experience and tradition) open the door to what I believe is a viable engagement of issues of a "religious" nature, one that values the historical contingencies and leads reflective individuals in different directions, for different, sometimes understandable reasons.

Surfacing Selfhood

The subject-constitutive emphasis in enecstatic philosophy of religious studies dovetails with the interests covered in this chapter, emphasizing subjective agency in the task. It joins with the "artistic thinking" of Pierre Hadot and Alexander Nehamas, who have reinstated the ancient practice of philosophy in the academy as a way of life and art of living. The gesture is toward a pre-Cartesian appreciation of philosophical inquiry that many a post-Cartesian philosopher echo. The pioneering work of Friedrich Nietzsche and his contemporary disciple Michel Foucault are good examples. One could enlist Søren Kierkegaard and Heidegger as well. My own sense about this artistry harks back—not uncontroversially—to the transcendental tradition, managing the contemporary preoccupation with critical reflexivity, stressing, while reconfiguring, the thinking of the self now overrun by problems of representation.

Avoiding the unnecessary controversy that often manifests in philosophical name-calling ("foundationalism" evidently takes pride of place), I imagine this self in terms of a singularity, an irreducible hypertranscendental. This approach to self means to service the individual, whose individuality may be compromised and in some real sense is always under threat by an object-constitutive emphasis (see postscript). At the risk of stating the obvious, the point is to negotiate a tendency, not some intrinsic travesty. I do not need to adumbrate how often object-constitutive inquiry has come to the rescue of the self by deliberately muting the self. The negotiation of self never happens in isolation. It absolutely needs the other, the object under consideration, to literally self-transcend. How often would our concerns and cherished beliefs, ideas, norms be served by aphasia! A self closed off to the world offered by object-constitutive discourse is tragic. Indeed, this is a value of inestimable worth in academia. However, like all things, precariousness, connoted by "constitutive" in the compound term, is always present. "Constitutive," in different terms, signals an element of exclusivity of the vector in question. Because an *object*-constitutive discourse fixates on some thing, some topic (whatever the aim), the subject, elicited in subject-constitutive determination, is taken to be secondary at best. The subject may be implicated in the discourse but is parenthetical to the main objective. Subject-constitutive inquiry removes this paralysis of engagement by disengaging the subject from object-constitutive fixation, its force, its logic, its reason. The importance of the activity, in other words, presupposes that the self to be disengaged has been vanquished by a specific discourse, through no fault of the discourse itself. The subject is simply overrun by a certain kind of tunnel vision. Were the object overwhelmed in lieu of the subject, an object-constitutive focus would need to be invoked to render the situation more fluid.

What does all this mean more concretely in the context of religious studies? The fact that this area of study consists in explicit examination of the *religious* dimension at least involves issues of deep human concern. Michel Foucault may not know what faith is (Carrette 1999, 107), but his preoccupation with what Jeremy Carrette (2000) identifies as "spiritual corporality" certainly does not exclude horizons with which "faith" overlaps. I understand this to mean the intellectual, moral, religious, and political horizons of the inquirer who arbitrates an objectified relationality of concerns: text to self, politics to self, transcendence to self, alterity to self, and what have you. One would not be wrong to call it a form of personalism,[27] even if, in continuity with my programmatic aims, I prefer to stick to "enecstatic," a disposition that signals a post-Heideggerian ontic preoccupation (see chapter 1). In addition to those just mentioned, the thinking of Bernard Lonergan and what he calls self-appropriation has been particularly serviceable.[28] Self-appropriation means precisely what it says: taking possession of one's self, but in the sense of taking responsibility to engage the self as one engages and is engaged by the other, whether that other is an object or a subject. It is a decisive and uninterrupted personal act. An important outcome is to recognize that "genuine objectivity is the fruit of authentic subjectivity" (Lonergan 1972b, 292). I translate what Lonergan means by "authentic subjectivity" in a context that reflects the current nonfoundationalist climate in philosophy of religion and religious studies.

Enecstasis provides an opportunity for students to negotiate their own sensibility regarding objects that they are often (rightly) encouraged to examine dispassionately. Nevertheless, in this *epochē* of the personal, the desire to be engaged attaches to an object that disenfranchises students from self-awareness and involvement. Their voice is never really lost, of course, but it resonates as though from another room. Taking possession of it is not something students of religion think of, because the room they find themselves in invariably averts their attention. And yet the alienation is experienced deeply, often viscerally, confusedly. Enecstasis, then, disrupts certain ideological-philosophical commitments in religious studies, those whose object-constitutive presuppositions and methods marginalize a holistic and personal mediation of meaning. As such, enecstatic analysis provides a space for participants to decide for themselves how to implement the level and relevance of their engagement. A sociologist will have a different appreciation of how he is implicated in the construction of a religious phenomenon than the historian constructing religious meanings. A philosopher of religion will have to decide for herself how her understanding of mystical experience impacts and is impacted by her being-in-the-world. Theologians must do the same, but vis-à-vis the norms of their tradition and the scales of dislocation embodied in the God before whom they learn to dance.

Enecstatic philosophy of religious studies includes—and indeed, has been generated by—the issues and concerns of analytic and continental philosophies of religion. However, enecstatic philosophy of religious studies aims to bring something different to the table, the personal negotiation of one's intellectual, moral, religious, and political foundations. Philosophy of religion, religious studies, and theology provide the content and methods of such a focus, enecstasis the contemporary ability to sense their relevance in a personally appropriated subjectivity formed by academic concerns. In an age where student indifference is at an all-time high, the importance of such an exercise in the modern university is warranted. I see it in undergraduate and graduate students each time their eyes light up in the realization that they matter, that they have a voice and ought to develop it critically, that is, with a heightened sense of self-awareness.

Before developing this further, it behooves me to make one last stop en route to a direct engagement with the philosophical heritage that has charged me with my enecstatic aims. I turn to the philosophy of religion of Jacques Derrida who—it is no exaggeration to say—inspired the very heart of enecstasis in search of a constructive approach to subjectivity that has made peace with systematic reflection.

Chapter 5

Derrida's Philosophy of Religion for Religious Studies

The term enecstasis, as I have been developing it throughout this study, earmarks a post-Heideggerian tendency in philosophy that features deconstructive and constructive phases of what I call agential self-possession. In prior chapters I have accented the disposition in connection with recent developments in philosophy of religion and religious studies. Currently I wish to expand on the philosophical tradition that has contoured something of the spirit of enecstatic reflection. As a style of philosophizing, enecstasis is concerned less with a system of knowledge, the "what," than it is with an opportunity to root oneself in critical self-awareness in a world, the "how," that cares to embrace or reject this or that system. But before actually turning to the philosophical tradition more generally, I feel it necessary to begin with an instance of it in the person of Jacques Derrida, whose ideas have been referenced sporadically till now. His manner of deconstruction exemplifies enecstasis in a roundabout but very real way in terms of its basic comportment. Thus, my analysis will aim to show how Derrida's post-Heideggerian critique of religion illustrates an ethos of enecstatic involvement that the student of religion can appreciate. I look to his perhaps most important article on religion for inspiration, "Faith and Knowledge: The Two Sources of 'Religion' at the Limits of Reason Alone," published originally in 1996, and for the obvious reason that it

---

This chapter is a revision of a paper presented at DEREE—The American College of Greece, Athens, Greece, May 17, 2012.

falls in line with my search for a philosophical manner of inquiry apropos to religious studies currently.

Any discussion *about* deconstruction inevitably empties deconstruction of its power, which is tantamount to what happens when one explains a joke. However, while whimsical, deconstruction is no laughing matter. The careful reader will detect a seriousness in Derrida's effervescent style. Since my purpose is to explain Derrida's rib-tickling manner and accompanying cryptic, colossal allusions, I must resort to comparatively boorish antics.

Derrida's known for dabbling in many different areas of thought. As a philosopher of religion, I am interested in what he himself confesses is his obsession: religion. In fact, Derrida's at the forefront of a lot of contemporary thinking surrounding the "return" of religion in modern society and consequently in philosophy.[1] "Religion" is like a life force in him that impels Derrida to think its essence spontaneously in machine-like manner. In "Faith and Knowledge," Derrida recounts an exchange with a colleague while trying to figure out the theme of a conference they planned to host on an island near Naples: Capri. " 'I need,' " Derrida's colleague tells him, " 'we need a theme for this meeting in Capri.' In a whisper," Derrida writes, "yet without whispering, almost without hesitating, machine-like," Derrida blurts out: "Religion." "Why?" he asks himself.

> From where did this come to me, and yes, mechanically? . . . The response that I gave almost without hesitation . . . must have come back to me from afar, resonating from an alchemist's cavern, in whose depths the word was a precipitate. "Religion," a word dictated by who knows what or whom: by everyone perhaps, by the reading of the nightly news televised on an international network, by the everyman we believe we see, by the state of the world. . . . Today once again, today finally, today otherwise, the great question would still be religion and what some hastily call its "return." To say things in this way and to believe that one knows of what one speaks, would be to begin by no longer understanding anything at all: as though religion, the question of religion was *what succeeds in returning*, that which all of a sudden would come as a surprise to what one believes one knows: man, the earth, the world, history falling thus under the rubric of anthropology, of history or of every other form of human science or of philosophy, even of the "philosophy of religion." (Derrida 2002, 75–76)

This is not simply literary flare, although, thankfully, it includes it. Derrida stands in a long line of thinkers, "masters of suspicion," who recognize the unconscious forces at play in life that resist mastery by some isolated ego. What is intriguing is how he gives himself over to such forces in his thinking, how he allows them to take precedence in his thought over his desire to dominate them. For this reason, he does not begin his critique of religion in the typical Enlightenment fashion of, say, the four horsemen of the so-called New Atheism (Christopher Hitchens, Richard Dawkins, Sam Harris, and Daniel Dennett) and their minions, who warn of the dangers of religion, irrational as it presumably is. No, Derrida recognizes the overwhelming presence of religion in practically every manner of discourse. His quip to John Caputo at a roundtable discussion at Villanova University in 1994 is telling in this regard. Wanting to steer the conversation from philosophy and politics to theology, Caputo asks, "Can we talk a little bit about theology?" Derrida (1997, 19) responds: "We have started already, but we could continue." In other words, religion (one could include theology) is an integral feature of language itself linked to the Indo-European tradition, namely Latin. His neologism for this is "globalatinization" (*mondialatinisation*). I will return to this later.

When discussing Derrida's thoughts on religion, it is important to recognize that he does not simply think religion as a believer or theologian or scholar.[2] As a philosopher, he distills it through a kind of quasi-transcendental search, as he does with most of the things he deconstructs. As I mean to suggest in my opening remarks, religion and/or theology hold something of a special place in his thought. For example, as early as at least 1972, Derrida, in his article on "Différance" (with an "a") (1982), feels compelled to address a religious school of thought, even if it is to distinguish it from deconstruction.[3] Heidegger, you remember, did something similar when insisting that Being is not just another name for the Christian God or the *causa sui* (self-caused) of metaphysics nor is *Dasein* just another name for the *res cogitans* (thinking thing) of Descartes. What is especially interesting about Derrida's approach is how he manages to affirm and negate religion while distinguishing deconstruction from it. It is a parenthetical gloss on Heideggerian *Destruktion*, de(con)struction, but without his (Heidegger's) idiosyncratic form of what Derrida (2002, 56) calls "prophetic prefiguration."[4]

For the purposes of this discussion, I want to break it down to three categories of irreducible components that I characterize as the locus, form, and aim of Derrida's deconstruction of religion. The "irreducible" features that aspect of deconstruction indebted to phenomenology, that is, some properly basic notion that founds a system like substance, God, subject, consciousness, Being, and so on—in a word, the transcendental signified. Of course, Derrida is at pains to disengage such notions from a system, his own included. In his earlier work he is committed to tracing the contours of this tendency, "logocentrism" he calls it: a rationalistic tendency to confiscate properly basic notions in an act of self-legitimation. Empiricists, for example, do this regarding sense data; idealists do it with some privileged concept; semiologists some differential of meaning. This early preoccupation got Derrida all the bad press for which he is famous. And yet he always keeps a watchful eye over the tendency, even in deconstruction, to propose a covert program of emancipation, perhaps some relativism to free us from logocentrism. Actually, the reverse is his aim. He wants to forge a strategy that allows a discourse's properly basic notions to destabilize the discourse in question. But not only that—and this is where it gets interesting! One also performs deconstruction to render oneself vulnerable to the irreducible burden of a discourse; to keep in check one's desire to pull rank on a discourse (the logocentric focus of a discourse), which hankers the discourse itself. For years individuals thought that Derrida wanted to supplant logocentrism, when in fact he has a profound respect for it. That is why deconstruction is a duty to him. As Tyler Roberts (2004, 158, n20) writes, Derrida "affirms over and over that logocentrism and metaphysics are inevitable aspects of human discourse. The point, then, is not to see deconstruction as 'dismissing' anything but, rather as opening—over and over, for they will always close again—inevitably logocentric discourse to difference or . . . 'singularity.'" That covers the "irreducibility" factor. It is time to turn to my threefold characterization of Derrida's treatment of religion: locus, form, and aim.

Locus

By locus I mean where and how Derrida positions himself when deconstructing. The framework is always textual and linguistic. After all, he did author the provocative statement: *Il n'y a pas de hors-texte.*[5] There's no outside-text. In the case of "religion" (*religio*) this linguisticality is tied to the coincidence of speaking Latin. "For everything that touches religion in particular," he writes, "for everything that speaks 'religion,' for whoever speaks religiously or about religion," even Anglo-American, "remains Latin. *Religion* circulates in the world . . . like an *English* word that has been to Rome and taken a detour to the United States" (Derrida 2002, 66). In this way he locates our involuntary interest in religion linguistically and geopolitically to the language of the Abrahamic traditions (Judaism, Christianity, Islam), to the phenomenon of globalatinization, which is "essentially Christian" (67). Derrida's not excluding other traditions, of course. His point is clear: the very term "religion" points to a specific linguistic tradition that will form how we engage religion. Thus, even the most radical critiques of religion protract the religious gesture in seeking to outbid religion or other philosophies. This is an unavoidable dimension of critique. Kant did this in his "reflecting faith" which he opposed to "dogmatic faith." Strangely, despite Kant's philosophical broadside on Christianity, he winds up stating that the Christian religion is *"the only truly 'moral' religion"* (50). Voltaire, too, concluded similarly despite those, as Derrida observes, who *"sloganize Voltaire and rally behind his flag in the combat for critical modernity"* (60). Even Heidegger, for all his talk about ontology as more originary than religion or faith, *"seems unable to stop either settling accounts with Christianity or distancing himself from it—with all the more violence,"* Derrida adds, because it is hard for Heidegger to deny *"certain proto-Christian motifs"* in his ontology (51). We could multiply examples from Hegel to Nietzsche, but we would only be making the same point: in inquiry, in a critique, we are always already in complicit relationship with what we critique. Giving up this complicity means giving up the critique we are directing against this complicity.[6] Perhaps Nietzsche, despite himself, is getting at something similar when he writes in *Twilight of the Idols* ([1889] 1998, 19): "I am afraid we are not getting rid of God because we still believe in grammar."

Derrida (2002, 51) is wary of this *"infinite spiral of outbidding, a maddening instability among these 'positions.'"* He locates deconstruction instead in a place that ironically cannot be placed, a place that is not your run-of-the-mill, four-dimensional spacetime that admits of observation and conception: *Khōra* (Χώρα). Derrida gets it from Plato's *Timaeus*. Χώρα is the receptacle from which all becoming arises. The notion is controversial, which does not prevent Derrida from playing on Plato's exposition, especially the description of χώρα as a substratum of change that is neither intelligible nor sensible but a little of both.[7] Quickly, χώρα is like the forms in that it has a kind of eternity: it is neither born nor does it die; it is always there, and as such is beyond temporality; it's the presupposition of temporality. And while it cannot be perceived by the senses but only by the mind, it is *not* an intelligible object of mind, like the forms. That's why Plato says χώρα "is not a legitimate son of reason but is apprehended by a spurious or corrupted *logos*, a hybrid or bastard reasoning" (Caputo 1997a, 84).

These irreducible qualities of χώρα capture Derrida's imagination. As a consequence, he recruits χώρα as the topological metaphor of deconstruction. It suits his purposes because deconstruction is a hybrid reasoning absorbed by the heterogeneous. Taking its stand in χώρα, like the demiurge in Plato's *Timaeus*, deconstruction makes it its business to consider χώρα and the heterogeneity of all its brood. He compares it to being in a desert, which is totally opportune since the desert is an important spatial metaphor of monotheisms. It marks a place of retreat for the religious ascetic, a withdrawal to a barren wasteland in preparation for divine revelation. Χώρα is like this desert. However, as "an utterly faceless other" (59), χώρα resists the determinations of this desert, its doctrines, its teachings. The desert is one "*of the revelations and the retreats, of the lives and deaths of God, of all the figures of kenosis or of transcendence, of* religio *or of historical 'religions'*" (59), namely, the locale of all practice and thinking influenced by the beliefs and expectations of religion. As the faceless container, χώρα is, by contrast, *utterly* barren, "the desert in the desert," Derrida calls it. "*It is neither Being, nor the Good, nor God, nor Man, nor History*" (59). Χώρα resists these desert retreats (Heideggerian, Platonic, Judeo-Christian, Hegelian) as their condition of possibility. Although not mutually exclusive, keeping these two deserts separate is crucial to Derrida if we are to make any headway in a positive critique of the determinations in question, their traditions and history.

Χώρα is Derrida's retreat without remainder. This means he can "position" himself constructively, critically, in an aporia that has haunted thought since the spread of Christianity: on the one hand, you have the irresistible frame of globalatinization, a world that speaks religion, speaks Latin, and, on the other hand, you have the maddening "spiral of outbidding" philosophies symptomatic of globalatinization; they protract the religious inclination, even when resisting it. Χώρα is the interstice that locates Derrida's deconstruction. It remains to discuss it further in terms of three key concepts that sustain Derrida's *response* to the aforementioned aporia: faith, messianicity, and justice. Earlier I called this the form of his philosophy of religion.

Form

Derrida gets to the nitty-gritty of religion when he deconstructs common etymologies that equate "the essential traits of the religious" (2002, 63) with determinate or positive religion. Quickly, two competing etymologies. The first, supported by texts of Cicero, links *religio* to *relegere*, "bringing together in order to return and begin again; whence *religio*, scrupulous attention, respect, patience, even modesty, shame or piety" (73). The second, relying on early Christian authors, Lactantius (ca. 240–320) and Tertullian (ca. 160–225), links *religio* to *religare*, to obligation, to debt either between human beings or between human beings and God (73). Derrida's next move, while difficult to follow, is crucial. It inaugurates a sighting in Derrida of the χώρα between these two etymologies. It forms how Derrida disassociates faith from religion

Clues are provided by the prefix "re-" in *re-ligio*, *re-legere*, *re-ligare*. "Re-" signals an act of repetition, a *re*turn to something, a *re*statement of something, a *re*enactment, and finally, most significantly: a *re*sponse to something. Derrida ingeniously ties this to the responsibility and obligation implied in the etymologies of *religio*. He follows the lead of French Indo-European linguist Émile Benveniste, who makes the connection—in an example of religion no less—between *spondeo* (promise) and *respondeo* (response): a sworn act of faith, a promise to tell the truth.[8] For Derrida, this at bottom constitutes an act of "religion," an act of faith: a response that consists in telling the truth, a promise to tell the truth, whether what is sworn is actually true or not. This pure act of faith is and is not religious. It *is* religious in the precarious sense that you find references to this pure act in any given religion, but its form is not specifically Christian or Jewish or Muslim or Buddhist. It is *not* religious in the equally precarious sense that faith cannot be reduced to the specific beliefs of a religion. It is absolutely universal and transrational, according to Derrida; it falls in the interstice, the χώρα, between belief and knowledge. Faith, in this "pure" sense, is response to the other, a testimony without the certainty of knowledge. Here's how Derrida explains it:

> You cannot address the other, speak to the other, without an act of faith, without testimony. What are you doing when you attest to something? You address the other and ask, "believe me." Even if you are lying, even in a perjury, you are addressing the other and asking the other to trust you. This "trust

me, I am speaking to you" is of the order of faith, a faith that cannot be reduced to a theoretical statement, to determinative judgment [religious, political, juridical, anthropological, etc.]; it is the opening of the address to the other. (Derrida 1997, 22)

Recall the episode between Derrida and his colleague with which I opened, about a conference theme. Derrida's knee-jerk *response* ("Religion") was a "religious" act in this sense; it sprang from a place of pure faith. He could not quite explain the origin of his spontaneous response. He could only express the conviction that the conference should be about religion, why it should be so important today and whether it should be circumscribed by our common understandings or determined by sectarian beliefs. In fact, the way Derrida cryptically narrates his analysis (in the post-scriptum of "Faith and Knowledge") suggests that this high priest of deconstruction is purposely conducting a religious ceremony, a peculiar one, mind you, molded, necessarily, by a litany of Latin terms.[9]

I said three key concepts basically form Derrida's philosophy of religion. The first is, as I have discussed, faith as promise, as response, as addressing the other. The second and third concepts are inextricably linked in this structure of faith/promise: messianicity and justice.

Derrida argues that addressing the other implies an openness to the future, an expectation of something to-come (*a-venir*). Although not entirely clear at first, a simple reflection on what "promise" denotes provides the missing link. When you promise something, you declare that you will do a particular thing or that a particular thing will happen. Since "every speech act is fundamentally a promise" (Derrida 1997, 22), this implies a relation to the future, a desired advent of the other. Interestingly, Derrida develops the idea in his book *Specters of Marx* (1993), where he provides a reinterpretation of the tradition of the Messiah, a future deliverer in Judaism and Christianity. He introduces the term "messianic" to distinguish the structure of faith from the messianisms these traditions represent.

If the structure of faith is distinct from determinate beliefs or expectations about a future deliverer, what, then, is expected or desired in this messianic structure? Justice, in a word. Justice, which Derrida gets from Emmanuel Levinas, is all about the relation to the future, to what *is* future and thus elusive, totally other. Paradoxically, it is the advent of the future as a future that cannot be known in advance, which is why the messianic is equated with desire, the desire "to be just with justice, to respect this relation to the other as justice" (Derrida 1997, 18). This precarious relation resists the assurance that the desire to be just is the same as being just or ensuring justice. Justice is heterogeneous. As messianicity cannot be reduced to sectarian beliefs and hopes about a future state, whether inaugurated by the Messiah or the classless society, justice cannot be reduced to the law or the history of legal structures (Derrida 1997, 17–18). A simple example from Derrida makes the point concretely:

> If someone tells you "I am just," you can be sure that he or she is wrong, because being just is not a matter of theoretical determination. I cannot know that I am just. I can know that I am right. I can see that I act in agreement with norms, with the law. I stop at the red light. I am right. That is no problem. But that does not mean that I am just. To speak of justice is not a matter of knowledge. . . . A judge, if he wants to be just, cannot content himself with applying the law. He has to reinvent the law each time. If he wants to be responsible, to make a decision, he has not simply to apply the law, as a coded program, to a given case, but to reinvent in a singular situation a new just relationship. . . . That may be right or in agreement with the law, but that is not justice. Justice, if it has to do with the other, with the infinite distance of the other, is always unequal to the other, is always [finally] incalculable. (Derrida 1997, 17–18)

The messianic structure and justice, like χώρα and faith, are heterogeneous. They are traces of a singularity in our experience, in our language, that cannot be reduced to determinate forms; they are the condition of determinate forms, they point to the structure of determinate forms. Deconstruction is all about cultivating this experience. Reflection on the structure of faith implied in religion has provided Derrida with an important means of doing this, which leads me to the question why Derrida would offer such a program, such a strategy of reading, thinking. This is the third and final characterization of my overview.

Aim

Deconstruction as a 'religious" act is the desire for justice. We may give this proposition our nod of approval, but think about it for a moment:

How different is stating this from stating what prompts actions like, for example, those of Jules, God's henchman in the 1994 cult classic *Pulp Fiction*? Jules, you remember, is a thug who goes around quoting the Bible ("Ezekiel 25:17") before he picks people off in the name of a higher justice.[10] Or what about the sentiment of the fanatical friar Jorge in Umberto Eco's masterpiece *The Name of the Rose* (1980)? Jorge perpetrates crimes inside a medieval abbey to protect Aristotle's legendary "lost" treatise on laughter. He defends his actions, like Jules, in the name of a higher justice responsible for the values of Christian civilization supposedly threatened by the discovery of this lost treatise. Derrida himself adds to the list when he describes "new 'wars of religion' . . . and military 'interventions,' led by the Judaeo-Christian West in the name of the best causes (of international law, democracy, the sovereignty of peoples, of nations or of states, even of humanitarian imperatives)" (2002, 63)—all of which prompts his own interest in the return of religion. In other words, is "the desire for justice" in deconstruction essentially any different from the desire that perpetrates well-meaning but unjust activity? Is it exempt from the logic that can lead to activity we would agree is unjust? No, of course not! There is no escaping the possibility, which is why Derrida makes the case for a deconstructive "religiosity."

Is it any wonder, then, that Derrida identifies religion as a discourse on salvation with respect to oneself and what is holy or sacred, that is, "*the safe and sound, the unscathed . . . the immune*" (2002, 42)? In the same breath he connects salvation with evil, in the sense of redemption from evil, "radical evil" even, "*which seems to mark our time as no other*" (43).[11] Given that for Derrida all positive discourse is a sworn act of faith, a "promise to tell the truth—and to already have told it!—in the very act of promising" (67), every discourse is implicated in a process of immunity: immunity from some detected threat because of what is believed to be holy or sacred, something safe and sound, something unscathed. Philosophy, politics, jurisprudence, and so on, are as susceptible to this as religion. The necessity is demonstrated by the mutual outbidding mentioned earlier (Kant, Voltaire, Heidegger, Nietzsche, etc.), a predicament, incidentally, Derrida is not very hopeful can be transcended. Vigilance—hypervigilance, even—is required.

However, none of this suggests that immunity is a bad thing. As in biology, discursive immunity has a very positive function necessary for development and growth. It defends a system against foreign objects that stunt growth and lead to the demise of an otherwise healthy system. Just a moment's reflection reveals the benefits of, for example, Greek philosophy, Christianity, Kantian thought, Marxist thought, liberal democracy, and so on. But also, as in biology, an immune system can be overproductive, "protecting itself against its self-protection" (80, n27). This mechanism, known as autoimmunity, marks the self-destruction of the immune system. Derrida imagines discourse to be hardwired this way, the universal structure of faith, of the promise, no less. "The auto-immunitary haunts the community and its system of immunitary survival like the hyperbole of its own possibility. Nothing in *common*, nothing immune, safe and sound, *heilig* and holy, nothing unscathed in the most autonomous living present without a risk of auto-immunity" (82).

I have already provided examples of discursive immunity (i.e., the outbidding philosophies discussed earlier). The examples of Jules and Jorge exemplify autoimmunity in specifically politico-religious terms.[12] They embody a rationale produced, appropriately enough, by two warring principles: "the absolute respect of **life**, the 'Thou shalt not kill,'" on the one hand, and the requirement of "sacrificial vocation" on the other hand (86). You find both in the monotheistic traditions and arguably in every (religious) tradition. The sacrificial vocation comes in forms that range from ecology: the disruption of nature, "large-scale breeding and slaughtering, in the fishing or hunting industries, in animal experimentation," to human sacrifice. Obvious examples of the latter include the famous witch hunts of the past and the suicide bombings of the present. "It always involves sacrifice of the living . . ." (86). The logic functions based on a simple mechanical principle: "life has absolute value only if it is worth *more than life*" (87). Thus, "sacrificial" behavior at odds with the absolute respect of life can be justified, made just, by a life believed to possess more value than life, something more absolute than absolute respect, that is, the holy, the safe and sound, the unscathed. This kind of qualification simultaneously protects and destroys. Derrida says that it is "what opens the space of death . . . ," the "death-drive . . . silently at work in every community . . . its heritage . . . its tradition" (87).

This mechanism, this contingency, is at the heart of all discourse, all faith, Derrida's included. He calls it the possibility of radical evil without which, paradoxically, nothing good could be done or done well.[13] If readers are detecting indictment and endorsement at the same time, they are detecting correctly. This is the "great risk" of communication. "Otherwise," writes Derrida, "that of which [radical evil] is the chance would not be faith but rather programme or proof, predictability or providence, pure knowledge and pure know-how, which is to say the annulment of the future" (2002, 83), death. There is no immunity from this, and deconstruction is certainly no silver bullet. It functions, rather, as an immunosuppressant, alerting us to what we *naturally* suppress in our self-protection. It does not pretend to alter the unalterable, namely that which comes naturally to us, but exposes us to alternative possibilities at any given moment. That is why deconstruction is a task and not a method per se. What deconstruction advocates does not come naturally to us since deconstruction threatens "everything within us that desires a kingdom" (Derrida 1982, 22), the desire for justice no less. *In fidem. A fide. Ita nobis Deus!*

The Specter of Deconstruction in Enecstatic Philosophy of Religious Studies

As a philosopher of religion who teaches in a religious studies environment, my interest in Derrida is not limited to his otherwise intriguing reflections on religion as a philosopher. I find his philosophy timely, not only for how it addresses the specific issues and concerns of the philosophical community. Derrida's contribution to continental philosophy and so-called postmodernity is established and needs no argument from me. (Gone are the days when his thought would inspire uprisings like in 1992, when a band of philosophers attempted to stop Cambridge University from granting Derrida an honorary doctorate.) Particularly promising is how Derrida's philosophy encourages students and scholars of religion to engage in their subject matter more personally and without sacrificing the descriptive task of their specialty. The scope of religious studies has become so culturally diverse and specialized that "the religious dimension itself," whatever we imagine that to be, has become contentious, if not largely irrelevant to some. Students have become very proficient in analyzing disparate cultures, their practices and beliefs, but are at a loss when pushed for a little self-awareness, namely how they are implicated in the study of the religious dimension. And this is the case, not only when considering their role in constructing an object like religion (orientalism) but also as participants in the human community.

It is quite understandable why this should happen. Religious studies has fought long and hard to sever ties with theology or anything that smacks of it. Comparing it to a messy or failed marriage is not a stretch: it makes every effort to avoid contact with the estranged partner. Rather than embrace the scholar's role as construing culture, and not simply observing it, scholars of religion interested in questions of theory and method resort to arguments for neutrality and objectivity—daring to call itself "postmodern" or "poststructuralist." (I actually consider it to be hypermodern.) While there are benefits to this, when cut off from the personal, it ostracizes students who desire some self-conscious, self-critical agency.[14]

Derrida's philosophy of religion is at the interstice of scholarly inquiry (religious studies) and determinate religious reflection (theology). It does not encroach upon either discipline. It positions a controversy, invites us to engage critically and self-critically in our cultural productions, and to do this without simply outbidding one another in an agonistic of self-legitimacy. Deconstructive philosophy of religion is part of a development in current philosophy of religion that sees religious discourse not simply as self-authorizing and ideological, which causes many in religious studies to categorically exclude the personal from a study of religion. Rather, deconstruction reintroduces the personal vis-à-vis religion by a disruptive logic with both positive and negative moments. It is positive in that deconstruction disrupts accepted norms and meanings, providing a space for new understanding and hence self-realization through personal engagement of extant cultural forms. The messianic and Derrida's notion of the universal culture of faith are just a couple of examples. This kind of disruptive engagement is negative in the sense that iteration is the focus and not simply reiteration of determinate religious beliefs. It does not simply affirm religion in this or that form. It is a strategy that potentially complements traditional religious discourse, which has taken off in the past decade or so.

In an explicitly enecstatic form of philosophy of religion, deconstruction contributes to a disposition desperately needed in religious studies. It offers courage to walk the plank of descriptive and normative engagement amid an open sea of understanding. Derrida's deconstruction contributes to the cultivation of critical self-awareness and personal involvement in a post-Cartesian environment of academic vigilance. Enecstasis may not be an explicit preoccupation, but it is an important presupposition in deconstruction. In the next series of chapters, I consider some explicit treatments in the heritage of transcendental philosophy whose problematization has informed my configuration.

Part III

The Heritage and Modus Operandi of Enecstasis

Chapter 6

Theorizing Religion Enecstatically

The Transcendental Gesture in a New Key

The phrase "enecstatic theorizing" seems like an oxymoron. Theory typically attaches to disengaged analysis while enecstasis, a highly reflective activity, is at the same time highly personal. In arguing for their close proximity, I imagine *theoria*, not in the modern sense of impersonal objectivity, but rather in the Aristotelian sense of a life of contemplation (*bios theoretikos*)—a way of life that overcomes the subjectively disenfranchised ideal of neutral knowledge. By attaching "religion" to the phrase "enecstatic theorizing," I am also alluding to the disposition, rooted in early Greek thought, that the life of the intellect may be seen as "a participation in the divine way of life"; as "the actualization of the divine in the human," requiring not only "inner transformation and personal *askesis*" but also the transformation of thought based on this interiorly differentiated apprehension and concern (Davidson 1995, 29). Enecstasis, like Pierre Hadot's *théorétique vie*, is "not a pure abstraction, but a life of the intellect, which, no doubt, can use a theoretical discourse [*discours théorique*], but nonetheless remains a life and a praxis, and which can even make room for a nondiscursive activity of thought, when it is a question of perceiving indivisible objects and God himself by noetic intuition" (Hadot as quoted in Davidson 1995, 29).

An earlier version of this chapter was presented at the 27th Annual Fallon Memorial Lonergan Symposium, West Coast Method Institute, Loyola Marymount University, Los Angeles, California, 2012.

Without quibbling over what "noetic intuition" is, we can at least acknowledge Hadot's sentiment that while (for the sake of argument) the religious dimension may not be integral to *theoria*, there is no reason to render it inadmissible except for biases of *théorique* that *théorétique* seeks to disarm. Moreover, the form of *theoria* in this chapter manages current developments that have passed through the sieve of the transcendental tradition. One individual in particular interests me: Charles E. Winquist (1944–2002). His theorizing of religion has impacted many of the philosophers of religion featured in this book. If it is a testament to the perspicacity of St. Augustine that the *Philosophical Investigations* (1953) of Wittgenstein commences with him, surely the same can be said about Winquist being memorialized at the outset of Gabriel Vahanian's *Praise of the Secular* (2008). My own interest in Winquist centers on this influence as well as his perceived relevance to issues in post-Heideggerian thought. I see him as an important bridge between the current climate in philosophy and the programmatic *théorétique* of a remote thinker in the field, a theologian by trade, whom Winquist numbers among his formative influences: Bernard Lonergan (1904–1984).

Whereas Winquist looks to Lonergan (among others) to redirect Kant's notion of the transcendental imagination for "desiring theology," I look to Lonergan to redirect Winquist's "emblematic vocable" (Vahanian 2008, viii)—desire qua desire—for philosophy of religious studies. Winquist's critical appreciation of Lonergan speaks to the potential of the transcendental gesture that has undergone a deconstructive baptism by fire. While I subject Winquist's critique to critique, his restatement nevertheless provides for the conviction that something approximating the *summum bonum* of Lonergan's transcendental method, the *théorétique* of self-appropriation, still holds promise for scholarship today. This is the rationale for my proposal of an enecstatic theorizing whose figuration takes shape here to base the claims of the two closing chapters. But first, a ghost story.

The Ghost of Transcendental Philosophy

Ghosts are everywhere and so are their exorcists. The specter haunting Europe survived, according to Marx and Engels, the exorcism of a "holy alliance." Derrida (1994), in our own day, writes that the specter of Marx continues to survive despite the demise of communism in the wake of the

Western triumphalist ideal of liberal democracy. While interesting, this specific ghost story is not my concern; the survival of ghosts is! And my ghost story extends further back, to the incantations of Kant that Marx may be seen as reversing in the company of what we might be forgiven to identify as an "unholy alliance." The specter, obviously, is transcendental philosophy, and it has survived in one form or another the exorcisms of the Marxian alliance and, more recently, the incantations of the postmodern anti-priest. The transcendental procedure fell into disrepute, to embellish J. Aaron Simmons's (2011, 118–119) recent retelling, because it led to totalistic notions such as the "transcendental unity of apperception," the idealist fantasy of the "absolute ego," and the phenomenological narcotic of "pure consciousness." And as if that were not enough, Simmons adds in parenthesis, "philosophical and theological arrogance" that can lead, in turn, to political violence.

Enter Nietzsche, Heidegger, and Wittgenstein. Their particular expellant discourses are said to have leveled transcendental accounts, rendering them inoperative in much of contemporary continental philosophy. If one turns to French poststructuralism, the disenchantment becomes even more profound with the intricacies of the discourse being nothing short of mind-numbing. And yet the specter of "conditions of possibility" looms large. It animates this dialectic much like Hegel's Absolute Spirit animates history. Nor can Kant claim sole rights to this aprioristic search any more than individual authors can over their work. If, as Ricoeur reminds us, "to read a book is to consider its author as already dead," rendering the relation to the book complete and intact, then one could argue that to read the transcendental project is to consider it free of its author's particular form. "Simply put, the transcendental method is not necessarily linked to the Kantian metaphysics in which it was first given shape" (Simmons 2011, 119). Although I cannot make the case that this represents the going consensus, it is a view I find compelling and generally sound.

The Transcendental Gesture Reassessed: Charles E. Winquist

Charles E. Winquist, an important figure for us in more ways than one, has been making this case for some time now. What interests me about Winquist is how he has done this with a sympathetic eye on the shifting foci of postmodern theory unencumbered by its "sham solution to an unresolved set of experiential problems" (Winquist 1995, 21). The Husserlian preoccupation with descriptive phenomenology that "gave Continental philosophers a license to continue to gather experiences in a signifying play discerning and thematizing patterns of meaning within that play" (Winquist 1995, 21–22); the Heideggerian preoccupation with ontological difference that "transformed the frustration of an epistemological separation from things-in-themselves into the despair of a separation from Being" (Winquist 1995, 24); the Nietzschean, Marxian, and Freudian preoccupations with the fluctuating forces of "distortion, disguise, and deceit" decentering the "matrix of consciousness" (Winquist 1995, 28–29)—in all these approaches "the similarity with Kant is the persistence of the transcendental project" (Winquist 1995, 23). And what of Foucault's fixation with the conditions of possibility of discursive formations, protracting the Nietzschean "radical troping of truth" (Winquist 1995, 31)?[1] What of Levinas's concern with the conditions of possibility of morality as an existential reality, a procedure that moves *"from the experience of totality back to a situation* where totality breaks up, a situation that *conditions the totality itself"* (Levinas as quoted in Simmons 2011, 119, emphasis his)? Or even Derrida's quasi-transcendental insistence on the exigence of thinking the impossible made possible through deconstructive humility and affirmation? Yes, even in these instances a "transcendental interrogation of thinking" is, dare I say, present.

Winquist is able to see this because of his investment in the importance and quandary of experience that he inherits from Kant, a quandary to which no "obvious solution" (1995, 20) exists: knowledge independent of experience that is nonetheless thoroughly enmeshed in experience (1995, 19). The twists and turns that take place after Kant, concerned with meaning rather than reality (hence the preoccupation with aesthetics, literature, the visual arts rather than empiricist, idealist, phenomenological epistemologies), espouse "heterology rather than unity in ordering experience" (Winquist 1995, 29). Still, while this accent on the discontinuities in experience pertains to the "changing surfaces of the phenomenal world," the concern continues to be with experience, what Winquist calls the "phenomenality of experience," specifically the "rules that in any specific situation regulate the differential play of appearances" (1995, 25). Failure to recognize this constitutive role of experience arises on account of equating experience with "a construct of subjectivity that values a vision of the world exhausted in reasonableness" (Winquist 1995, 21). Thus, antagonists of the hermeneutics of suspicion, both classical and contemporary, cannot but view the latter as offering "nihilistic augmentations to the Kantian problematic" (Winquist 1995, 21). On the other hand, protagonists, bent on a diagnostic of the unconscious forces constructing the phenomenal world, charge that the former merely extend the pipe dream of Cartesian rationalism. Against both extremes Winquist warns that "[a] loss of interest and the waning of a sense of importance in experience seem more nihilistic and a greater danger than the drift of subjectivity into ambiguities and indeterminacies. That the world may be more complicated than its Cartesian reconstruction is a relief and a hope. Depth, reality, and importance reside in the complications of experience" (1995, 21).

Winquist, it is true, inherits this appreciation of experience from Kant, which he sees as the fulcrum of contemporary quests for meaning. However, were it not for the lens provided by Bernard Lonergan, I doubt the intelligibility of experience would have assumed the shape and permanence it does in Winquist's thought. Nor is the observation pedestrian, if a conversation I once had with John D. Caputo has any bearing. Caputo, Winquist's now-retired successor at Syracuse University, expressed great astonishment at Lonergan's far-reaching influence on Winquist. It must have seemed "wild conjecture" only a few years earlier to involve Lonergan in "serious dialogue" over postmodern themes as Caputo faced off with James Marsh and Merold Westphal on modernity and its discontents (Marsh, Caputo, and Westphal 1992). I certainly do not mean to suggest that Caputo, as a result, would enlist Lonergan among the "luminaries in postmodern theology." His intrigue, rather, thanks to Winquist, consists primarily in Lonergan's conception of the "desire to know" grounded in a dynamism of intelligence whose term is God. This complements Caputo's own postmodern resistance to ideologies and reductionisms that embrace "simple and straightforward" connotations of the death of God, which he understands to be the death of desire, the death of questioning, "God being the name of what we desire" (Caputo 2004, viii). Nevertheless, Caputo would continue to fault Lonergan for an excessive intellectualism, couching it in the terms of Winquist, who evidently faults Lonergan "for attaching an ontological reference to the word 'God'" (2004, ix). Winquist's (2003) specific complaint, however, is that Lonergan confuses "the act of knowing with the content of knowing," which presumably comes as a result of "limiting himself to intellectual patterns of experience" (33). It's a "dialectical illusion," Winquist asserts, to which Lonergan naturally succumbs because "he overestimates the power of reason and improperly extends its use to the realm of transcendent being" (Winquist 2003, 32).

What this amounts to, for Winquist, is Lonergan limiting the broader perspective of being through an intellectualist reduction of ontological inquiry to objective and subjective poles of metaphysics, with Lonergan's preference in the order of inquiry being the subjective pole. And yet this reduction of ontological considerations to objective and subjective poles, Winquist suggests, is symptomatic of an overextended intellectual pattern of experience. While Lonergan acknowledges "the pluralistic dimensions of meaning resident within our experience," his actual practice, "limited to intellectual patterns," does not allow one to probe "below the separation between subject and object" (Winquist 2003, 34). Winquist wants to retain Lonergan's phenomenology of consciousness, with the basic importance Lonergan attributes to consciousness as experience. But one of Winquist's many desires is to subsume Lonergan's so-called epistemological considerations under ontological considerations.

Reassessing the Reassessment: Bernard Lonergan

Particularly unfortunate in Winquist's reading of Lonergan is the misleading claim that Lonergan confuses "the act of knowing with the content of knowing," which is patently false unless you understand it in the Kantian sense in which Winquist (2003) means it, that is, "making the subjective conditions of our thinking objective conditions of objects in themselves" (32). However we may feel about Winquist's complaint, it is common enough to be shrugged off as understandable. It betrays a philosophical eclecticism guided by a personal concern or research program that no one philosophy can be expected to accommodate. In any case, I am not of the opinion that the complaint is a reaction to a chimera. Lonergan's hard-won respect for intellect and rationality is clearly evident in his intentionality analysis. Is it a logocentric bias? What isn't, according to the diagnostician who came up with the term? Indeed, the desire to escape logocentrism is a symptom of logocentrism. It turns out that the otherwise laudable campaign advised by Hume needs some redirecting. And if all the fuss over foundationalism and critical modernity is any indication, it appears some postmoderns have missed the memo. The reconnaissance spearheaded by Derrida is literally closer to home and for that reason "infallibly dreaded by everything within us that desires a kingdom" (Derrida 1982, 22).[2] Hence the value I see in deconstruction, which is minimalist and strategic rather than alarmist or constitutive.

Without suggesting Winquist missed the memo, I do think he overstates his case against Lonergan. The historical contingencies surrounding Lonergan's transcendental method need to be considered. It may be true that Lonergan "resists any form of reductionism" in an effort "to preserve the richness of possibilities in the subjective pole of our intellectual life" and thus "resists subsuming epistemological inquiry under metaphysical methods" (Winquist 2003, 35). However, I like to think that Lonergan, if pressed, would be pragmatic about the specific form of self-appropriation. As he states, admittedly offhandedly, in a footnote in *Method in Theology* (1972b, 7, n2): "The process of self-appropriation occurs only slowly, and usually, only through the struggle *with some such book* as *Insight*" (italics added). I am not arguing for a "pragmatism" on the part of Lonergan. His attitude, rather, reflects an ancient practice that sees the self-reflective venture, what Foucault calls "practices of the self" (*practiques de soi*), as a way of life whose truths "must be lived, and constantly re-experienced" (Hadot 1995, 108). It involves taking up, "from scratch, the task of learning to read and to re-read . . . 'old truths'" (Hadot 1995, 108). If one can achieve such an end through some other means, so be it! However, the central role Lonergan attributes to the "virtually unconditioned" as intellectually apprehended and his own personal struggle with the "flight from understanding"—let alone his desire to deflect suspicions regarding his program as modernist—may explain the infrequency of such admissions.[3]

Gerard Walmsley (2008) has tackled concerns such as Winquist's through a close reading of Lonergan's notion of polymorphic consciousness, which Lonergan describes as "the one and only key to philosophy" (Lonergan [1957] 1992, 452). It is a richer analysis of what Winquist does incidentally recognize: Lonergan's important emphasis on "diverse patterns of experience." But Walmsley includes Lonergan's "levels" and "differentiations of consciousness" as integral to the patterns of experience.[4] This is a terribly crucial step lost on many because it avoids errors like Winquist's that confuse the *summum bonum* of Lonergan's phenomenological program with the particular determinations of the patterns featured in *Insight* (i.e., the intellectual, commonsensical, dramatic, and biological). In a word, it is to confuse, equate even, the self-appropriation of the polymorphic dynamism of intentional consciousness with the (determinations of the) intellectual pattern of experience. Winquist's practice of referring to Lonergan's program as "epistemological" unwittingly discloses this tendency.[5]

The magnanimous aspect of Walmsley's work is that it does not dismiss reactions such as Winquist's as chimerical: "Lonergan's own account of polymorphic consciousness is not always sufficiently developed or integrated," and "while Lonergan gives a good account of philosophical difference in the modern period, he is not able to give an account of philosophical pluralism that would address the postmodern context or culturally based differences in philosophy" (2008, 4).[6] And so Walmsley proffers that "only when all the modalities of consciousness are considered, in an integral account of polymorphic consciousness, is Lonergan's basic claim found to be convincing. Only then do we find a claim to possess a key to philosophy that is adequate to the postmodern philosophical context" (2008, 4). I join Walmsley in his basic affirmation, having articulated a version of it myself (Kanaris 1997, 2004, 2005a). Presently its validation comes indirectly through consideration of Winquist and a string of thinkers in his train. They would fain look to Lonergan for inspiration, of course. And yet traces of self-appropriation as *théorétique* haunt their work, thanks to Winquist. I turn now to this development.

Enecstasis: Reenchanting the Transcendental Gesture

Winquist's overtly epistemological retelling of the Kantian story is a distillation of Lonergan's cognitional theory.[7] It is largely guided by a theological concern about a methodological crisis of meaning that is primarily self-referential. "The crisis has occurred because we experience a distance between our way of thinking and religious experience itself. We are frustrated by not being able to explicate thematically the anomalous quality of religious experience that resists extinction in an otherwise secular world" (Winquist 1980, 47). This anomalous quality of religious experience is anomalous because of a disconnect between contemporary disruptions of meaning that form lived experience and the traditional language of objects now alien to that experience. Nietzsche's "death of God" was the initial outworking of this realization developed into a paso doble of affirmation, stubbornly, joyously, bewilderingly engaging the oncoming bull of existence. In Winquist's terms, relying on Langdon Gilkey, these objects alien to experience consist in "talk about talk of God that was sensed to be totally disrelated to life and experience" (Winquist 1980, 47). Doubtless the aspect of self-appropriation in Lonergan's philosophy is what tugs at Winquist since self-appropriation centers meaning methodologically in rational self-conscious personal experience. I have already discussed why Winquist cannot fully endorse Lonergan. Lonergan's so-called overestimation of reason in organizing "larger dimensions of meaning" is out of step with the lived experience constituted by "the literature and philosophy that have loosed the irrational furies of human existence in the affirmation of life" (Winquist 2003, 32). A new modality of self-appropriation is thus suggested, one in which the virtually unconditioned is grasped according to the dictates of disruptive, artistic rather than systematic, ordered meaning.

According to Lonergan, experience, understanding, judging, and deciding are patterned biologically, aesthetically, artistically, intellectually, dramatically.[8] Four-tiered consciousness in an artistic pattern is configured differently from the *explanatory* dictates of an intellectual pattern governed by classical and statistical methods of inquiry.[9] Judgment, that constitutive level of consciousness Lonergan makes so much of, is what connects understanding and emergent reality as concurrently known. While Lonergan in principle allows that the aesthetic and the artistic are interested in making true judgments, his practice suggests that, as an endeavor unconcerned with the explanatory as such, the artistic pattern is unqualified to judge the truth or falsity of explanations. The assumption is fine, of course, if the issue is judging the explanatory import of, say, a scientific theory governed by the intellectual pattern. It becomes problematic when "slippage" occurs and the arbitration of truth and falsity equates with a general pattern (in this particular case, the intellectual) whose contours are defined by and reserved to a specific manner of inquiry, that is, the scientific and the logical. It is here where Lonergan's preference of explanatory knowledge is, to put it diplomatically, a personal choice whose extrapolation to the universal raises flags when negotiating his phenomenological insights in the context of poststructuralism. This is also why I invoke Walmsley as a corrective to Winquist, who, as noted, recognizes that "Lonergan's own account of polymorphic consciousness is not always sufficiently developed or integrated" and that "while Lonergan gives a good account of philosophical difference in the modern period, he is not able to give an account of philosophical pluralism that would address the postmodern context or culturally based differences in philosophy" (2008, 4).

In my estimation, this is a crucial juncture in the discussion of Lonergan's philosophy vis-a-vis poststructuralist insights. The aforementioned is the problematic logocentric (intellectualist) element in Lonergan's system. When foregrounded it tends to barricade a comprehensive negotiation of so-called postmodern concerns. Walmsley detects this, too, when he states, "Only when all the modalities of consciousness are considered, in *an integral account* of polymorphic consciousness, is Lonergan's basic claim found to be convincing. Only then do we find a claim to possess a key to philosophy that is adequate to the postmodern philosophical context" (2008, 4). The aim is not to substitute the aesthetic for the intellectual but to cultivate an "integral account," one that is context specific, refusing mediation rights (when it comes to truth and falsity) to the explanatory alone.

The element of the subversive in the artistic pattern is what I have been running with. For me, it is the primary configuration of judgment in the artistic pattern. It need not constantly disrupt the flow of attention in the intellectual pattern. But it can provide a constructive means by which to displace and/or negotiate, ex parte, classifications of explanation, which can be self-authorizing. In the context of the current discussion, I connect the artistic pattern with a wave of thinking that combines Derridean deconstruction and Levinasian ethics with Winquist's transcendental search for theological epiphanies formed and rooted in the "ambiguities and indeterminacies" of our times.[10] It subscribes to a "religious theorizing" that subverts the ever-present danger of its own discourse as self-authorizing and what it takes to be the exclusionary, stogy conceptions of theories of religion exemplified in religious studies, that is, *disengaged*, naturalistic analysis of the religious *object*.[11]

Winquist's formative role in this development is tokenized in an epigraph in a fairly recent article by one of the movement's key players. The epigraph features Winquist's postmodern transcendental "personalist" theology: "A postmodern theology is not defined by the object of its inquiry. It is a textual production in which the author is written into the work as a theologian by implicating the text in the exigencies of the unrestricted scope of theological inquiry" (Winquist as quoted in Taylor 2005, 1). What we have here is a form of the "unrestricted desire" to be (in love) matted to Nietzschean critiques of religion, which contain resources for reimagining religion. According to Tyler Roberts (an important figure in this form of religious theorizing), these resources constitute the affirmative dimension of Nietzsche's work that refrains from "casting traditions and spiritual virtuosos commonly called 'religious' in terms of belief in God or gods, or in terms of faith in the ultimate salvation of the individual beyond his or her worldly, temporal life" (1998, 11–12). It is a peculiar form of faith, Roberts continues, that "cultivates the passionate, eternal affirmation *in* and of this life through a certain—both critical and affirmative—*practice* of the limit of the human" (Roberts 1998, 12, emphasis mine).

It is no wonder that Nietzsche respected Buddhism, a tradition Lonergan understands to emphasize *nontheistic* (i.e., nonpersonalistic) unobjectified mystical *experience*—practice, to use Roberts's expression. However, resources exist, too, in so-called Western apophatic traditions that similarly disrupt theistic objectifications that Lonergan characterizes as germane to a personalistic orientation (Gregson 1985, 70–71). This affirmative yet transgressive function of theology converges with Winquist's transcendental reading of philosophic "'heterologies' associated with figures such as Nietzsche, Freud, and Heidegger" (Roberts 2004, 160). It also connects with the scholarship I have singled out that identifies with Winquist and, by association—and so unwittingly and indirectly—with self-appropriation as artistically patterned, as disruptive, openly creative being-in-love. The invitation is to "encounter singularities in our own experience," this "surplus of being, this existential exaggeration that is called being me," "not to explain or decipher singularities but . . . to open discourse to them, to interrupt or disturb ordinary ways of communicating and interacting with others and ways of 'being ourselves' in order to attend to disturbances caused by that which is ordinarily, and necessarily, excluded from consciousness or occluded by various discursive strategies" (Roberts 2004, 162). Carl Raschke (1999), whom I also view as a playing a key role in this development, describes it as a semiotic way of thinking religious semiosis "wherein the 'object' signified is neither visible nor recognizable," wherein the 'sacred' has no entitative status" (7–8). Lyotard speaks of it as the *differend*, "the speaking of the unspoken," which Raschke (1990, 674–675, 678) expropriates from highly formalized theories about mass culture ("grand hotel theory") and restores it to popular culture. Raschke (1999, 5) sees divination of the *differend* as the programmatic "counterdiscourse" of theorizing religion.[12]

All this stands at the basis of my many-pronged thesis. First, that the basic gesture of transcendental method is evident in radical forms of contemporary continental philosophy; second, that Lonergan's version, via the influence of Winquist, can be seen to be at the basis of an important current in this style of philosophizing qua theology and philosophy of religion; third, that theorizing religion, the brain child of the recent development that I have been tracking, specifically provides evidence of two aspects of Lonergan's notion of self-appropriation: (a) *engaged* self-critical reflexivity and—risking a configuration of terms in Lonergan that does not appear as such—(b) the *nonsystematic* process as *artistically* explicated.

Enecstasis earmarks these two aspects in deference to Heidegger. It also sounds this new key to transcendental method in deference to Lonergan and Winquist, however disparate their views. To reiterate, enecstasis, like Heidegger's ecstasis, signals a disposition of personal involvement. This covers the standing-in aspect of the term, specifically the *en* and *stasis* parts (what I have been calling "agential self-possession" in the book). The standing-out aspect, the *ek* and *stasis* parts of the term, consists in cultivating an openness toward the "other" of discourse ("singularity" of self, neighbor, God, etc.). When enecstasis appears in Heidegger's work—for example in his treatment of the *sum* of Descartes's "I think" (Heidegger [1927] 1962, 46, 122–134)—it is seen in light of his ontological aims. I let the enecstasis of Descartes's "I think" *stand* there,[13] with its there-*being* left to Heidegger, from which even he moved later in life. The creation of the term, in other words, marks a break with the early and late Heidegger, although not a violent one. I see enecstasis, rather, in solidarity with programs of ontical reflective selfhood represented by self-appropriation and contemporary theorizing religion.

In the next chapter I trace this gesture explicitly in the context of self-appropriation, how it is indebted to Lonergan's idea but also how it differs from it. This should provide some insight into the function of enecstasis as the culmination of a development that combines the insights of the continental tradition and elements of Lonergan's philosophy into what I hope is a unique philosophy of religion, one germane to current ideas of religious studies and academic theology.

Chapter 7

Enecstatic Philosophy of Religious Studies

A Sidelong Bow to Self-Appropriation

Toward the end of his career, Lonergan poured energy into the formulation of a philosophy of religion that would unite his transcendental method with developments in religious studies. It enhanced his early philosophy of God, which his later model of religion would nip and tuck, by shifting from knowledge of God to the foundational orientation and methodological presuppositions of the religion scholar (see Kanaris 2002). The linchpin of both "philosophies of" (God and religion) continued to be his general theory of religion, outlined, for example, in chapter 4 of *Method in Theology* His philosophy of religion, however, managed a different set of concerns that continue, in my estimation, to have value for a special class of scholarship that I imagine to be philosophy of religious studies. It is this aspect that I develop in this chapter.

Two issues arise when determining the value of Lonergan's offering in this context. The first pertains to the idiosyncrasies of his philosophy of religion that are remote from the field of the same name, whether analytic or continental. Identifying why provides some perspective as to how it relates to the conversation. David Burrell (1986) offers some clues that expand on larger issues directly pertinent to my concern with philosophy

---

An earlier version of this chapter was presented at the 30th Annual Fallon Memorial Lonergan Symposium, West Coast Method Institute, Loyola Marymount University, Los Angeles, California, 2015.

of religious studies. This overlaps with the second issue. The short of it is transcendental method and the problems it poses in our age.

In chapter 6 I discussed the philosophical controversies surrounding these issues. Two of my main presuppositions are as follows: (1) transcendental method, while problematic in an environment determined by poststructuralist philosophies, is far from dead, and (2) self-appropriation, vis-à-vis an integral account of polymorphic consciousness, can create constructive opportunities to rethink the role of subjectivity in academic reflection. As I have been proposing throughout the volume, "enecstasis" is my means of doing this. It accepts the "position" in current debates while reversing the "counterposition" in the immanentist bias against subjectivity. I develop this more fully in this chapter in terms of the practical configuration of enecstasis as philosophy of religion in Lonergan's sense but in a new key, as the former chapter states it.

The Current Climate of Philosophizing in Religion

By the practical configuration of enecstasis I mean my personal engagement in self-appropriation coupled with the indirect but very real influence of Lonergan's philosophy in my work as a philosopher of religious studies. Burrell (1986, 1) recounted a similar situation over thirty years ago when he noted that "Lonergan did not have a *line* on philosophy of religion as a subject, nor do his writings give us one." Burrell offsets this admission with an equally insightful claim: "There is no better training for one exploring issues germane to philosophy of religion than the discipline of *Insight*—understood *not* as a competing theory of knowledge but as a performative document issuing an exciting if demanding invitation" (1986, 2). The vocational and contextual clarifications Burrell offers separate Lonergan, not only from the guild of philosophy of religion—of which Burrell is a card-carrying member—but also from the idiosyncratic form of philosophizing about religion germane to religious studies. It's as if Lonergan is twice removed from the environment in which I find myself as a professor of religious studies practicing philosophy of religion. And yet in Lonergan's idiosyncratic idea of philosophy of religion is a clue for a more proximate relationship.

"Philosophy of religion," Lonergan (1974, 204) states, "reveals how basic thinking relates itself to the various branches of religious studies. Thereby it offers theology an analogous model of the way it can relate itself to religious studies." Notwithstanding the fact that philosophy of religion, let alone theology, means specific things to Lonergan (see Kanaris 2002), his definition is programmatically useful in a field that has radically changed since he penned these words. I will risk a brief outline to contextualize my claim.

In religious studies there are basically two species of "philosophy of religion."[1] The negotiation tactics of one resembles the philosophizing of the analytic tradition. It combines an interest in language theory, often operationally nonrealist, with philosophies of science. A principal theme tends to be religious experience vis-à-vis controversial issues of method such as reductionism. Somewhat representative are the philosophies of the later Wittgenstein and Imre Lakatos (see Taliaferro 1998; Segal 1983; Wiebe 1984; Pals 1987; Segal and Wiebe 1989; Pals, Segal, and Wiebe 1991; Smith 1978). The other species of philosophy of religion is as eclectic, but more complex on account of a cultural upheaval in ambivalent relationship to the modern differentiation of consciousness presupposed in the analytic species. It rummages through the continental tradition for philosophical "footing" (perhaps an unfortunate metaphor to describe the postfoundational enterprise). Here poststructuralism dominates. Its manner of critique splinters into strategies of analysis rather than systematic methodologies, which nonetheless "rests in the longer philosophical tradition of epistemology" (Carrette 2010, 277). As such, poststructuralism and reliant philosophies of religion develop the critique of the Enlightenment, in its suspicion of such thinking, "by extending the critical platform of knowledge to the problem of representation" (Carrette 2010, 277). It embodies a shift of examination that moves from what Terence Hawkes (quoted in Carrette 2010, 278) terms "the object itself" to a world made up of "relationships *not things.*" Bell's inequality theorem is an example of this that comes to us from the world of science.

Poststructuralism deploys a new lexicon for this disposition. Its adherents concern themselves with how objects are framed rather than what they are purported to be. The famous and humorous umpire reference may help to communicate this point. For purposes of my analysis, I will limit the well-known skirmish to two umpires. The first umpire, obviously (naive) realist in inclination, states, "I calls 'em like I sees 'em." The second umpire, of idealist leanings, rebuts, "They ain't nothin' till I calls 'em." A poststructuralist umpire, were she present, would peer at her colleagues and say, "I sees you as you calls 'em." The preoccupation, in other words, shifts from the object to the subject, but not just any subject. The shift pertains to a peculiar manner in which subject and object relate. In the context of poststructuralism, this relationship is superintended in terms of "strategies of critique" and not proper methods per se (Carrette 2010, 282). Carrette breaks it down to ways of reading texts, exposing ideological structures, uncovering the historical formation of ideas, revealing the hidden desires, and the construction of subjectivity.

Scholars of religion with a philosophic penchant embody these strategies in their approaches as they rethink categories of language and text, religious authority, and questions of alterity involving the body and the subject (see Carrette 2010, 282–286). The discourse is politically charged, with a strong undercurrent of normative theorizing. But it is a normative theorizing, if we follow the characterizations in Carrette, that is *object-constitutive*, that is, it arbitrates an objectified relationality of concerns. The programmatic is reflexively self-critical, but as formed by the power dynamics of "object relations": text to self, politics to self, alterity to self, and vice versa. One detects a structural similarity, too, in the analytic strain of reflexivity in religious studies, where the accent falls on an empirical arbitration of theorizing and what one scholar describes as "the politics of nostalgia" (McCutcheon 1997). This opens the door, oftentimes contrary to the intentions of those embodying these dispositions, to finding analogies to theology and interpreting aspects of such reflexivity in terms of "doing religion."

Were one to press for such a correlation in religious studies, as I often do, only the broadest of terms suffice. "Academic theology" (Davaney 2002; Cooey 2002), "pluralizing theology," "Reflective Studies" (Smart 1996) have been thrown into the ring. The designation comes from those wishing to negotiate the nagging antipathy toward theology or any type of personal involvement that has been with religious studies since its inception. As a designation, I am partial to what fellow religionist Tyler Roberts (2005, 371)—featured frequently in my search for enecstatic forms of thinking—relying on the categories of Raymond Guess, calls "ideology critique." Traded in for the pejorative use of the concept ideology—which consists in "the critical task of contrasting illusion with truth"—is the more descriptive sensibility of "gaining self-consciousness about human meaning in the making" (Roberts 2005, 371). In the descriptive sense of ideology, the task of critique involves intentional cultural construction, which is simultaneously interlaced with "metaphysical," trans-empirical commitments; to put it in Lonergan's (non-Kantian) terms: intellectually patterned consciousness governed by foundational horizons (religious, moral, intellectual). The idea here is that "ideology," personal or otherwise, directs theorizing, and is not, as pejoratively thought, the false consciousness—call it what you will: the subjective, the religious, the moral, the nonobvious—which theorizing is supposed to stamp out.

Currents in religious studies, appreciative of this nuance and of developments in poststructuralism, make the case for self-critical reflexivity in an object-constitutive configuration of subjective involvement. Thus, fellow inquirers are invited to critically and constructively *participate* in the making and unmaking of central religious *concepts* such as God, Nirvana, Sunyata, Bhakti, Yoga, and so on (see Cooey 2002, 178–179; Smart 1996, 23). Unlike some colleagues, such currents of religion scholarship see this as a complement to the no less ideologically driven task of explaining or historicizing theology. In sympathy with these developments, I, too, am compelled to personalize self-critical reflexivity *but as subject-constitutive*, for which I quite contently blame Lonergan and others.

Self-Appropriation:
Focusing the Issue of Philosophy of Religious Studies

Ever since accepting the "demanding invitation" of self-discovery in Lonergan's "performative document," I have been unable to shake the preoccupation of being personally self-aware in academic inquiry. The invitation is issued in *Insight: A Study of Human Understanding*—Lonergan's magnum opus—as a process of identifying one's own rational self-consciousness through a personal appropriation and objectification of that "structure" which opens out into a concrete universe of being, "the to-be-known toward which that process heads" (Lonergan [1957] 1992, 398). By distinguishing what Burrell calls the "discipline of *Insight*" from its other features, I have followed Burrell's lead in viewing Lonergan's relevance to philosophy in religious studies as fundamentally indirect. And yet the structure of Lonergan's definition has influenced me directly in forging a contemporary vision that is quite literally philosophy of religious studies.

Recall Lonergan's (1974, 204) definition: "Philosophy of religion reveals how basic thinking relates to the various branches of religious studies. Thereby it offers theology an analogous model of the way it can relate itself to religious studies." What this can mean in light of my earlier outline is how normative "basic thinking"—which is subject-constitutive, performative, and indirectly relevant—relates to the normative theorizing in religious studies, which is, for the most part, object-constitutive, relational, and increasingly highly political. The quality of the personal dimension of the task also divides according to the type of "self-consciousness" gained about human meaning in the making, that is, the type of ideology critique involved. Such an understanding disentangles the significance of self-appropriation from the contingencies surrounding Lonergan's objectification, contingencies, incidentally, that are problematic and of a delicate nature in the ether of religious studies today.[2] While I am not personally scandalized by these contingencies, which boil down to the language and times of Lonergan's project, I have found the "shortcut" I am proposing to be productive in my pedagogy and research in religious studies.

The *indirect* but paramount relevance of Lonergan's work to what I am calling philosophy of religious studies is, of course, the actual practice of self-appropriation "through a struggle with some such book as *Insight*" (Lonergan 1972b, 7, n2)—that is, *Insight* ideally read together with other such works. Here, the personal and irreducible "private practice" of self-discovery is properly basic and ongoing as one intimately faces the human condition of the "flight from understanding" (Lonergan [1957] 1992, 9). The *direct* relevance of that normative task is nonetheless a *mediating* act. It transposes the accent in self-appropriation, which highlights the presence of self to self, in terms apposite to the context and primary difficult concerns of the field in question. In religious studies, as I mentioned earlier, the scaffolding of poststructuralism is prominent. For this reason, I have settled on a term that fleshes out the postfoundational character of personal involvement qua critical self-reflexivity, that is, what Lonergan calls the "positional" in the largely "counterpositional" resistance to the self-appropriating venture. Enecstasis is the term. It tables the counterpositional, a misfortune of timing (my earlier "contingencies") and looks instead to inculcate the transcendental precepts in a system frozen by unnecessary anxieties about subjectivity.[3]

Enecstasis, as reiterated numerous times in this volume, is reminiscent of the early Heidegger's *ekstasis*, standing in the openness of and for Being. It hooks up with the Heideggerian concern of engaged agency but moves the discussion from the ontological to the ontical. Although the Greek prepositions *en* and *ek* in *enec*stasis are congruent with Heidegger's intentions, their unprecedented combination in a proper term means to indicate a point of departure from his ontological concerns. In this way, the term also connects with the disruptive forms of thinking in poststructuralism that hark back to the "spiritual practice" of Nietzsche's philosophizing and ultimately the early Greeks (Roberts 1998; Nehamas 1998; Hadot 1995; see also chapter 2). Enecstasis attunes the subject-constitutive practice of self-appropriation to this "deconstructive" sensibility, a thematic focus of relationality that tends to be object-constitutive, for lack of a better term. The constructive aspect to it, especially as regards the reversal of the counterpositional, is finally left up to practitioners. This is what I mean earlier by 'tabling" that part of the discussion in the determinate guise of straightforward transcendental method. It remains now to outline the specific form of this enecstatic trope in connection with religious studies.

The Contours of Enecstatic Philosophy of Religious Studies

As an ontical preoccupation connecting selfhood to the science of religion and theory (see McCutcheon 1997, 192–214), enecstasis lives and breathes in a second-order discourse in religious studies that has two phases. It addresses itself to the tradition of religious studies, first vis-à-vis the discursive formation of "religion" (the history of the concept of religion), and second through a characteristically philosophical engagement of the tradition's scholarly presuppositions (its theories and methods). In the first phase the analysis focuses the discussion on a descriptive overview of the tradition that takes seriously the famous pronouncement of historian of religion Jonathan Z. Smith (1982, xi), that "religion is solely the creation of the scholar's study." In a second phase the analysis morphs into a negotiation of the ideological underpinnings of such statements. Here, the student of religion moves from an enecstatic preoccupation with the history informing her horizons to explicit "foundational" engagement with the normative claims in theorizing about that history. Put otherwise, in the self-realization occurring at the descriptive level is a latent opportunity to engage at the philosophical level or, if you prefer, the metamethodological. It consists in disrupting methodologically self-serving claims such as Smith's, which argue that, whatever else religion is, it cannot be the totally other (*tout autre*) in religious discourse. Of course, the same applies to the nemesis of scholars like Smith in the tradition, who argue conversely that religion is sui generis and elides the social scientific gaze, history, and politics.

The enecstatic in the exercise is an attention to and for the self, attendant to the object-constitutive theorizing in religion discussed earlier. At that level, it differs from Lonergan's programmatic in that it is not modeled on the laudable desire for a subject-constitutive explanatory heuristics. If, as I have argued in the past, we are looking for a near equivalent in Lonergan, it would also be subject-constitutive but as artistically patterned (see, e.g., Kanaris 2003). To cast the artistic in explanatory terms, in my estimation, is to conflate its manner of *thinking* as creative, subversive, disruptive, and whatnot, with that of the intellectual pattern, which tends to be systematic and scientific. This is the point I was making in chapter 6. That's why I prefer to keep the aims of self-appropriation in generalized empirical method separate from those in enecstatic philosophy of religion and, more specifically, philosophy of religious studies. It is also what allows me to view them as complementary. What the one should not be expected to achieve, the other may be able to supply. Conflating their different aims and methodological concerns forces a conversation, which in my experience and in a wider context is stifling and awkward.

The type of attention to self called for in enecstatic philosophy of religion is of the reflexive order that, at the empirical end of the spectrum, resigns itself to implement the methodological perspective best suited to the task in hand. If, for example, the desire is to assess the role of myth as an occasion for thought concretized by religious practitioners, a phenomenological (read: Eliadean) resolution in terms of the primal truth of the myth separate from its application is bound to disappoint. As Jonathan Z. Smith (1978, 307) writes concerning the Indonesian myth of "The Coconut Girl," *Hainuwele*, "The setting of the myth is not in the 'once upon a time' but in the painful post-European 'here and now.'" At the normative end of the spectrum is attention to self through a process of critique and intentional construction. Ontologizing and thus self-authorizing our methods is the ever-present danger being disrupted here. It is one thing to say that fertility symbolism reproduces androcentric assumptions serving socially repressive functions, and quite another to say that a phenomenologically based commentary, let alone a theological one, invariably authorizes those functions. Ergo, all analysis of religion should be naturalistic, reductionistic, and historicizing (McCutcheon 1997, 40–41, 192ff.). This self-consciously descriptive ideological rhetoric masks a pejorative sense of ideology that truncates discussion of the disruptive potential of phenomenological and theological discourses (see Roberts 2004, 2005).

Enecstatic analysis consists in the personal negotiation of such standoffs. It disrupts ideological commitments in religious studies whose "foundations" marginalize a holistic and personal mediation of meaning. As such, the analysis provides a space for enecstatic participants to decide for themselves how to implement the level and relevance of their engagement. A sociologist will have a different appreciation of how he is implicated in the construction of a religious phenomenon than the historian constructing religious meanings. A philosopher of religion will have to decide for herself how her understanding of mystical experience impacts and is impacted by her being-in-the-world. Theologians must do the same but vis-à-vis the norms of their tradition and the scales of dislocation embodied in the God before whom they learn to dance.

Enecstasis and self-appropriation can coalesce at this point at a tertiary level, implied earlier in my invoking Burrell. The enecstatic intentional construction, which attends to self in object-constitutive fashion (i.e., as artistic and relational in the preceding senses), can only be aided by an attention to self in subject-constitutive involvement. Lonergan's (1972b) project of discovering and appropriating for oneself the "normative pattern of recurrent and related operations" (4) of consciousness yields a momentous opportunity to be explicit to oneself about oneself and that which qualifies as an attentive, intelligent, reasonable, and responsible intentional construction. It is a metamethodological exercise extrinsic to enecstatic philosophy of religion whose form as extrinsic is appreciated on its own terms. The constituted self that emerges as a result settles the philosophical implications of the exercise for oneself in mediating the enecstatic preoccupation in, our case, religious studies. The process, maybe even the proposal itself, may sound tenuous. However I cannot imagine *self*-appropriation without such risk. For what is this if not to pluck Lonergan's ([1957] 1992, 13) general phrases from the world of thought that informed him to set them in the pulsing flow of one's own professional life?

It has taken me a long while to learn how to perform the balancing act proposed here. It was occasioned in me through circumstance, which I expand on in the postscript. Suffice it to say here that the experience has precipitated a differentiation of consciousness that straddled disparate worlds of meaning. Toward the end of his career, Ninian Smart (1996, 24) opined that the world of religious studies needed a general theory "in the style" of classical European phenomenologists such as G. van der Leeuw (1890–1950) and Nathan Söderblom (1866–1931). Such a theory, he continues, would not be the grand theorizing of his contemporaries, which he describes as "epistemological and skeptical" (read: relativistic, postmodern), but "empirical and generalizing." Smart, thankfully, is noncommittal about the theorists he names, as the phrase "in the style of" suggests. Were he not, few in the current climate of religious studies would take him seriously. Still, his reading of "grand theory" no sooner placates the suspicion than raises a new one. This compels me to qualify Smart's otherwise commendable reference to a generalizing empirical theory but in the style of Lonergan and others glossed enecstatically.

Because the point at issue is theory, the engagement is largely philosophical. As such, Lonergan offers a philosophy of religion. Because I am concerned with the less controversial part of Lonergan's philosophy of religion, basic thinking as it relates to religious studies, I bracket his model of religion in this discussion. Lonergan offers that model *in the style of* phenomenology of religion, which exemplifies the religious pattern of experience. Such a discussion *is* in the order of generalized empirical method and self-appropriation, but as proper to theology, not ideology critique per se as discussed here (i.e., germane to postphenomenological religious studies).

Enecstasis is my means of negotiating that context focused by the tendenz of Lonergan's concerns, authentic subject-constitutive knowledge, and refurbished by "positional" elements in contemporary poststructuralism. This has yielded a programmatic apposite to religious studies that elicits a critical self-reflexivity concerning the "foundational" orientation of scholars. At a descriptive level, the normative engagement in the programmatic addresses the tradition of the science of religion, its concepts, theories, and methods, developed since the nineteenth century. This provides for the effective historical consciousness that sets the terms of relation and correlation discussed at a subsequent level of normative analysis and disrupts truncating ideological commitments.[4] The personal involvement of the analyst, the philosopher of religious studies, is the feature at both levels, levels in which self-appropriation is indirectly relevant. Self-appropriation becomes directly relevant—that is, in the autonomy of its peculiar sphere of discourse, which is a formidable undertaking in itself—when scholars of religion qua philosophers of religious studies embark on a rationally self-conscious quest of intentional construction.

The dividends of this practice far outweigh the deficit of the theory. Clearly, I want my cake and eat it too! But all kidding aside, the true test has been to see the benefits of the practice as I maneuver students and colleagues, often tacitly, through stages of analysis and to see the joy, especially in students' faces, as they discover their voice.

Chapter 8

The Normative Impetus of Enecstatic Philosophy of Religious Studies

Dialectic and Foundations

We are all quite aware that the field of religious studies approaches questions about the human condition in stark contrast to theology. We are equally aware that, as a far younger sibling, religious studies, in its desire to distinguish itself from theology, has insisted on the social-scientific and historical nature of its approach as the academic ideal. As a result, religious studies casts an intensely suspicious eye on cousin approaches such as comparative religion and phenomenology of religion, which are not ready to dispense with the humanist concern of treating religion as sui generis. Interestingly, theologians such as, for example, Karl Barth, would share in this suspicion, but for completely different reasons. Still, alternatives such as his would do little to cull support from either family member. Religious studies, it is true, did emerge from Protestant and deistic distillations of Abrahamic religion. But however much this is commemorated, it would be wide-eyed to assume that an appreciation for theological reflection attaches to this. Indeed, even classical phenomenologists of religion, far more sympathetic to theology than the wider scholarly community, were painstaking in taking a distance from theology.[2] The rush toward aca-

---

An earlier version of this chapter was presented at the 34th Annual Fallon Memorial Lonergan Symposium, West Coast Method Institute, Loyola Marymount University, Los Angeles, California, 2019.

demic legitimacy led both currents, social scientific and humanist, down different but related paths. Theology would cast a long shadow on both trajectories, suggesting—in Ray Hart's (1991, 732) terms—that theology is the bête noire within religious studies.

I mention theology here to spotlight my main theme: how a normative preoccupation in the study of religion continues to be a significant point of tension. I take an interest in this because religious studies happens to be my field, which, incidentally, can be as precarious when it comes to my own area of specialty, philosophy of religion. And although most religion scholars jettison ideas of "complete" neutrality, the tendency is still to evaluate theology and "metaphysics" as speculative and subjective.[3] This is an indication of how deep-seated the bias is. Lonergan (1972b, 276) calls it an "impenetrable wall," one that scholarship builds between the normative discourse of theology and its historical sources. This also explains why, as noted earlier, social-scientific and historicist approaches flag analyses approximating the phenomenological derogatorily, as crypto-theology and self-authorizing. It is religious discourse, according to Bruce Lincoln (2005, 8) and, unlike historical analysis, "speaks of things eternal and transcendent with an authority equally transcendent and eternal." Mircea Eliade is archetypal, the scapegoat of this "new materialist" attack. Incidentally, Lonergan, specifically his model of religious experience (outlined in chapter 4 of *Method in Theology*), would also come under fire.[4] The basic charge is that the category of religious experience, guarded by methodologically descriptive tools such as *epochē*, works to conceal and license an underlying confessional agenda (see Prus 2016, 40). Donald Wiebe, of the Toronto School of Theology, is representative. He argues that phenomenological strategies grant religious reality an ontological status impervious to scientific explanation and theory (Prus 2016, 36–41). Unlike Wiebe and Lincoln and others who follow in their trail, I do not believe the issues to be insuperable. The answer offered by Lonergan almost fifty years ago is basically correct. It consists in migrating "from a basis in theory to a basis in interiority" (Lonergan 1972b, 276).

Lonergan roots this in his transcendental method, which allows him, ultimately, to foreground a series of functional specialties that could eventually disassemble the notorious wall just mentioned. His principal objective is to refashion theology as integral to the acquisition and dissemination of composite realms of meaning in mediating and mediated phases. Insofar as a systematic exigence intrudes into the realm of common sense,[5] the mediation of objects of meaning successfully correlates with the intentionality suffusing the realm of theory. In the language of *Insight*, it moves us from a preoccupation with a description of the relation of things to us to an explanation of the relations between things themselves. The layperson communicates daily with the God of Abraham, Isaac, and Jacob. The scholar, on the other hand, wishes to ascertain the *conditio sine qua non* of this communication, that is, the historical veracity and hermeneutical significance of what provides for the experience. Both realms, that of common sense and theory, have their validity. They become truncated, however, when riveted to an exclusivist perspective that oversees their objects. Even in the happy coincidence of an object-constitutive differentiation, which mitigates the individual concerns of common sense and theory, a blind spot remains, one that obstructs a critical exigence that leads to a rounded negotiation of inherent, neglected norms or their performative contradiction. If common sense is not to devolve into common nonsense; if the mediating phase of realms of meaning is to avoid becoming a necrology of data and facts, the move to interiority, which grounds the authentic functioning of both mediating and mediated phases, is advisable.

A main preoccupation of Lonergan in *Method in Theology* is to issue an invitation to restructure the theological task along the lines of this migratory basis. What Lonergan (1972b, 83–84) calls "the transcendent exigence," which leads "beyond the realms of common sense, theory, and interiority into the realm in which God is known and loved," is proper to a full-blooded theology, as he imagines it. I wish to argue for the unpopular view that something similar may also be the case for a full-blooded study of religion, one serviced by Lonergan's philosophy of religion. The issue is rather complex, bedeviled by nomenclature about which it is important to have some clarity.

Lonergan's Philosophy of Religion

As Lonergan worked on a method in theology, he was also devising a philosophy of religion, which he understands in terms of "how basic thinking relates itself to the various branches of religious studies" (1974, 202). An important theme in basic thinking, interiority, is as pivotal to philosophy of religion as it is to theology. What it offers theology is "an analogous model of the way it can relate itself to religious studies" (Lonergan 1974, 204). What it offers religious studies (something Lonergan is not explicit about) is an analogous model of the way it can relate itself to theology.

Crucial here are the mediating and mediated phases that direct the normative reflection of interiority vectorially. Allow me to discuss this as I clear up some terminology.

By philosophy of religion Lonergan means philosophy of *religious studies*. The material components of this philosophizing are the methods and theories that religion scholars bring to bear on religious phenomena. It is these components that offer theology an analogous model for relating to religious studies—which, incidentally, Lonergan understands rather conventionally, as a discipline principally concerned with the functional specialties one finds in the mediating phase (i.e., research, interpretation, history, dialectic).

The religion scholar might describe it more broadly—disengaged analysis of religion as object, for instance—but the functional sensibility is virtually the same. Lonergan qualifies this, however, by adding the personal dimension interiority signals, "philosophy of religion" being a gloss on its dialectical character. Dialectic is all about engaging the implicit and explicit assumptions that shape methodological inquiry. Implicit in dialectic is something welcomed today in religious studies in terms of "self-critical reflexivity." Self-critical reflexivity basically connotes what the natural scientist calls the personal equation. Lonergan gives it philosophical content by identifying and formulating operations of consciousness that scale for us the worlds of meaning into which we are thrown or in which we deliberately and oftentimes tenuously participate. This kind of reflexivity pushes a self through mere being to taking possession of the self merely being; the norms, in other words, are already operative in the self, in you, in me, whether heeded, appropriated, or ignored. As they provide for their formulation in transcendental method, these norms of conscious inquiry provide for their formulation in philosophy of religion. What this means for a philosophy of religious studies is that religion scholars subject the philosophical presuppositions of their research programs to the normative constraints of consciousness, their consciousness. Pertinent questions include (among others): Do my notions of meaning, truth, objectivity, and value skew the religious reality I am mediating? To what degree do my philosophical assumptions determine (in Poincaré's terms) "the scale that makes the phenomenon"? How this approach differs from an ordinary philosophical approach can be seen by quickly comparing it to the procedure of Ninian Smart (1996), a savant of religious studies. Smart's approach, while insightful, is, dare I say, superficial by comparison. He relies on what functionally resembles commonsense rhetorical logic to trigger suspicion concerning scholarly superstructures that disturb him. Lonergan, by contrast, plumbs consciousness to surface the normative operations imminent in such superstructures, whether they are yielding cumulative and progressive results or whether they are being blocked by a variety of biases (dramatic, individual, group, and general). In Smart's approach, dialectical engagement is limited to the exposure of philosophical biases, biases one accepts only to the degree to which one shares the assumptions of the undermining rhetoric. In Lonergan, not without a rhetoric of his own,[6] a dialectically constituted philosophy of religion exposes the methodological biases that block correct anticipations about the object of religious studies, primarily by engaging the self in the conversation (Lonergan [1985] 2017, 16). Insofar as dialectic "philosophy of religion is the foundational methodology of religious studies" (Lonergan 1994, 128), scholars are encouraged to bring this level of awareness to bear on the superstructures, their own and others', informing the mediation of religious phenomena. To what degree this is done is an interesting question.

As in dialectic, the functional specialty—the point of philosophy of religion in Lonergan's sense—is to "line up opposed positions" and decide about partiality levels managing scholarly objectifications. That's it! To the extent that the activity displays implicit levels of authenticity, intellectual, moral, and religious, philosophers of and scholars in religious studies are doing their job with respect to dialectic. The migration into interiority need not, in other words, be total, which will doubtless allay the concerns of some scholars, philosophers now of religious studies, who are wary of "theological" engagement.[7] To return to my Smart example, hopefully worthy of the name. Smart's criticism of so-called relativists and reductionists displays signs of positionality, in Lonergan's sense. To the extent that Smart is involved in pointing out shortcomings of polymorphic human consciousness (Lonergan 1972b, 268), elements of conversion (better: positionality) are present, "its operation is implicit." In this way, we can suspend judgments about the underdeveloped and therefore potentially counterpositional nature of Smart's viewpoint and enlist his dialectical insights into our philosophy of religion.

I consider this the minimalist dimension of Lonergan's philosophy of religion. It complies with the conventional understanding that religious studies is predominately a mediating activity in the realm of theory. The dialectical component does indeed introduce elements of interiority that constitute Lonergan's *Destruktion* of "the wall"—it is no accident that conversion is a central theme in the "Dialectic" chapter in *Method in*

Theology. But the full functionality and implementation of interiority qua interiorly differentiated, converted consciousness, is reserved to foundations in *Method*. Still, I believe the case can be made that interiority, as foundational preoccupation—that is, as "a fully conscious decision about one's horizon, one's outlook, one's world-view ... illuminated by the manifold possibilities exhibited in dialectic" (Lonergan 1972b, 268)—attaches to the broader methodological activity of philosophy of religion, both in Lonergan's sense and my own. Philosophy of religion is, after all, "*foundational* methodology." The self it foregrounds is central to mediated "religious" meanings. In my book *Bernard Lonergan's Philosophy of Religion: From Philosophy of God to Philosophy of Religious Studies* (2002), I provide an overview of this development in terms of functions and stages of meaning, Lonergan's categories.[8] Here I simply assert the connection to dialectic and foundations, making a case for my peculiar application that deals with a different configuration of religious studies than Lonergan was familiar with.

Beyond the minimalist dialectic function, I believe Lonergan advocates—if not in word, then in practice—a philosophy of religion that manages questions surrounding the positions and counterpositions laid bare by foundations as we move into the mediated phase of interiorly differentiated, authentically subjectively centered, reconstructed religious meaning. This entails an explicit preoccupation with an "established, universally recognized criterion of proper procedure ... which aims at decreasing darkness and increasing light and keeps adding discovery to discovery" (Lonergan 1972b, 268, 270). Normative reflection does not get more explicit than this! For this reason, I think it is prudent to designate the minimalist function of Lonergan's philosophy of religion as "philosophy of religious studies" and to reserve the term "philosophy of religion" to all the elements in his thinking, including philosophy of religious studies, which overlap with themes in religion and in which foundational preoccupation comes to a head. Lonergan later came to see this regarding general transcendent knowledge, to which we can also append, in his philosophy of religion (in our broad sense), special transcendent knowledge and his model of religious experience. These are explicitations of Lonergan's intellectual, moral, and religious foundations, apropos, as philosophy of religion, to normative discourses as philosophical theology and certain forms of phenomenology of religion. They are broached by the individual intentionally constructing meaning and not merely mediating it. To put it in the terms of parts 1 and 2, foundations extends the reach of dialectic in the "spiritual practice" of the second-order tradition to a plane of personal negotiation of mediated meaning.

To bring Smart back into the conversation, Lonergan's philosophy of religion (broad sense) would press Smart (1996, 16) on the issue of conjoining dialectic procedure with what he (Smart) calls Extended Religious Studies, Extended Theology, and so forth—"extended" because it does more than conventional science of religion and confessional theologies. Extended Religious Studies or Extended Theology is "philosophy plus the religions . . . competing in truth and value" (Smart 1996, 16). If proposals such as Smart's are to avoid confusing the role proper to mediated meanings, furnished by critical and transcendent exigences, with the role proper to mediating meaning furnished by a systematic exigence, more is needed, much more, than an object-constitutive rhetorical logic for what is, operationally, a subject-constitutive task. As my younger self likes to say, Smart's Extended Religious Studies "doesn't cut it"! But will an explicit preoccupation with an "established, universally recognized criterion of proper procedure" supply what is needed? People are not exactly lining up for it. Not that they ever did, of course, but the reasons for continued disinterest are even more subtle now. I need not rehearse them here. I will simply state how I imagine a way forward in deference to what James Marsh (2014, 3–12) calls "Lonergan's pearl of great price."

When the anvil of Lonergan's philosophy of religion (broad sense) fell on the science of religion, the principal objectives of studying religion boiled down to polemics between academic approaches fixated on impartial mediation of a cultural object. It reflected what to many religion scholars was the hard-won separation of scientific study from theological reflection. There was no going back! The appearance of phenomenology of religion made some inroads, but its empathetic treatment of religion as religious unfurled sails that would direct the academic vessel in different directions. The foci of analysis changed as critiques of structured mediations preempted examination of the object "religion." In structuralism and poststructuralism—the winds in these sails—"the world is made up of *relationships, not things*" (Hawkes as quoted in Carrette 2010, 278, emphasis his). What matters, in other words, are the frameworks of representation (*Vertreten*)—how, for example, religion(s) is represented rather than what religion is. In the context of discourse analysis, deconstruction, psycholinguistics, and what have you, it is "to suspend the structures we construct to critique the structures we despise as constructions" (Carrette 2010, 287). This is not relativistic gobbledygook. It develops, in the words of Jeremy Carrette (2010, 277), the "critique of the Enlightenment—even in its suspicion of such thinking—by extending the critical platform of knowledge to the problem of representation. It arguably rests in the longer philosophical tradition of epistemology."

Lonergan anticipated this shift, captured in his phrase "the end of the age of innocence" ([1985] 2017, 151), but his critical realism—configured to take "things" more seriously through a proper grasp of what it means to grasp the virtually unconditioned, to endorse, if you will, a structure to critique a despised structure—does not elicit the interest I believe it deserves. Still, my aim is not to recapitulate his diagnostic but to clear a way for it, to provide, more specifically, a propaedeutic in my field that loosens the grip of a certain reception history of poststructuralism—new materialism. The work of figures such as Steven Katz and J. Z. Smith gave it momentum. They also gave it a platform for categorical elimination of "religious thinking" from religion scholarship.[9] The two, in their estimation, are to be kept separate since religious thinking is, presumably, not cognitive, scientific, and critical but existential, humanist, and ideological (see Wiebe 1991, 2000). This is not *functionally* counterpositional per se. But it is dialectically problematic, especially in its assumption that interiority concerns are or should be absent in the mediating phase. For that reason, it *is* counterpositional in the partner assumption that, contrary to what it holds, mediating meaning is a view from nowhere. Thus, dialectic becomes confused with foundations where mediated meaning, the new materialist's, hijacks foundations (ill-conceived to be sure) for an exclusivist mediating phase. If "genuine objectivity is the fruit of authentic subjectivity" (Lonergan 1972b, 292, 265), the produce here is overripe.

This desire to fence off objectivity is complex, not least because of supporting poststructuralist philosophies. It is also ironic given new materialists advocate self-critical reflexivity. And yet the expropriation of foundations for mediating purposes makes perfect sense when one considers that their posture is object-constitutive—and, incidentally, not in the best possible sense. Religion scholar Ivan Strenski (2006, 340) suggests this when he calls out Russell McCutcheon for his "naturalist metaphysics" that he (McCutcheon) links to his "naturalist approach to religion." In the second edition of *Understanding Theories of Religion: An Historical Introduction to Theories of Religion*, Strenski (2015, 244–245) is even clearer in his rebuke by identifying McCutcheon's foundational metaphysics as nothing more than mere "thinking *about* religion." Strenski's alternative, however, "thinking *with* religion," is, unfortunately, no less object-constitutive, wary as Strenski (2006, 340) is of any "metaphysical foundation, supernaturalist *or* naturalist . . . for doing the study of religion."[10]

Enecstatic Philosophy of Religious Studies

What we are faced with is a combination of issues configured in a variety of ways that reacts to a category, that of "subjectivity." On the one side is the poststructuralist or postmodern rejection of that category as "too compromised by the modern ideals of autonomy and disembodied consciousness" (see Roberts 2013, 103). The other side of this ethos is "an antihumanism that declares the death of the subject." Enecstasis is my "X" that "marks the spot,' my *khōra* that strategically locates a subject-constitutive discourse designed for the current critical platform of representation. It cloaks interiority concerns such as Lonergan's, accenting intellectual, aesthetic, and mystical motifs with specific permutations determined by personal interest and the interest of others (see Morelli 2015, 170–309). What enecstasis spotlights is participant awareness, the importance of owning the singularity of one's own irreducible voice (*parole*) notwithstanding the constitutive role of language (*largue*).[11] That is why I turned to Heidegger when searching for a portal into the Being of this world. His appreciation of the all-pervasive role of language, which provides for the basic presupposition of the critique of subjectivity, is second to none, bar Derrida. And yet the way language transmits the call of Being in Heidegger's *Destruktion* of the scientific *Subjectum* can still manage a concern like the care of ecstatic *Dasein*, "standing in" in the openness of Being, "of enduring and *out*-standing this standing-in (care)" (Heidegger [1949] 1992, 255, italics mine). The *en* of enecstasis releases this particular standing-in and out-standing from Heidegger's ontological thinking, locating it in a milieu of ontic concerns that I understand self-appropriation to service. In the context of our discussion, this means a philosophy of religious studies centered on the intellectual, aesthetic, and mystical motifs of a singularity dialectically and foundationally engaged, both in mediating religious meaning and in the intentional, mediated construction of it. I have discussed this in reference to Lonergan's method in theology and his overall philosophy of religion. I wish now to conclude with some thoughts about what it means for enecstatic philosophy of religion as such.

The move to new materialism in religious studies—the desire, let us call it, to expunge foundations from religious studies—was serviced by what was perceived to be the religious, "crypto-theological" intentions in phenomenology of religion. The work of Wayne Proudfoot is important here. Proudfoot (1985, 129, 132) discovered how the grammatical rules of mystical discourse, which aim to prescribe and evoke religious experience rather than to describe or analyze it, function analogously in the purportedly descriptive intentions of phenomenologists. As adepts in a particular religious tradition circumscribe ineffable experiences through the language rules of their tradition, one finds religious thinkers and religion scholars doing the same through notions such as religious feeling (*Gefühl*) and the numinous. When you put this on a representation footing, prescription becomes "theological" and evocation problematic in so-called truly descriptive science of religion. In enecstatic philosophy of religion, this charge or fear is mitigated by acknowledging intentional construction at all levels of meaning. To put it in the terms of this chapter, "foundations" is operative, if implicitly, in the establishment of standards and norms that direct the desideratum of fully mediating meaning. Dialectic surfaces this need (i.e., explicit engagement of implicit foundational activity), since mediating meaning involves "dos and don'ts" and mediated meanings are not the exclusive right of theologians. Religion scholars may be strangers to "doctrines," "systematics," and "communications," but only in word. They are quite familiar with the practice, as is apparent from their ideals of mediating meaning and in-house debates surrounding the role of "metaphysics" in the study of religion.[12] These are issues of foundations.

Religion scholars of the new materialist caste are simply mistaken in thinking that meaning construction is inconsequential to their manner of theorizing—it is an integral component of their gaze. Still, I am not sure I want to go in the direction of some who argue that everything is really theology in disguise.[13] I have my doubts about disarming one caricature by another. In any case, foundational engagement in philosophy of religious studies invites normative reflection, theological and phenomenological, where issues of interiority surface either object-constitutively or (ideally for enecstasis) subject-constitutively. What do I mean? Allow me to explain by distinguishing my programmatic efforts from the excellent kin offering of the late philosopher and religion scholar Tyler Roberts.

Roberts did much to disarm the academic phalanx of new materialism in religious studies.[14] His first book, on Nietzsche—*Contesting Spirit: Nietzsche, Affirmation, Religion* (1998)—was something of a foray into the discussion. It served him, I believe, as my treatment of Heidegger serves me: as a useful, if what on the surface seems counterintuitive, choice for

The Normative Impetus of Enecstatic Philosophy of Religious Studies | 125

our twin tasks. Nietzsche, being seen as the enemy of religion, hardly qualifies, many would assume, as an important resource for dismantling the wall "between 'secular' and 'religious' discourses" (see Roberts 2013, 20) or for blurring "the boundaries between philosophical and religious thought" (2013, 18). And yet this is precisely what Roberts does with Nietzsche. Some might think the same about Heidegger, the enemy of the subject, inspiring a retrieval of subjectivity with ontic purpose. And yet that is precisely what I do with Heidegger. The aim of our individual selection acknowledges an ethos, often dubbed "postmodern," which Nietzsche and Heidegger helped create. Our selection is a cipher, a way to think past aspects of this ethos that reduces everything to self-interest. Basically, Roberts learned from Nietzsche, his asceticism, how to navigate two extant forms of suspicion, the suspicion of religion and the suspicion of modernity, which are "converging in our culture in an interesting and perhaps radical way" (2013, 19). He thinks this "may lead us to what Rowan Williams describes as the 'suspicion of suspicion' and even to what Paul Ricoeur called the 'hermeneutics of affirmation'" (Roberts 2013, 19).[15] That is, to thinkers "citing religious ideas, practices, and figures not as false consciousness or illusion, but as means to move through or around some of the dead ends of a critical consciousness," as we find in new materialism, "that has emptied concepts such as 'responsibility,' 'ethics,' 'freedom,' and 'subjectivity' of critical and emancipatory force" (Roberts 2013, 19). If, Roberts (2013, 82) continues musing, "we as scholars of religion stopped viewing theology and the religious heritage of the study of religion with embarrassment, as the relic of a past we must overcome so that we can start doing what we think our colleagues in other fields are doing, we might in the spirit of such experimentation [how Nietzschean!] come to see this heritage as a resource that can help us think differently and creatively about knowledge and criticism." This revalorization of normative reflection for religious studies Roberts (2018) calls "reverence as critical responsiveness."

Roberts's task is, in my estimation, an instance of foundations concerned with "self-consciousness about 'religion.'" He does not describe himself as religious. "I am not a Christian, a Jew, a Buddhist, or an adherent of any other 'religion'; for all sorts of reasons, I would never describe myself as 'spiritual'" (Roberts 2013, 5). Fair enough! But he is nevertheless compelled "by the depths of beauty and insight" he sees in religious writings such as Williams's *Writing in the Dust* (2002), spending much time "wondering and thinking' about how he (Roberts) "might respond to it and other instances of religion like it" (Roberts 2013, 5). He is compelled "by Williams's humanity . . . whether, and if so how, religious beliefs and practices are a force for cultivating such humanity" (Roberts 2013, 5). In the same breath, Roberts asks whether he, as a scholar and teacher of religious studies, should "even be thinking about religion in such apparently vague and ideologically loaded terms as 'beauty,' 'insight,' and 'humanity'?" (Roberts 2013, 5). If this is not foundations, I don't know what is.

Whether Roberts is religiously converted in Lonergan's sense is not my concern. I simply point out how his superstructure, whose very basic intentions I outline here only to demonstrate an identification, represents an important contemporary instance of foundations *in and for religious studies*, which, additionally, pivots toward *a mediated phase of religious meaning*. I should like to go even further and say that Roberts offers religious studies something functionally like Eliade, serving us now as another cipher. "History of Religions" may have been pitched as a discipline, but it offered (and Eliade knew this) more. The fact that it raised and continues to raise the ire of religion scholars ideologically, who are strictly invested in mediating meaning, is the only indication required of a clear methodological fault line.[16] What Eliade offered is a foundational discourse, "a discourse of resistance" (Roberts 2013, 7). But whereas his is poised against elements of modernity (i.e., tyrannical historicism), Roberts's resists an element dominating in our milieu: a politics of exclusion, which insists that religious discourses be treated exclusively "as *objects of* study" and never, on principle, "as potential methodological *resources for* the study of religion and for cultural criticism" (2013, 20). I am not conflating their individual discourses, for how different they are! I only wish to point to their foundational aims—at cross-purposes, perhaps, but united functionally in using religious resources for cultural critique—and, moreover (and here is the rub), as embodying dispositions indispensable to the study of religion.[17] They represent "religious thinking" apropos to religious studies as philosophy of religion. But Roberts's version is arguably much more enecstatic.

Roberts's desire for *self-consciousness* is why I call his program enecstatic; he operates in a thoroughly poststructuralist frame, but with an important qualification: the problem of representation is thought to open out into self-awareness rather than to forestall it. Enecstasis presupposes this frame as well as such a qualification. His desire for self-consciousness *about religion* in an academic setting is why I call it object-constitutive in the best possible sense of the term for my enecstatic aims.[18] It may be a far cry from inculcating "the transcendent exigence," but that does not detract from the authentic way it recognizes the exigence as integral to self-discovery in academic discussions about religion. Religious discourse as religious is given agency in Roberts's philosophy of religion. He allows his data (contra new materialists such as McCutcheon) to talk back.[19] Now, to enecstasis as subject-constitutive.

It was approaches like Roberts's, among others, that shaped my understanding of the importance and possible role of self-appropriation in religious studies, an environment irreversibly impacted by the ethos I have been describing. Self-appropriation assumed new form, as "care of the self," if you will, which, with a little "nip and tuck," could alight on the field of religious studies in a meaningful way, that is, without compromising the positional aspects initially ushering religious studies into the plane of immanence. Can philosophy of religious studies ask for more?

Enecstasis utilizes this movement of care as a peculiar form of dialectic and foundations. It performs, as it also looks to, such object-constitutive tasks as Roberts's. Its primary contribution, however, is in signaling an explicit preoccupation with self-making. As dialectical, it looks to the scholarly objectifications providing the context that edges one toward foundations. As one engages mediating viewpoint X, contrasting it with mediating viewpoints Y and Z, one is confronted by disputes and discrepancies concerning which one must decide. "Always historicize, never theologize" (an axiom of new materialism). "Religious phenomena are best explained by an appeal to other religious phenomena" (an axiom of phenomenology). Are these the only permutations available to the religion scholar? Do they mask an ideological agenda or are they intrinsic to the mediating data? An answer to these questions will depend on the dominant motif, to use Morelli's terms. If dramatic, the presence of my department head will force a specific response, hopefully cautious. As Lonergan once said, "You never want to be stupid"![20] If intellectual, the blindsiding axioms will be thrown into relief and eschewed in their exclusivity. If religious and/or artistic, the reflex concerning "otherness" will influence the decision concerning the mediating "metaphysic" either way.

The role of the object is apparent in this dialectic configuration. As enecstatic, however, the focus turns to issues of interiority attending to the mediating, the motifs of attending, if you like. Once one starts asking why one chooses position X regarding object Y, one's foundations come to the fore. Roberts (2018, 202) mines the work of Williams to determine how faith as dispossession of God, the condition of the possibility of opening ourselves to God's love, disrupts caricatures such as Lincoln's, where theology is always self-authorizing, speaking of things eternal and transcendent "with an authority equally transcendent and eternal" (Lincoln as quoted in Roberts 2005, 147). It also shows how a disposition of reverence as critical responsiveness can enliven religious studies much like, as Martha Nussbaum argues, love stories can enliven philosophy (Roberts 2018, 198). An alliance of what it means to be human with "philosophical or scientific cognitive determination" is desirable. As with dialectic, foundations in an enecstatic key takes this from resource (for the study of religion) to explicit personal preoccupation (in the study of religion). How do such ideas implicate me? Why do they (not) resonate with me? Do I need a change of heart, a change of mind, a moral compass? As program for the explicitation of these concerns, enecstasis as subject-constitutive guards the experience as irreducible. It does not commit one to the terms of an overt philosophical system for explicit rendering. It is withdrawal for return, but on the terms of the singularity so engaged. If the intellectual motif dominates, exemplified by the transcendental turn, the directives of something like generalized empirical method are more than expedient. However, because enecstasis was coined to serve a context shaped by the problem of representation, the artistic motif is emphasized in it, which is experiential and disruptive. The "doctrines," "systematics," and "communications" that result will be based on an enecstatic explicitation of the intellectual, moral, and religious foundations one sees as apropos to philosophy of religious studies. The issues outlined in this chapter, in this book finally, serve as an example of what it might look like. The dividends for a philosophy of religious studies cannot be overemphasized. Since I have discussed these in chapter 2, I will only note them in passing. Students are invited to negotiate their complicity in the study of religion without committing to specialized philosophical programs; the integrity of scholarly research is kept intact by a general philosophizing that does not compromise the goals and techniques of specific areas of study.

Sailing Enecstatically

The face of "foundational methodology of religious studies" has changed but its function is virtually the same. The normative impetus of interiority is central on this vessel as it monitors the tides of representation. Dialectic as that which invites one—as hired hand on this ship—to decide about mediating meanings opens up onto decisions regarding one's foundations where the desired end is to be captain of this vessel. In terms of enecstatic philosophy of religion, this means responsible citizenship in a community and area of study threatened by illusions of a kind of spectral normativity. Religious studies is an ideal testing ground for changing such a perception, for it deals with a deeply personal dimension of human culture, the study of which has never ceased being informing (mediating meaning) and forming (mediated meaning) individuals. Enecstasis is agential self-possession toward that aim.

Conclusion

A principal objective of this work has been to formulate a programmatic of philosophy of religion that accommodates the pedagogical, methodological, and research concerns of scholars of religion and academic theologians on the one hand, and the personal intellectual and religious foundations of the inquiring individual on the other hand. Such an objective aims to cultivate a sense of philosophy that, ideally, is aware of the needs and concerns of particular philosophical traditions but limits itself to none. For this reason, in my *philosophy* of religious studies I have relied on that part of the tradition that conceives the task of philosophy, not as a specialty per se, but more generally as an "art of living" open to anyone concerned with the self and being (see Hadot 1995, 83). This also explains why, as regards the *religious studies* part of this philosophy, I have consistently relied on a class of scholarship that aims to correlate the methodological concerns of religion scholars with the religious and theological (ideological) dimensions typically marginalized or critically disregarded in the pursuit. The preoccupation is admittedly metamethodological, according to which focus falls on specific issues in religious studies insofar as they illustrate the general need for broader methodological considerations that include the existential as central, determinative.

Thus, enecstatic philosophy of religion serves as a catalyst to bridge an ideological divide in and for oneself primarily at the level of method. The divide pertains to the chasm separating naturalist and phenomenological exclusivists as well as theological inclusivists. Enecstatic engagement facilitates explicit self-reflection on the ways in which ideological commitments in this divide impact methodological choices in religious studies. I have been describing this space of self-reflexivity as subject-constitutive to distinguish it from current contributions that tend to be object-constitutive, whether naturalistic or humanistic in orientation. As such enecstasis expedites a negotiating tactic that is context specific and, literally, self-determining: it leaves to the scholar's discretion, insofar as the scholar is personally engaged and critically self-aware, the extent to which otherwise exclusivist and inclusivist methodological insights are applicable. Enecstasis is a precondition of method, I might even say a companion to method. It entertains a notion of self always already emergent and not the sum total of insights about its basic "structure," transcendental or otherwise. Maieutic in intention, it operationally fixates on the singularity of the self that emerges. It disrupts to integrate. As such enecstasis is bound to dissatisfy individuals on the lookout for a method modeled on the otherwise exemplary approaches of science. The aim here, in other words, is not a reflexivity whose procedures and precepts provide a stable means by which one arrives at truth. Rather, the preoccupation is of an elusive self that adjusts, as a matter of course, to the needs and demands of a research community at any given time. A guiding presupposition is to care for the self, one's own self, being constructed in the intentional construction of culture. As critically reflexive, it is philosophical. As engaged, it is ideologically self-critical, not ideologically neutral or ideologically descriptive in a subtly pejorative way.

What does this mean in terms of philosophy of religion? As touched on in chapter 3, philosophy of religion is a complicated affair, with a complicated history of overlapping philosophical and religious traditions. The subject matter varies from philosophies about God and suffering to philosophies about religion as a dimension of human life. Within this spectrum, in the Western tradition, are philosophical styles of exploration conveniently described as analytic (Anglo-American) and continental (i.e., German and French). These styles emerged out of a history of looking at the aforementioned themes from the perspective of scholastic natural theology, an early to late medieval attempt to consider the truths of faith within or as opposed to the horizon of reason. The "logical" preoccupation with God and human suffering is typically identified as philosophical theology, which in modern dress is predominately analytic and metaphysical. This form of "philosophy of religion" differs from the philosophical pursuit that intersects with the social sciences that emerged in the continent in the nineteenth century. Philosophical analysis of religion would thus center on human experience, which explains why the continental approach often identifies, broadly speaking, as phenomenological. Religious studies, as a by-product of this development, is characteristically continental in inclination, housing a phenomenological manner of philosophizing that distinguishes it from the metaphysics of philosophical theology one finds in philosophy departments and seminaries.

Enecstasis, by definition, owes itself to the "effective historical consciousness" occasioned by and in the continental tradition. It is thus a response to the problematic of analyzing human experience qua the notion of subjectivity—with all due deference to Heidegger. For this reason, enecstasis also correlates with the philosophical practice in religious studies. When explicit, that philosophical practice can identify with a number of different schools within the tradition: transcendental idealism, phenomenology, genealogy, deconstruction, feminism, or what have you. When implicit, it is more generally "critical thinking," which is idiosyncratic and often informed by a variety of philosophical assumptions typically of analytic descent. In this we see both the technical and pedagogical aspects of enecstasis. Enecstasis is fundamentally about pedagogy, and in that respect it offers nothing new to models of education already in abundance. However, it serves as a cipher in pointing to a tradition in the philosophy of education that cements knowledge acquisition to self-care and the element of technique that dovetails with ancient spiritual practices (see Hadot 1995, 81–144). In this the technical aspect of enecstasis becomes readily available. It is a response to our exasperation, so ably diagnosed by Heidegger, Foucault, Derrida, and others, with representational thought and the foundationalist enterprise. Enecstasis is a thematic retrieval of the ancient concern with the self, ossified in systems about the subject (ὑποκείμενον) but as a singularity, as the essence of the modern enframing of subjectivity (see Heidegger 1977, 68n9, 79, 83, 88, 128, 147–148).

The technical aspect of enecstasis is topological. It precipitates a space of discourse where the ancient concern with the self coalesces with poststructuralist self-consciousness. But whereas poststructuralist projects—both wittingly and unwittingly—guard the irreducibility of self in object-constitutive fashion, enecstasis foregrounds that self-consciousness in hypertranscendental, subject-constitutive terms. We have learned much from Derrida in this regard, who in turn learned much from Heidegger. But he (Derrida), perhaps more than anyone, in my opinion, has alerted us to the equiprimordial grandeur and inherent danger of our discourses manifested most effectively in a process of outbidding (see chapter 5). Because we are all inescapably implicated in this process, vigilance is required. But vigilance itself easily becomes regressive, soft cushioning us into the belief that we have achieved success, however self-effacing our epistemological models. Hence, vigilance of this "hyper" variety is what is on the table. Enecstasis is my cipher for this thinking space that connects the essence of the transcendental gesture with the irreducibly personal in the academic enterprise. To eliminate confusion with the standard phenomenological conception of irreducibility, I should perhaps mention that I mean irreducibility along the lines of a Derridean hypertranscendental. It signals the personal dimension as a function of and trace in discourse, which tends to identify the irreducibly personal in terms of a fixed or universalizable set of properties or operations that legitimate that particular discourse.

In chapters 1 through 4 the contours of this practice are explained in the context of methodological debates in religious studies. When discussed in this connection, philosophy of religion becomes a concern with the field as an academic subdivision.[1] However, as already discussed, enecstasis intersects with this particular metamethodological instantiation of philosophy of religion with a different aim. It intersects with the "religion" element in philosophy of *religion*, in that the academic subdivision of philosophy of religion (i.e., philosophy of religious studies) addresses itself to issues of ideology that inform method. Enecstasis also intersects with the discourse about "religious studies," that is, with the concern about how religious studies is conducted—rather: the one conducting the study. So, where philosophy of religious studies, on this reckoning, includes philosophical theology and philosophy of religion (see chapter 3 and figure 1), its enecstatic instantiation, as subject-constitutive, moves the discourse to a level of engagement explicitly concerned with the self qua self in any one of these modalities. A visual may be in order.

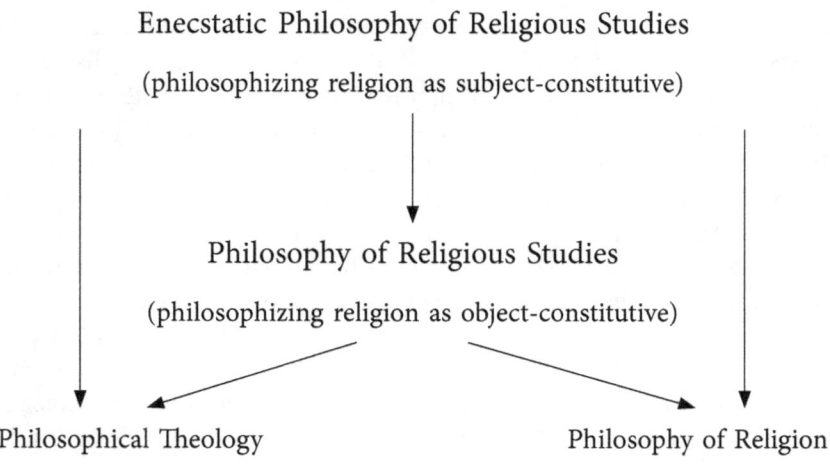

Figure 1. A Taxonomy of Relations. *Source*: Author's own material.

Whereas both philosophies of religious studies can include reflection on the themes of philosophical theology and philosophy of religion, they are independent of each other as proper procedures of analysis. Not all, in other words, will feel that enecstatic reflection is necessary for a sound philosophy of religious studies, and they are certainly not wrong to think so. However, enecstasis aims to elicit a sphere of engagement in philosophy of religious studies, as I conceive it, which is existentially authentic and critically self-aware. As a special preoccupation with the self in relation to religion and its study, enecstatic engagement moves freely among the three "philosophies of." This is important to note, too, since chapters 3 and 5 may leave one with the impression that enecstatic philosophizing is pertinent only to the continental tradition in philosophy of religion. On the contrary, as I hope to have shown, enecstasis is pertinent to the negotiation of analytic-like concerns—as evidenced, for example, in the new materialist philosophy of religious studies, despite this new materialism being "postmodern" in tenor—as well as to the general analytic ethos in philosophical theology. In the hopes of formulating a unique dimension of philosophy of *religious studies*, I have not tackled the latter in this work. And yet, the enecstatically charged analyst cannot but be interested in the self under construction in the philosophical and theological venture of philosophical theology. This is a project for future analysis.[2]

Perhaps a concrete example from my own teaching experience is appropriate given the personal and pedagogical nature of enecstasis. A subtle interplay occurs between the two levels of philosophy of religious studies discussed. The context is undergraduate and graduate methodology seminars that deal with the history and concept of religion since the nineteenth century. At one level I provide students with the various approaches to and theories of religion that constitute the critical reflexivity of modern scholarly traditions. This elicits a philosophical sensibility that directs attention from the religious phenomena under consideration to the intersubjectivity of the scholarship in question. This for me constitutes philosophy of religious studies as distinct from what usually passes as philosophy of religion in academia. As a concern with the agency of scholarship, this scholarly form of philosophy of religious studies pertains to subjectivity in the enecstatic sense outlined in chapters 2 and 4. The arbitration, in other words, is object-constitutive with the mediating tactic being an objectified relationality of concerns: how texts, rituals, and politics form our intersubjectivity, scholarly and religious. The concern is with an object of study and its various power dynamics and ideologies informing consciousness. If philosophy of religious studies is concerned with subjectivity in terms of critical reflexivity, enecstatic philosophy of religious studies is concerned with subjectivity in terms of critical self-reflexivity.

At the level of enecstatic philosophy of religious studies, experience trumps theory as an abstract system disconnected from experience. The space opened up by philosophy of religious studies invites a participatory dialectical conversation with one's self. In enecstatic terms, philosophy of religious studies precipitates an experiential self-theorizing that urges the self to be a self while being relationally engaged. This elusive, personal dimension is captured nicely by Charles Taylor (1997, 101) when he states, "Each of our voices has something unique to say. Not only should I not mold my life to the demands of external conformity; I can't even find the model by which to live outside myself. I can only find it within." The personal nature of the exercise is what I mean by experience trumping theory. Aristotelian *phronesis* is at issue here, which goes beyond *episteme* and *techne*. This kind of theorizing is left to the participant and is hence irreducibly agent-based and experiential. It would not be surprising, then, were my theory to be perceived as disconnected from the experience of one attempting to be similarly self-engaged. That is why the pedagogical aim of enecstasis necessarily trumps my particular theory of it. It is a conduit for self-discovery and self-expression. Stated otherwise, the theory is my approximation of a happenstance, serving to express the elusive nature of what I take to be a crucial missing component in object-constitutive discourses that lack enecstatic significance. The theory, then, is to facilitate a discourse with oneself within a domain of experience occasioned by any one of the three "philosophies of" itemized earlier. The quality of theorizing implied is programmatically distinct from foundationalist ideas of theory.

This particular problematic lurks in the background of chapters 6 and 7. The contours of the *théorétique* of enecstasis have been provided by the transcendental gestures of Lonergan and Winquist. Together they supply the significance that I attach to the preposition *en* forming my neologism. Recall Heidegger's characterization of ecstasis as a "standing in" in the openness of Being, "of enduring and out-standing this standing in (care), and of out-braving the utmost (Being-toward-death)" (Heidegger [1949] 1992, 255). Lonergan, specifically his notion of self-appropriation, provides the general outline for recasting the "standing in" element gestured by Heidegger in an ontic frame. It commends the positional in poststructuralism. Winquist provides the fold that brings this concern in line with the "out-standing" element that attaches to the *ek* in Heidegger's ecstasis. In effect, by appending the *en* of enecstasis to the *ek* of ecstasis, I am extending the critical platform of knowledge past the problem of representation, augmenting the critique of the Enlightenment.[3] Chapters 6, 7, and 8 demonstrate my rationale, that is, who informs it and how enecstasis is both like and unlike these progenitors' aims. To this end I offer my scaffolding, which I can only hope will serve the reader as well as it has served me over the years.

Postscript

At the end of this journey, I feel compelled to provide more context to the twists and turns embodied in these chapters, something more personal that conveys my own enecstatic experience as I struggled to foreground the strangeness within. If the reader has reached enough clarity regarding my principal aims, he or she is not required to read any further. However, a nagging sense of incompleteness consumes me without formulating what I include here. Contentment is highly individual, which I can no more decide for the reader than I can the importance and utility of this entire project.

One of the most challenging aspects of teaching is the bewildering spectrum of interests and experiences of students and teachers alike. It is especially challenging when one's area of specialization is remote from the concerns, informed and uninformed, in that spectrum. Because educators desire, ideally, to be engaging, they aim to alleviate the dissociation students and colleagues experience when faced with their subject matter. This is an important aspect—let us call it, the extrinsic aspect—that focuses my research on a teaching strategy apropos to my field, religious studies, specifically philosophy of religion. The other aspect, more intrinsic, involves the idiosyncrasies surrounding my academic formation, what Bernard Lonergan calls "intellectual conversion." Various elements I wish to feature from this idea are captured well in Plato's Allegory of the Cave.

The storyline is well known. Shackled in a cave observing shadows on a wall, a prisoner, driven (let us imagine) by discontent and curiosity, escapes discovering the blinding truth that awaits him outside. The reality to which he was accustomed as a prisoner was an impoverished version of the truth, what we often call appearances. Inhabitants of the cave are unable to grasp this epiphany chained as they are to their perceptions and inclinations. Once outside, slowly, painfully, acclimatized to what previously escaped him, he takes pity on his fellows and ventures back into the shadowy cavern to communicate his epiphany. A new challenge confronts him, perhaps even more challenging than what he faced previously. The obstructions of inexperience (largely the prisoners') and the medium that passes as truth inside the cave, namely "opinion" (*eikasia* and *pistis*), distorts his liberating message. Combined with the elements of fragility, trial and error (his), he finds himself in a ring of competing commitments that ancient Greeks appropriately describe as *agon*, a contest.

There is no shortage of this *exitus-reditus* theme in religious literature and practice. The bodhisattva reaches nirvana but vows to continue rebirths to assist others; after encountering the risen Christ, Saint Paul, exemplifying the Great Commission (Matt. 28:18–20), desires to depart and be with Christ but evades death to lead others to Christ; the yogi and the yogini master the self-discipline of meditation as they teach others to overcome bondage to samsara; and so on.

Whether philosophical or religious, this emancipatory impulse and trajectory—from darkness to light, from *inferno* to *paradiso*, from ignorance to wisdom—are integral to teaching, or at least should be. That is why the combination of terms in the phrase "intellectual *conversion*" is apropos. Not only does it suggest a close connection between the intellectual pursuit and what drives all emancipatory discourses, but it also removes the teaching activity from connotations of disengaged communication, the infamous "sage on the stage" education model. Amanda Fulford and Áine Mahon (2018), two education scholars, have been addressing these issues recently in support of the now unpopular institution of the lecture. Teaching, they rightly argue, is "deeply dialogic" (2018), a rather classical assumption. It is an encounter in which one commits oneself to "an active relationship with students" (2018). Fulford and Mahon characterize this in terms of a self, the teacher, "rendered vulnerable to the other's [students'] reproof" (2018). They add that such a relationship "might lead to awkward and messy moments," but that such moments are the "mark [of a] genuine and meaningful encounter" (2018).

This captures the emancipatory aim and bewildering elements of pedagogy in Plato's famous allegory. It also, incidentally, captures the foundational element of this work, which explicitly integrates research and the "process of inquiry" into an admittedly idiosyncratic teaching philosophy centered on agential self-possession—*enecstasis*—a technical response to a highly personal and explicit way of being self-aware in today's world, in one's role as a teacher, a student, or simply as an inquiring mind. The program I have been advancing recognizes a self, "the self," to be an irreducible singularity. Such a view presupposes plurality, individuality, and difference as orienting principles. My teaching platform has been directly shaped by this network of ideas. It places inestimable value on the other while being (in)formed by the dialogic space identified by Fulford and Mahon and the scholarship upon which they rely.

Focusing on these aspects of teaching, extrinsic and intrinsic, has kept me from wandering outside the confines of my cave, always in search of an *Anknüpfungspunkt* (point of contact) with those forced to listen to my proposed escape route: my students. With the publication of this volume, the audience widens, as will the variables surrounding its appreciation. Despite the tenor of this difference, my intentions remain unchanged: a research program shaped by a concrete spectrum of aspects (my teaching environment), hopefully serviceable to the wider academic community.

This book, as noted in the preface, documents a personal journey, but the chapters are not unlike others found in academic books. The topics are specialized with overlapping themes engaging, largely contextualizing, the work of others that have framed the problematic. The problematic is subjectivity in a post-Cartesian world, "post" being a precarious term given the continued preoccupation with the Copernican revolution and its aftermath[1]—a preoccupation that would lead to the transcendental method enhanced, if not overturned, by phenomenology, toppled outward by dialectical materialism on the one hand, and catapulted "horizonward" into the Open through hermeneutical philosophy on the other hand. Poststructuralism would further fragment the situation, featuring diagnosis as the interminable condition. The term "minefield" would be far from exaggeration to describe this mental landscape. Every step calculating, without many of the luxuries of calculation, how to proceed with vigilance, hypervigilance, in search of I know not what. "I" indeed! "What" indeed! Such a post-Cartesian notion of subjectivity—this substance without substance, without the convenience of a naive view of substance—in a word, functions. A substance that is function. Here the "conditions of possibility" are conditioned, not in the sense that the conditioning as condition is "already out there now real," to use Lonergan's ([1957] 1992, 178, 181, 184, 260, 275–277, 408, 413, 414, 437–440, 449–450, 523–524, 529) quaint phrase for common sense and formal philosophies aiming to circumvent the constitutive role of judgment. The sense here is of a conditioning whose conditions are late determinations, academic formulations, based on a functioning, the significant contours of which are future-present. That is my sense of the function of the to-come (*a-venir*) in Derrida, which means to keep our determinations open, which means to instill a deep appreciation of, responsibility for, the functioning of self in knowing.[2]

This bifurcated erasure of "the real" as preconstituted or independent—indifferent, as some wish to imagine it—contours the liminal space toward which enecstasis gestures: the "reality" of the self as a singularity, irreducible, hypertranscendental, a differential of mediation and negotiation. It (to speak of the self impersonally but entirely with personal dividends) opens toward positive content as a purely formal category in the designation of things. But it itself (if pronouns work here), not out-there now, not in-here now, resists categorization as its condition of possibility. As such the self looms in the language it finally resists.[3] Caught in the straits of binary determinations, whether celebrating or disrupting them, the self assumes different qualities and operations. An ontic class of thinking, to put categories of Heidegger to use, will be typically resolute about sizing things up in terms of positive entities, an "I," a "subject," *the* subject, consciousness, and so on. A characteristically artistic treatment, for lack of a better term, will, by contrast, insist on such categorizations as purely formal to disrupt all-too positive characterizations. A good example of this is two well-known meditations: Descartes's *Meditations on First Philosophy* (1641) and Samuel Beckett's *The Unnamable* (1953).

Even if these discourses are classified differently—Descartes's being a philosophical tractate, Beckett's a novel—thematically they are similar. The narrators, transparent in one (*Meditations*), purposely obscure in the other (*The Unnamable*), manage the lever of doubt about the self toward different ends. Descartes, aiming for certainty, dials up doubt through a calculating calm of imagination ("let us suppose," "I suppose," "suppose," etc.). Here substance thinking—if the term is permitted—gets to substance, the thinking I, discursively in translucent spacetime assuming an equally translucent idea of language, where the signified is targeted as "out there" (*res extensa*) or "in here" (*res cogitans*) now real. Despite his idiosyncrasies, Descartes's rationalism, with most of its underlay of relations, captures the common sense regarding subjectivity (an "I," "you," "them" qua *res cogitans*) and objectivity (an "I," "you," "them," "it" qua *res extensa*). Its independent intelligibility is made possible, but not constitutively, through a convenient marriage of reason and its principal instrument: language.

About such things Beckett, by contrast, achieves only greater and greater obscurity in the deliberately frenetic monologue of *The Unnamable*.[4]

His omniscient narrator, like Descartes in the *Meditations*, is "disembodied," if that term even means anything in the context of Beckett's novel. However, it is important to note that the narrator in *The Unnamable*, the third installment of a trilogy,[5] occupies a narrative spacetime immobile ("I can't stir") and in limbo (yearning for "the true silence") as he considers the language, beliefs, and "hypotheses" ("all lies" to help one forward) that constitute his speech. A complex relation ensues that constitutes the debonding compound of the narrator's words to speak of himself as though "for the first time" in the trilogy: the voices of characters, stifled in the story, whose adhesion to him obtains in memory; the voice(s), the impersonal voice of language, indifferently binding the two, characters to narrator and vice versa; and the narrator's voice, strenuously attempting to withdraw his adhesion from his characters, however failingly. Nothing can be too clear with these sets of assumptions and their context. This is all to disengage a contesting will forced to "go on," to speak, despite the thirst for the true silence of which silence knows nothing.

What a stark contrast to Descartes's disembodied mind, which reasons dependence on God in reconstructing the world through thinking. The protagonist in *The Unnamable* balks at the process, inverting the prized pole of relations, "voice" to "mind" ("you can't call that thinking"), "words" to "things" ("with no ground for their settling"), and "going on" to "being" (a timeless stream with no thought for being, "as if there could be no being but being conceived"). Once Descartes discovers the cogito, like a gust of warm air lifting a lake fog, the evil genius disappears. In *The Unnamable*, thanks to the increasing dew point of questioning, the "threat" reappears, never to disappear.

This is a good snapshot, albeit oversaturated by abridgment, of the problem that birthed my notion of enecstasis. The references adequately pinpoint a different ethos and mood regarding the delineation of the singularity in question: Descartes's, representative of the turn to the subject, and Beckett's, representative of the turn to language. Agency in the one is transparent, provided by the deliverances of and assumptions about reason, and in the other, obscure, provided by disruptive artistry denuding self-sufficient reason. Both embody an experience determined by different aims. Descartes gets to the cogito to thwart assumptions of things hitherto entertained, that is, to support a vision of objectivity that must pass through the "I think," as well as to disarm doubts concerning the possibility of objectivity, that is, the "Nouveaux Pyrrhoniens." Beckett's protagonist throughout the trilogy deems it fit to ridicule reason, the pretensions of which are furnished by an overconfident thinking reflex. He does not simply dismiss *thinking* to *speak* of himself—the dichotomy is not lost on us. He is pragmatic about it. The activity is an ingredient of the debonding compound lacing the narrative, a workhorse, if you like, pulling the cart of indefatigable becoming, "going on," which amounts to speaking, storytelling, making sense, however absurd the idea that we are making sense of anything. That is why the protagonist regularly qualifies otherwise reasonable views (his, society's, traditional ways of thinking, etc.) with refrains such as "I have no opinion," "I don't know," "I don't see how," "I don't know why," and so forth. Such views, we are told, are hypotheses used "to scratch [his] arse with," that is, they allow him to "complete [his] views, before [he] shit[s] on them."[6]

I have purposely selected these examples to highlight radically disparate aims that seem irreconcilable. By saying this, however, I do not mean to suggest that these differences are reconcilable or that they should be reconciled. My aim is different. The example of Beckett is invoked to feature a modality of intelligence that narrates an experience overshadowed by formal philosophy (what passes as such) and the common sense that sustains such philosophy; it subverts common sense in the service of a purportedly truer common sense, one having overcome common nonsense. Beckett's narrative, in his trilogy as a whole—I have featured *The Unnamable* on account of its place in the trilogy and the radicality of its pronouncements—frustrates both, common sense and philosophy, its repackaged common sense. He does this by surrealist narrative storytelling. The difference was alluded to earlier in the asymmetric use of imagination in both writers. Descartes, like a mathematician, a scientist, asks us to *suppose* various things that initially sound strange to eliminate their strangeness, notwithstanding how strange his proposal sounds to the contemporary ear: a world exposed to the soulish gaze of the cogito grounded in the most perfect being. Beckett takes us on a journey whose main protagonist laboriously strips away everything he knew, everything he knows, from his insubstantial self who is unnamable and must keep his wits about him under the irresistible force of "going on." The imagination involved in cogitating, which thinks of substances and accidents, being and becoming, is not welcomed here, in a narrative where one freely moves from disjointed story to disjointed story, disjointed monologue to disjointed monologue, in a place that is no place, from a place where it is absurd to think one is stirring or seeing; from a place, finally, where it is absurd to think one can know things with the slightest certainty.

Beckett's gesture can be expressed philosophically and indeed has been in poststructuralist offerings. One need only mention Derrida, Alain Badiou, and Slavoj Žižek, all of whom settle on aspects of Beckett's sentiments qualified in their respective philosophies.[7] However, by tying it together via Beckett, I am isolating an elemental dimension philosophically minimalist in intention. It is an invitation to experience an agency where terms such as "agency" suffer from qualification upon qualification. "The subject doesn't matter, there is none." And again: "it's the fault of the pronouns, there is no name for me, no pronoun for me, all the trouble comes from that, that, it's a kind of pronoun too, it isn't that either, I'm not that either, let us leave all that, forget about all that." I agree with Badiou (2003, 55) that such an opposition is an inverted Cartesianism "to break with Cartesian terrorism," where, through the introduction of "some third terms, neither reducible to the place of being nor identical to the repetitions of the voice," "the subject opens itself up to an alterity and cease[s] being folded upon itself in an interminable and torturous speech." This, however, is a philosophical transposition, translation, of the narrative framework in question, to, as Steven Connor (Beckett [1953] 2012, preface) observes, "[reprove] a generation of critics who have found in *The Unnamable* what [Badiou] sees as a sterile model for self-replicating and ultimately self-satisfied scepticism."[8] To connect it with the denegation of Derrida (as Russell Kilbourn [2005] has done) or the Lacanian real (as Žižek [2019] has done) makes a similar move, whose legitimacy I am not contesting as such. "Enecstasis" purposely avoids the explicit philosophical extrapolation, aiming to capture the zeitgeist surrounding alterity, which Beckett here artistically services. As I argue in the book, this is expedient in the context of religious studies, where the role of philosophizing, especially as metamethod, is seen as secondary at best. If philosophy *in* religious studies is to become philosophy *of* religious studies, it cannot do so effectively in the traditional sense of a stand-in, of whatever variety, adjudicating rules for rational conduct, let alone proper topics for discussion.[9] The methods are too varied, the suspicions (regarding philosophy, especially of the regulating, transcendental sort) too deep. Michel Foucault's (1999, 95) attitude toward the cogito embodies the general ethos: "I do not deny the cogito, I confine myself to observing that its methodological potential is ultimately not as great as one might have believed and that, in any case, we can nowadays make descriptions which seem to me objective and positive, by dispensing with the cogito entirely." Philosophy of religion needs to function as consultant in such an environment, not as director, where inquiry as method, at least in the humanities, is still foundering.

Now to return to the overview and then back to my claim about the personal nature of this work. Enecstasis as a philosophical gesture pedagogically underscores the irreducible nature of both motifs represented by Descartes and Beckett. As noted, the service to which I put them embodies a tension I see as fundamental in contemporary philosophy of religion. Also crucial is that both point to a self to disturb a stasis of self, a commonality I nominate later as their elemental meaning. Put in my earlier terms, they exemplify the *arhat* of Plato's allegory who communicates a more truthful, bearable life, however disconcerting the activity appears to be. What educator worth her salt dismisses the need for critical inquiry, to manage, with whatever effort available, the shadows one cannot but see? We may, like Beckett, recoil from the self-confidence produced by otherwise indeterminable contingencies. However, if Badiou is right (and I think he is), the luxury of "third terms," rendering tolerable "interminable and torturous speech," protracts, if inversely, that which it aims to overcome, namely, the subject, one opening itself up to alterity and ceasing to be folded upon itself. This tension of a moving viewpoint that is nevertheless a viewpoint quite literally forced the term "enecstasis" from me. Chapter 1 is my Vesuvius. Enecstasis provided the space to negotiate both personally and professionally what I saw and continue to see as the impasse that threatens to shut down the desire for movement due to a contest between system and antisystem philosophies. Derrida's term "outbidding" is portentous.

More pointedly now. Enecstasis signifies something, call it what you will, that is fundamental—I do not say foundational (although personally I have no problems with the word)—for the negotiation of some x (insert what you will). It is not some privileged standpoint, although privilege is always already present in academic discourse. It is (and I say "is" guardedly) an important premise of discourse, of learning, of intellectual engagement in the refusal of truncation. Be that as it may, enecstasis nevertheless welcomes the insights emergent from what we may call the tragedy of truncation. It is the suspension toward self-formulation tethered inextricably to formulations. Erring on the side of good faith—the common expression is "caution"—enecstasis says "no" both to system and antisystem. It remains with experience to express itself here systematically, there artistically—to stick to only two of several possible motifs. In deference to the other, oneself as other, the other as other, enecstasis looks for wisdom to decide for oneself. Putting it a little differently, to be enecstatically engaged is to follow and appreciate a pattern of experience without universalizing its elemental meanings. Because I have detailed this connection elsewhere (Kanaris 2023), I will be relatively brief. Beckett will serve as the key example.

In *The Unnamable*, elemental meaning presents itself obliquely as experience of that which is ineffable, an experience of self that is no ordinary self. Indeed, to speak of it in these terms, as a self identical with itself, would be absurd in such a context. Beckett effectively demonstrates this in the framework of the story, which narrates disparate stories to facilitate the human project of "going on"—what *we do*, what *we see* as significant, how *we react*, *our* strangely incalculable *temperaments*, and so on. The trilogy is filled with instances of this to subvert our reflex about agency, often through tragicomic illustrations. Think, for instance, of Molloy, in the installment of the same name, recounting in painstaking detail the pointless enumeration of sucking stones in a juggling act between his greatcoat, mouth, and trousers. Methodical behavior and arithmetic, their uncanny benefit ("nothing more restful than arithmetic"), are a running anti-theme in the trilogy. It is not hard to imagine Descartes as the principal target. Each time such references appear, we see him staring down the barrel of Beckett's gun. The expectancy of meaning is of finitude, where the prospect of intelligence fixing the innumerable variables of existence is portrayed as comic. To introduce Descartes's scale of expectancy, where the presupposition is to provide a shelf life to knowing, would be to flub the cadence. As with the joke, once grasped, the attempt to explain it becomes "funnier" than the joke itself, as I attempt to do with Derrida in chapter 5.

As affirmed or negated, each of these dispositions works itself out into technical philosophies. Enecstasis as such stalls the need. It provides parameters for the negotiation of systematic formulation, not its resolution. The current environment, dominated by artistic thinking,[10] forced me to settle on enecstasis as a condition of plausibility, that is, a condition of plausible talk about the subject. Pinpointing Heidegger as an opening for the possibility (see chapter 1), thanks to a lecture on art by Lonergan (1993, 208–232), contributed to the contours of the preoccupation. He (Heidegger), despite himself, as arch critic of *Subjectum*, was my "green light" to reintroduce the tired but always crucial question of subjective agency. What this meant—which took over a decade to develop—is painstaking attention to elemental meaning, the hinge pivoting differentiated, critical self-reflexivity on self-reflexive awareness. A former teacher once effectively captured the aporia by the phrase "the outrageous proclamation of subjectivity" (McEvenue 1994, 61), which he endorsed and from whom I inherited the concern. It is useful to document how my preoccupation mirrors his, although faced with different challenges on account of our different fields.

Sean McEvenue was a literary critic and biblical scholar. He died in 2018. His principal contribution, for our purposes, is his hermeneutical approach to the Bible, or really any literary text. It is an invitation to interact with elemental meaning. Not incidental for us is how his hermeneutics facilitates a (enecstatic) sensibility to distinguish elemental meanings from their systematic formulations.

> In current culture, serious questions are formed in philosophically precise language, and are answered within philosophically complete systems. Religious truths in the Bible cannot be found in that manner of thinking. The fact is that theological questions have been asked within Western tradition which forms all of our thoughts whether or not we are believers. It is a tradition which begins with the Bible but continued through an evolution in which philosophically accurate modes of thought have translated biblical (and other) meaning into systematic meaning, have translated elemental preconceptual meaning into conceptualized meaning. (McEvenue 1994, 20)

As an exegete, McEvenue carefully disengages overwrought effective historical meanings from the horizon, the elemental meaning, of their sources. He does this not because those meanings are necessarily wrong. That is a different question. He does it finally to recircuit audience participation impeded by "philosophically accurate modes of thought." Does this not simply reintroduce the dead issue of original meaning? To mitigate this, one should distinguish between "elemental" and "original." The former pertains to a horizon of meaning or sense of expectancy ascertained through attention to style, pattern, rhythm, form, orientation, extant historical information, and so on. Original it need not be in the sense of origin in time: the closer one is to something the purer it is. If elemental meaning is "pure," it is so only in the sense of being decipherable from other horizonal ingredients and interpolations. All that pertains to elemental meaning is visceral, intelligence as trough between the crest of biological, intelligent reaction and that of conceptual system—"preconceptual" in McEvenue's terms.[11]

The correlation to enecstatic philosophy of religion is McEvenue's treatment of biblical meaning whose elemental stance of expectancy about meaning and human fulfillment is distinct from the preoccupation with theological truth. We gather from this that elemental meaning traffics in norms and is viscerally acquired, at least more rudimentarily than is the case with conceptual meaning.

> The foundational stance of an author as such is not his or her whole psyche. It is those aspects of the psyche which shape the writing. It is foundational in the sense that it underlines other psychic activity, directing choices without being a choice at the moment of directing, determining objectives without being one itself, enforcing criteria without necessarily being prepared to define them. It is a living value system, and an operative theory of knowledge, which could be partially articulated but which usually will not even be reflected upon. (McEvenue 1990, 58)

The elemental meaning of a biblical text, in other words, is more "compact" than in systems of meaning where, to retrace McEvenue's terms, the "whole psyche" is at play, directing and determining objectives while defining criteria. Because the form is different the elicitation of elemental meaning is conveyed and acquired differently. In terms of its acquisition, McEvenue provides the guiding question, "In what realm of human meaning or activity does this text expect meaning, revelation, salvation to occur? In war? In family life? In obeying the law? In prayer? and so forth?" (McEvenue 1990, 153). The realms pertain to our commerce in life, the strategies for the attainment of their individual ends exemplifying their being. In the writer dubbed "Priestly" (P) by scholars of the Bible, to provide just one of McEvenue's many examples, the elemental meaning is faithful religious observance amid hopelessness and despair, Israel's during the Babylonian exile. This is wrapped up with the instrumentality of liturgy. "The stance of expectancy of the Priestly Speaker . . . is that God will not be revealed in social and political, or even family, institutions [the stances of other biblical writers, e.g., J, E, Dtr]. He is revealed in the order of nature, not of society. He is discovered and adored as creator. His glory will appear to us when we spend the money and effort required to provide an aesthetic and correct liturgy" (McEvenue 1990, 127). The takeaway is that elemental meaning is both horizonal and visceral with its peculiar realm of expression governed accordingly by the instrumentality of choice, material and ideational.

What about elemental meaning in a conceptual setting such as enecstasis hopes to plumb? As with McEvenue, the task is to distinguish the elemental from the conceptual. However, because enecstasis consists in the engagement of the elemental in the conceptual, the direction of the analysis, while functionally similar, shifts on its axis. The playing field, to put it differently, expands from elucidating forms of expectancy in compact consciousness, discriminating them from effective historical meanings (McEvenue's aim), to identifying forms of expectancy in conceptual meaning often at odds with itself. In his elucidation of elemental meaning, McEvenue faced the challenges of structuralism in literature. My attempts, archived here, faced the challenges of philosophical post-structuralism. Our "outrageous proclamation" is a polyphony of related though oscillating concerns.

The value of isolating elemental meaning in Descartes and Beckett consists in the personal negotiation of normative frameworks whose burden and significance are neither alleviated by nor resolved in systemic extrapolations. The burden consists in an awareness of self, communicated through different patterns of expression, as outlined earlier. This challenges us, in the clearing provided by the discourses, to revision our selves, the self. Like with McEvenue's subjects, the stance of expectancy in Descartes and Beckett will vary significantly, contoured as they are by their respective cultural contexts: the modern scientific revolution in Descartes, pre–death of God, and the *nouveau théâtre, nouvelle poésie*, in Beckett, post-anthropological. Descartes summons a resolution modeled on the mathematician's proclivity for clear and distinct perceptions. That is the only way to know anything worth its salt. Beckett ridicules the suggestion with an alternative stance of expectancy, minimalist at best when it comes to thinking. There the struggle of being trumps so-called clear and distinct perceptions. The evil genius is not so evil after all, nor good for that matter.

By focusing on elemental meaning, we need not decide between the foundational stances of the two, at least not in enecstatic appreciation of their patterning, their intonation, accent, what they communicate about the human condition. The only concern is with the condition of plausibility of a "we" at stake in the encounter. Perhaps it is useful to imagine this as treading water in a pool to avoid drowning. Moreover, our reaction may be one of endorsement or disapproval. As a pathway to such negotiation, enecstasis is the premise of judgment and not an excuse for it. McEvenue (1990, 45) observes how a spontaneous negative evaluation of a foundational stance elementally expressed can be improved upon with the onset of understanding and yet remain negative. He documents his reaction to Beckett and Dylan Thomas, whom he attempted to read for years. They "appear to have entered the canon, leaving [him] a heretic." Enecstasis acknowledges this as requisite but individual. McEvenue's reaction to Beckett is not mine, but not because I disagree with McEvenue. If cornered, I, too, would probably reject Beckett's foundational stance post-enecstatically, premised as it is on his "inverted Cartesianism," not to mention what seems to be an antipathy toward devotional religious horizons.[12] However, his manner, which annoys McEvenue, is not incidental to expressing the positional in Beckett that resonates with the zeitgeist about subjectivity, what makes it "outrageous" to some. To promote evaluation in systematic, exclusivist "Derridean" or "Lonerganian" terms in such an environment is ill-advised as well as a missed opportunity.[13]

Remaining enecstatically agnostic about systematic evaluations also has an added pedagogical advantage. It recognizes that a conceptual expression of elemental meaning need not constitute the terms of relationality between elemental meaning and frameworks of subjectivity and signification. Take Žižek's interpretation of *The Unnamable*, following Jacques-Alain Miller's treatment of the later Lacan, who delineates "the contours of One alone before the Other, of a hallucination before symbolic reality, of meaningless lapses prior to any signifying articulation" (Žižek 2019). The dividends of *The Unnamable* are filtered through a contemporary aporia of Singularity in which the couplet human/posthuman relate to Beckett's being born/not-yet-fully-born.

> Are we, humans, in some sense not yet fully born, a fuzzy and inconsistent intermediary state between animality and post-humanity (as the predominant ideology of Singularity implies)? Or, are we, as humans, in some sense fully human, and will the passage into post-human Singularity involve some kind of regression into a state of not-being-fully-born as human individuals? Our reference to Beckett's *Unnameable* points in this direction: will subjectivity that is immersed in Singularity not function as a version of the Cartesian cogito which remains stuck in solipsist hallucinations and fails to pass over into a

> Self that relates to a constituted objective reality? However, the opposite version holds as well: we exist as humans, embedded in our reality, precisely, as unborn, ontologically incomplete, i.e., insofar as our human existence is marked by a constitutive failure. And in post-humanity we get stuck in a limbo of not-yet-being born, precisely insofar as we achieve our identity in being immersed in the shared space of Singularity. (Žižek 2019)

The connections are obviously insightful and provocative. Note, however, the resolution regarding the cogito, a version of which "remains stuck in solipsistic hallucinations and fails to pass over into a Self that relates to a constituted objective reality." Now couple this stance to the assumptions of signification based on Lacan's "two axes": "One is the axis of the symbolic Unconscious where, in transference, the subject relates to an Other, where symptoms have a (supposed) meaning and, as such, wait to be historicized, integrated into a symbolic narrative. The other is the axis of the real Unconscious where the subject (or, rather, the subjectless Self) is all alone" (Žižek 2019). The Lacanian Real, as Žižek wonderfully explains in a YouTube clip, is

> a purely nonsubstantial formal notion. It is in a way nothing in itself. . . . It is just an obstacle, which is a kind of meta-obstacle. It is an obstacle to its own formulation. It is not that we have the Real, which is then too strong and some obstacle prevents contact with the Real. The Real is a kind of obstacle to itself in the sense that the Real is not what we cannot touch but it is at the same time the obstacle that prevents us to touch the Real. In this sense it is a purely formal category. (Žižek 2020)

The paradox is not lost on Žižek, which does not diminish in the least its constitutive, regulatory role in his philosophy.

Now to the crucial question for enecstasis. Imagining Beckett along the lines of Žižek's Lacanian Real is clearly appropriate, but it introduces a decision about (1) identifying the elemental meaning of the cogito as "stuck in solipsistic hallucinations," as unable to pass into a view of a correlation of Self and objective reality that is (2) best understood in Žižek's Lacanian-baptized Hegelian view of reality. As I have stated repeatedly, this is the right of every individual considering the elemental meaning in a foundational stance about the world. But the important question for us is to what degree that translation determines the significance of elemental meanings and whether it mutes alternative readings for their reasoned nonconformism. I may share Žižek's prophetic concerns about our so-called posthuman culture. But his foundational stance, filtered through the sieve of his amalgamation of Hegel and Marx through Lacan, is relatively foreign to me, my experience of the world. That may be a shortcoming on my part, but enecstasis grants it leverage. And although the condition of possibility of dialogue means performing some sort of *epochē* about the self, this need not entail a Kafkian metamorphosis.

Beckett captures a contemporary sense of self whose elemental meaning frowns on an alternative accent, Descartes's, much like the Priestly Writer when emphasizing the contrary elemental meanings of the Yahwist, Elohist, or Deuteronomist. The contemporary sense of self ridicules Descartes's accent, or a version of it, cognizant that the latter provides for the former. The artistic gesture, embodied for us by Beckett, is configured as such precisely because of perceived incommensurability *in actu*. Locating the issue at this level helps to distinguish elemental meaning from formalizations, which typically set the ground rules for inclusion or exclusion. The name Descartes (Cartesianism if you like) is not equivalent to what Descartes names through elemental meaning: the importance of self-critically, rationally, organizing the world. The name Beckett, too, the novelist, is not equivalent to what in his novels he (un) names. The elemental meaning of that activity anticipates meaning through an elevation of the discontinuities of classification.

By focusing on Beckett, we tap into an experience of the world, an elemental meaning, that may be continuous with formalizations that disqualify talk of the subject. But that is not grounds to dismiss subjective engagement qua enecstasis, since elemental meaning is a premise of formalization to invite a reaction. As such, the subject, you and I however fragmented, are summoned by discourse to discourse. Formalizing the procedure is requisite with formalizing decisions about the task disqualified as prerequisite. As a technical designation, enecstasis—in deference to elemental meanings as in Beckett and his formalizers—is fundamentally a pedagogical notion. It insists on elemental meaning as a plausible entry point for engaging oneself and another; I do not say oneself as another because such a designation implies a formalization premised on the realization of a self who happens to be relational. This tactic makes controversies surrounding ipseity and alterity, formalizations, secondary in the interstice of agential self-possession. McEvenue does the same with biblical (elemental) meanings with an accent on evaluation informed by a formalization (generalized empirical method), which I recognize as requisite but secondary in, and an individual achievement of, enecstatic engagement.

Despite appearances, this book is autobiographical. It recounts a personal journey struggling with the "right" of self-discovery, to honor those fluctuating elements of self, commonly called an "identity," toward fuller selfhood. This desire is desire itself, desire of self to self-transcend. In it I recount how I managed this challenge in deference to the voices that would speak my own, that would, through no fault of their own, have me speak. This *cri de coeur* issued from a place of deep respect and appreciation. But as sons and daughters must subjectively dismiss their parents in being parents themselves, a subjective dismissal needed to take place in me as well.[14] A *cri* that differentiates itself from *les coeurs* beating in it. Nothing negative is implied as if parents are always abusive. When self-possession is at stake, one must disabuse oneself of the expectation and temptation to remain a dependent. As such, enecstasis surfaces when strangeness surfaces. In a parking lot, after shopping, you stubbornly try to open the door of a car you think is yours. (Little effort to imagine this scenario is needed. Most busy consumers know the experience well.) The model, year, and color of the car dupe you into thinking it is yours. An uncomfortable moment of vertigo quickly disturbs the association. Enecstasis, if anything, is like that. You feel strange, standing before an object you think is yours but is not. The fit is wrong. A disconnect occurs that is increasingly mitigated as you move toward the vehicle your car key unlocks. The incompatibility forces a realization. The right car key in the wrong keyhole is ineffectual and dissociative. Enecstasis struggles with this, the movement toward a "proper" fit bedazzled by a plethora of options that simultaneously aid and confound.

All this is background to the problematic configuring my intellectual journey. I started with some thoughts on Plato's allegory, which flags the normative underpinnings and pedagogical nature of the enecstatic gesture. This ties the procedure to its heritage of philosophy and religion in the West, for good or ill. The specificities of the preoccupation, while applicable in other contexts with different histories, is unabashedly a product and answer to the specific issues arising from this heritage. Philosophy of religion is finally becoming more globally conscious, for which we can all breathe a sigh of relief. However, it boots nothing to demonize the heritage in hopes of establishing some vantage point unaffected by its concerns and limitations. I dare say that such a philosophy of religion is potentially more dangerous intellectually than what it seeks to dismantle. Mary Louise Pratt (2008) spoke of "contact zones" for a reason, which depressurizes the scholarly alchemy in our day. A philosophy of religion that is of Western origins and desires to be more global and self-critical must embrace this limitation through negotiation. Derrida has become a cipher for this, underlining the futility of escape routes with ramparts built from materials from their point of departure. Enecstasis circumvents this by embracing the normative exigence baked into the DNA of these respective gestures, philosophy and religion, much to the chagrin of philosophy and religious studies modeled after science. A principal issue was to disengage formalizations that lock the individual into a specific elemental meaning whose emancipatory inclination blights participant involvement. In the competition of formalizations, elemental meaning and individual foundational stances become subsidiary with the agent losing all sense of self under the strictures of a particular inclination, a particular philosophy, or school of thought.

Each chapter in this volume conveys my negotiation of issues specific to philosophy of religion in an effort to articulate an idiosyncratic appreciation of elemental meaning. Enecstasis, the term for this kind of engagement, stems from a personal intellectual formation not all will identify with. Notwithstanding this, hopefully the perspective can model alternatives to a situation regarding the subject often formalized as insuperable. My struggle occurred on account of a disconnect between my foundational stance regarding elemental meanings and a field configured in a way that makes such concerns remote at best. It tended to do this—and the reflex still seems to exist—by calling it "foundationalist" or "theological." The former label is finely sculpted and meted out by philosophers (of religion), the latter by scholars of religion. The literature featured in this volume provided for the form of negotiation enecstasis names, the principal aim of which is to mitigate disqualifying formalizations advancing a preferred elemental meaning over others. This means that the strategy of enecstasis is the focus and not the literature relied on. In other words, while important, how that literature has configured enecstasis as, for example, disruptive, is truly secondary to the task at hand. Such designations are merely a form facilitated by an appreciation of the gesture that has almost become commonplace in the social sciences and humanities, especially the latter. I have indexed Beckett because his elemental meaning embodies a purposely nonlinear disruptive artistry hardwired to dishevel the Cartesian brand

and everything in its wake. Enecstasis is an example of how agential self-possession is crucial and can still occur, despite formulations of elemental meaning championed by the likes of Beckett, which too readily dismiss such attention as Cartesian. Some other body of literature could furnish the enecstatic sensibility just as well along different lines, but the point of the volume is to be discreet, not exhaustive; to ascertain the importance of being so involved and the shape it may assume in the context of an academic environment ideologically opposed to it.

The configuration of philosophy of religion in such an environment is already bewildering. Why not just concentrate on that instead of introducing a procedure likely to be deemed tertiary at best? Leaving aside that such a possible objection is itself justification for the procedure, why I devised the notion in the first place, I do admit to the exigency being intellectually personal as well as professionally expedient. Teaching philosophy of religion in a religious studies context provides a host of challenges that exceed a simple decision between different species of philosophy and their respective concerns (see chapter 4). The philosopher of religion is faced with a highly specialized and diversified demographic almost unconsciously inimical to the highly specialized questions broached by analytic and continental thinkers. Even in a context where the social sciences predominate, the largely welcomed developments in analytic philosophy of religion, global in scope and trafficking in topical comparisons of religious worldviews, are arguably precarious; the relevance factor varies relative to the degree to which "speculation" and "metaphysics" are considered empirically worthwhile. The narrative is as old as philosophy itself. In the humanities, impacted by continental sensibilities, the situation is more complex. Science, usually appreciated as such, is not regarded as the benchmark of truth. How things are conceived or represented becomes the scale rather than the presupposition. Truth is earthier here, buried in the slop of history and culture.

Driven by an elemental meaning oscillating between Descartes and Beckett, I avoided professional suicide by accommodating students and colleagues ideologically vexed by classical forms of analytic philosophy of religion and phenomenology of religion. Incidentally, this does not mean a carte blanche for continental philosophy, although it does elicit greater tolerance compared to its older sibling on account of its direct historical impact on the field. My Beckettian sensibilities (let us call them) inspired a sense of solidarity, throttling my "Cartesian" affections. But those affections continued to exist, which meant alleviating the tension between professional demands and the concern for intellectual integrity tugging at my conscience (if the expression is permitted). I scurried about identifying ways to be useful to students of religion and to myself—a philosopher by trade, interested in engaging philosophically with the tradition of religious studies, specifically the historical contingencies surrounding the foundations that animate scholarly worlds of (elemental) meaning, religious, political, moral, social, and so on. The concern is admittedly metamethodological, metaphilosophical perhaps. However, it is so without being ideationally impositional, fashioned by the reflections of this or that philosopher, scholar, or theologian.[15] It is a clearing I have found to resonate with students averse to formal philosophy and yet enthusiastic about engaging in its diverse set of elemental meanings and formalizations. Students are encouraged to be explicit about their philosophical foundations, affording themselves the courage necessary to encounter their reflex of affirming and rejecting the extant meanings that provide for their reactions.[16] It is a "safe place," to use a perhaps imprudent term, for negotiating the crippling self-doubt that formalizations and their post-systematic configuration tend to sequester as a matter of course.

Enecstatic philosophy of religion, then, is not about religion per se, described and/or explained in its instantiations—whether religious practices are worthwhile given circumstance a, b, or c, whether religious ideas can be philosophically justified or repudiated given philosophy a, b, or c, and so on. As I argue in chapter 2, this undergirds an object-constitutive approach, which, incidentally, does carry enecstatic weight in certain offerings. However, to avoid the imposition, I choose to nominate enecstatic philosophy of religion as fundamentally, but certainly not exclusively, subject-constitutive. It (1) recognizes the problematic of subjectivity in today's world, its history, limitations, and whatnot, hence the need to locate the issue elementally rather than conceptually, formally systematically, or antisystematically; (2) dialectically negotiates the mediation of religion, the theorizing of religion, which is directed by normative philosophical assumptions about religious phenomena, explicit and implicit; and (3), because of (1), provides an opportunity, despite formal prescriptions favoring or discrediting the subject, to self-assess foundations vis-à-vis, but not at the expense of, others' foundations. The issue is a practical and pedagogical one en route to conceptual formalization. Too often in academia, it is the reverse: philosophy x formalizing how one is to think about a given subject matter. While there is nothing wrong with the approach as such—it is, after all, the baseline of education, research, and self-transcendence—it does tongue-tie or induce disadvantageous vertigo discombobulating the self in search of a fuller, more responsible self. I believe this is implied in Martha Nussbaum's (1997) version of the classical notion of "world citizenship." I learned this best in the lecture hall, where acuity to disseminate ideas is forced through the messy exchange of different viewpoints formed by a zeitgeist as elusive as the self itself. That is why my prefatory remarks begin with Fulford and Mahon, who make this properly basic to learning and growth. What this meant for me was to cultivate valuable formative influences without compromising the individuality of self-discovery and its dissemination. I wanted to impress upon students and interested colleagues the invaluable potential of philosophy of religion, despite its much-deserved reputation for being detached or the click track of a very select few. I was happy to discover that others channeled a similar sentiment but about philosophy more generally, thanks to Nietzsche and Foucault. To put it in the terms of this overview, the lesson to be learned was to do for students of religion what individuals such as Pierre Hadot and Alexander Nehamas were doing for students of philosophy: first, to retrace the elemental inclinations of the philosophical reflex made possible by the disclosures of the masters of suspicion, namely, their penetrating diagnoses of the conflation of these inclinations with effective historical meanings, their formalization; and second, to align this with the needs and concerns of highly specialized, splintered research groups under the catchall "religious studies."

This host of issues fed into my formalization of a discipline haunted by a specter of cynicism or bewilderment (perhaps a blend of the two) regarding notions of subjectivity and philosophical inquiry.[17] The formalization is more diagnostic than systematic or a formalized set of instructions to achieve consensus. It evokes rather than tabulates. In my professional settings it consists of organizing stages of the study of religion, from classical to contemporary, the proper object of enecstatic philosophy of religious studies, which broaches questions of normativity in theorizing (object-constitutive) to inspire self-awareness of the reflexively self-critical variety (subject-constitutive). What better place for such reflection than in a field devoted to a dimension of human experience, "religion" being the delicate signifier, saturated by peculiar normative questions? That is why I feel enecstasis, as outlined here, is relevant in a world that has, by and large, digested the poststructuralist challenge, which I continue to take very seriously.[18] The extent to which that challenge has been mitigated is a question for another occasion. I mention it only to level expectations regarding the scope and form of the present offering. The function of enecstasis, to put it pithily, has been contoured by that challenge. It, post-structuralism, informed the general ethos of my professional surroundings. This book documents my attempt to work through certain fundamental key issues, a by-product of which was a teaching platform designed not only to pique student interest but also to negotiate an amorphous inherited indifference, theirs and (to a far lesser degree) mine, toward theory and method. Indifference may not be the best word for this. Somnambulistic theorizing, which can be quite enthusiastic, is more like it. If enecstasis disrupts anything, it is that: a learned reflex of advocacy, object-constitutive formalizations swamping agency. A delicate dance needs to be learned even if stilted at first. It takes two to tango indeed! And where the movement is fluid, Beckettian defecation can bring relief rather than ruin.

Notes

Preface

1. For a protracted discussion of these terms, "dialectic" and "foundations," see chapter 8.

Introduction

1. See also "Translating the Untranslatable," *NPR Morning Edition*, January 19, 2005, http://www.npr.org/templates/story/story.php?storyId=4457805, which provides a summary of other terms from Moore's book.

2. In this study, I am noncommittal about "postmodernism" and all the perplexity and confusion surrounding the term. When and if used positively, I assume an ethos that has moved beyond all the negativity and cynicism wrongly associated with the French theorists supposed responsible for the trend. Two recent studies on theory and discourse have offered appropriations of "the canon" that differ from one another in terms of application; they agree, however, as to the utility of poststructuralist insights. Jason Ānanda Josephson Storm (2021, 6) fashions his appropriation after a "metamodernism" that aims "to move beyond deconstruction by radicalizing it or turning it inside out." Craig Martin (2022) turns deconstruction—among other approaches (principally those of Michel Foucault and Judith Butler)—"inside out" by welding its diagnostic aims to an antirealist empiricism that locks arms with the new materialism in religious studies. Both approaches offer insights to move past the essentialist-antiessentialist stalemate—Storm, I believe, more than Martin. However, both tend to take their projects down a path that commits one to their individual ontologies. The reader will soon discover why I am unable to follow them tout court. In Storm's case, it boils down to the fundamental issue in his (mis)handling of the notion of substance, essence, in support of his "process social ontology," which one gets the impression from his prose is the only way to transcend antiessentialism. In

Martin's case, matters are more serious. Suffice it to say that what Tyler Roberts (2005; 2013, 1–82) has diagnosed as a politics of exclusion, namely, a peculiar ideological rhetoric in academia configured to exclude phenomenological and theological discourses from academic study of religion, markedly directs Martin's aims in appropriating the poststructuralist tradition. He is keenly aware, in Foucauldian fashion, that his reading of it may be his "own ravings," his "own obsession" (Martin 2022, 13). He exonerates this, however, with a quip about failing to see such a tendentious posture absent in others. Indeed, as I argue in chapter 8, a crucial juncture in mediating and mediated meaning—taken broadly here in terms of interpretation—requires organizing "dialectic" and "foundations" together. But my sense is that Martin's foundations, that which earlier I said markedly directs his interpretation, calls for more care in dialectic.

3. James L. Marsh (2014) is another, although his, so to speak, enecstatic aims extend self-appropriation qua the intellectual pattern in a predominately social-political direction. That treatment of self-appropriation is, as I argue later, quite different from my offering.

4. For the most exhaustive treatment of Lonergan's patterns of experience with which I am familiar, the reader is invited to turn to Mark D. Morelli's (2015) excellent exposition, which discusses this in terms of "motifs of conscious performance."

5. See the postscript for a different take on this artistically patterned form of thinking developed in connection with the notion of "elemental meaning" and poststructuralism.

Chapter 1. Enecstasis: A Disposition for Our Times?

1. See Masuzawa (2005) for a detailed overview of this development.

2. Craig Martin (2022) is a more recent exponent of this position, which offers a more sophisticated reading of the tradition that informs it, namely, poststructuralism. However, as I suggest in the introduction, his position is subject to the same critique I offer throughout the book.

3. That Raschke changes his tone toward deconstruction in later work (e.g., Raschke 2012) does not frustrate this observation. It points to a reaction to a philosophically configured elemental meaning, which is not in keeping with that of the reaction itself. The perceived dire consequence elicits the solidaric *cri de coeur* in question. See the preface and chapter 8 for more.

Chapter 2. The Enecstatic Jig: Personalizing Philosophy of Religion

1. For more concerning Asad on Geertz see chapter 4.

2. The second edition of Strenski's work (2015) requires some qualification of this assessment. Retitled, with the content of the first edition significantly reworked, the second edition, *Understanding Theories of Religion: An Historical Introduction to Theories of Religion*, suggests something of a development in Strenski's thinking. Although it is not incorrect to say he "protracts the otherwise insightful social-scientific preoccupation with religion as object," his endorsement in the conclusion of the holistic phenomenological approach of Ninian Smart mitigates simplistic associations of Strenski with the new materialist strategy of confinement. He is actually more critical in the second edition of McCutcheon, who represents for Strenski a "post-modern vice" in religious studies, along with Timothy Fitzgerald, another "post-modern eliminationist" (see Strenski 2015, 243–244). Indeed, Strenski argues vehemently against those who want to eliminate the category "religion" in the academy—he includes, for instance, Talal Asad and Bruce Lincoln (232–238). Strenski quips that we should be "'Smart' about bringing 'religion' back in" (the changed title in the conclusion of the second edition). Ninian Smart, "one of the greatest contemporary religious studies scholars" (248), serves as an ideal interlocutor for Strenski in the task he considers requisite nowadays of thinking *with* religion and not just *about* it (244–245). Whether this is the case is beside the point here. My principal aim is to point out that Strenski is not fairly sized up as a new materialist. Rather, he becomes something of an advocate of what I might call neo-phenomenology in the sense of his desire to bring "classic phenomenology up to date in the work of . . . Smart" (248). And yet, also in line with my aim, is that Strenski continues to be preoccupied with religion as object supported by Smart's form of phenomenology of religion, which incidentally features a concept analogous to *epochē*: the Focus. Focus brackets normative discussion about transcendent reality in religious studies roughly in the same way Strenski proposes to think *with* and not just *about* religion (see Smart 1996, 20–21). And so, while clearly neither a new materialist nor a phenomenologist who lays out "the bits and pieces of religion—experiences, saviors, gods, powers, prophets, mystics, and such—as if they were items 'etherized upon a table'" (250), Strenski's brand of thinking that "brings 'religion' back in," that tries "to come to a 'common mind' about religion" (250), differs significantly from my proposal to be smart about bringing "religion," normative reflection, back into religious studies. It is an object-constitutive focus on religion, but short of the aims of thinking I later identify as object-constitutively *enecstatic*.

3. "Religion" is to be understood here vis-à-vis the distillation of the second-order tradition of religious studies. See chapter 4.

4. As I point out in the postscript, this feature of disruption, while significant to enecstasis, is only one aspect of the gesture. Its deconstructive element is emphasized here to displace the bogus charge that normative, "religious" thinking is always stabilizing and self-authorizing. In the next chapter, the constructive elements of deconstruction will be featured. While deconstruction is consonant with enecstatic reflection, enecstasis offers a different twist, which I attempt to

spell out in the postscript. In this way, I honor the uniqueness of Derrida's contribution while differentiating it from my own.

5. Here I share the views of Caputo regarding the function of "radical theology," specifically the interstice it inhabits as a philosophical perspective between traditional philosophy of religion, philosophical theology, and confessional theology (Caputo 2018). One sees elements of this as well in Roberts's idea of "critical responsiveness," an interstice of critical awareness where the focus on alterity encourages subjective involvement in a dispossession of the divine and disruption of the stabilizing (religious) self (Roberts 2013, 2018; see also chapter 8).

6. This is the procedure I took as I was working through/in my *khōra* of enecstasis in 2013. Tyler Roberts, Clayton Crockett, Bradley B. Onishi, Carl A. Raschke, John D. Caputo, among others, have championed the gesture, surfacing the religious, the sacred, the *tout autre*, and so forth, in contemporary thinking. The tactic I take at the time of this publication is more configurative in structure to orient students through various stages of the second-order tradition of religious studies and the space it provides for dialectical engagement and the negotiation of students' own foundations—in the sense argued in chapter 8. This is the matter of philosophy of religious studies, which provides the context for a wide variety of object-constitutive gestures, including the one noted earlier that I lasso to my subjective-constitutive, enecstatic aims.

7. See note 6, which provides a gloss on the history of this development, specifically the relationship of enecstatic philosophy of religion (object-constitutive) to enecstatic philosophy of religious studies (subject-constitutive). See conclusion, figure 1.

8. Note here the appropriation of Wilfred Cantwell Smith's category, which is typically tied to the study of the *externalia* of an explicitly religious tradition (what I call a first-order tradition in chapter 4), as a designation to refer to distilled religion occasioned by and in the second-order tradition of religious studies. This is shorthand for a bona fide form of "religion," which I release from the concerns, and constraints, of the Dasein of first-order traditions and attach it to the productions of the Dasein, cares and concerns, of the second-order tradition of religious studies. Given the context of these productions, the academy, I typically name the procedure "ideology critique" in Tyler Roberts's (2018, 192–196) sense of critique as reflexively analytic, transcendental, demystifying, and reverential.

9. In his valiant reconstitution of comparative method for religious studies, Oliver Freiberger (2019) discusses this in terms of "maximal reflexivity" that "explores the epistemology of comparison by taking a close look at the origin and genesis of the comparands (the items to be compared) and the *tertium comparationis* (the aspect with regard to which they are compared) as well as their mutual relationship" (3). This "third of comparison" highlights the comparativist's agency, his or her "personal and scholarly interests, cultural background, academic training, and individual decisions" that "shape the conjunction of comparands

and *tertium* long before s/he designs the actual study" (109). It points to the highly individual nature of research complexly directed by the pre-predicative, the horizonal. Freiberger (2019, 96–101) identifies three specific factors of this background knowledge: personal, cultural, and academic. Enecstasis recognizes these factors but renders the process for their reflection explicit (subject-constitutive) in terms of dialectic (academic) and foundations (personal and cultural) (see chapter 8). Freiberger (2019) provides concrete examples of these factors in the work of scholarship (object-constitutive).

Chapter 3. Philosophy of Religious Studies: The Changing Face of Philosophy of Religion

1. Harman (2018, 6) observes: "Socrates' famous name for his profession, *philosophia*, means the *love* of wisdom rather than the possession of it. This attitude differs at its root from mathematics and the sciences, which aspire to obtain knowledge rather than merely to love it, though this difference is ignored by the many . . . who urge philosophy to follow the sure path of a science." See also 46–47, 171–177.

2. Derrida (2002, 51) makes a similar point when he writes that Heidegger is seemingly "*unable to stop either settling accounts with Christianity or distancing himself from it—with all the more violence in so far as it is already too late, perhaps, for him to deny certain proto-Christian motifs in the ontological repetition and existential analytics*" (italics in the original).

3. Harman's favorite example is fire and cotton: "OOO fully accepts the Kantian thing-in-itself, and merely denies that it is something that haunts human thought alone. Fire and cotton are also opaque to each other even if they are not 'conscious' in the same way as humans or animals" (2018, 259). For a fairly detailed discussion of these points of overlap and dissention, see Harman (2011, 136–143).

4. Interestingly, scholars of religion aim to do the same. This says more about current "metaphysics" and issues of method than it does anything intrinsic to the relation of thinking and religious themes. More anon.

5. While the differences are real, the Abrahamic faiths nonetheless share the "complication" of relating the "extra" in their knowledge, knowledge of God made available by God, with the assumptions and conclusions that those in search of a so-called dispassionate, autonomous discipline, *philosophia*, do not have. See Stead (1994, 79–81). See also El-Tobgui (2020, 23–77) and Shatz (2003). Of course, the issue of complication pertains largely to those who entertained a high view of *nous* or *intellectus agens* and the philosophic quest. Pannenberg (1991, 2) makes the important point that, at least regarding Christian theology, this issue correlates with "a recognition of theology's constitutive correlation with revelation [which] remained intact in the discussion of the High Scholastic period even among the

more Aristotelian theologians and notwithstanding the usual differences between the Augustinian-Platonist and Aristotelian camps." He continues, "The knowledge of God that is made possible by God, and therefore by revelation, is one of the basic conditions of the concept of theology as such" (2).

6. As Westphal (1997, 116) splendidly puts it: "Religion must be the knowledge of God, and while Hegel finds Kant's theology unconvincing, he finds Schleiermacher's, to which he is more sympathetic, simply confused."

7. "Religion is the elevation of finite spirit to absolute or infinite spirit. In its religious form, this is (mis)understood as encounter with Someone Other. In its philosophical form it is the discovery that the highest form of human self-awareness is the sole locus in which the infinite totality . . . comes to self-knowledge" (Westphal 1997, 116).

8. Incidentally, I do not see the emphasis on Kant in the exchange between Wolterstorff and Westphal as contradicting my claim that it is Hegel who is key to the bifurcation of philosophy of religion. Just as knowledge of Kant requires knowledge of Hume, knowledge of Hegel requires knowledge of Kant. The same cannot be said, in other words, about Hegel and Hume. Hegel's dependence on Kant, although a negative one, is nonetheless part of the Kantian tradition. His thinking style, specifically as regards the historicality (*Geschichtlichkeit*) of thought, is what marks him as weightier for the continental tradition than Kant himself, although we would want to qualify this with respect to others in his shadow (e.g., Jacobi, Fichte, Schelling). Kant is a transitional figure from Hume to Hegel, although his strong and continued influence on contemporary continental philosophy is undeniable. The emphasis will vary depending on the degree to which foundationalism and nonfoundationalism are being espoused.

9. What Paul Griffiths (1997) identifies as "structural analysis," a rubric of comparative philosophy of religion, may be the exception. Structural analysis "will treat not so much the truth or desirability or meaning of [particular doctrines, rituals, exegetical activities], as the logical or conceptual structure of the phenomena in question and their possible uses" (721).

10. See the discussion in chapter 2.

11. Others who deserve mention include Robert Segal, Bruce Lincoln, Gary Lease, Donald Wiebe, and Willi Braun. See entries in the references of their work for further reading.

12. The postscript documents a later development, devised in preparing the manuscript for publication. It isolates "elemental meaning" as the point of departure of enecstatic involvement.

13. See my more focused discussion of Roberts's contributions in chapter 8.

14. The aporia in this particular instance is to try to articulate, through language, what is not language.

15. "The analytic post-modern should be construed as the formalist re-appropriation of the anti-metaphysical propensities within modernist culture

and thought . . . The 'metaphoric post-modern' . . . harks back to the desire of Nietzsche's Zarathustra to *dance*. [It] rests on a profound post-metaphysical insight—what the Czech novelist Milan Kundera has called the 'unbearable lightness of being.' The metaphoric post-modern is Eco's 'travels in hyperreality.' It is the transcendence of nihilism" (Raschke 1990, 681–682).

16. Raschke has progressively toned down his antipathy, toward Derrida at least. From "Fire and Roses: Toward Authentic Postmodern Religious Thinking" (1990) to *Postmodernism and the Revolution in Religious Theory* (2012), the tone is notably more eirenic and even emulative. For example, Derrida is promoted from indulging in "two-dimensional . . . wordgrams with their curious, Dadaist messages of inconsequentiality" (Raschke 1990, 685) to being the "most visible envoy of postmodernist belles lettres" (Raschke 2012, 15) whose semiotic revolution "has been betrayed repeatedly by partisans of various ideological persuasions . . . who utterly confuse the deconstructive project with some kind of constructive critique of long-held or normative positions" (4). The Derrida of Raschke's "Fire and Roses," unable "to intuit his own nihilism" (1990, 674), sets in motion a revolution that "can be belatedly set right if we begin to examine closely what he has wrought in terms of postmodern philosophy as a whole, which can serve also as the launchpad for a *revolution in religious theory as a whole*" (2012, 4–5, emphasis original).

17. When found in philosophy departments this kind of thinking is simply continental reflection. It does not have to deal with the burden of connecting it with thinking in religious studies or vis-à-vis religious topics.

18. Examples of this would include works from Charles Taliaferro and Arvind Sharma.

19. Cooey is specific about this assumption being held about "nor theological scholars of religion." My selective quotation means to broaden it.

Chapter 4. Philosophy of Religion Religious Studies Style

1. See chapter 3, which provides an overview of these different thinking styles in philosophy of religion in terms of discordant tribes.

2. See the important study of Tomoko Masuzawa (2005), which provides a detailed overview of the intellectual history that has heightened this awareness in religious studies. In philosophy of religion, a noteworthy appreciation of the situation can be seen in Hendrik M. Vroom (2006), who seeks to inculcate developments in what is often called "world philosophy" in a post-1990s appreciation of the category of pluralism. The earlier work of the late philosopher of religion John Hick can be flagged as a significant pioneering attempt, which, incidentally, Vroom rightly criticizes. Another example of the current awareness, also critical of the earlier pluralist posture, but in theology, is David F. Ford (2007, 2010)

and Michael Barnes (2002, 2010). Closer to the field interests of philosophers of religion, mindful of the religious studies context, is Steven M. Wasserstrom (1999) and a recent contribution from Bradley B. Onishi (2018). My project differs from theirs in being explicitly subject-constitutive, which I explain later in this and other chapters of the book. What I find valuable in works such as these is the enecstatic potential of their respective object-constitutive critiques of secularism in the study of religion. Onishi's work in particular offers some positive directives concerning the dimension of sacrality in the secular broached in continental philosophy and its "turn to religion." Analogous to this, in the terms of this study, is the "foundational" preoccupation one finds in the work of Tyler Roberts and his notion of "critical responsiveness" (see chapter 8).

3. The observation of Jeremy Carrette (2010, 277) in this regard is perspicacious. He puts an epistemological face on the poststructuralist concern with representation. In other words, the epistemological tendency of the Enlightenment—to focus on the impartial mediation of objects—changes with the advent of poststructuralism; it is not eliminated. It changes into critical awareness of the cultural-linguistic-psychological-political saturation of mediation. This element is crucial for understanding the form and accent featured in enecstatic "epistemological" self-awareness. It caters specifically to students of culture, where the method they consciously or unconsciously entertain is managed by an artistry whose conscience is guided by the problem of representation.

4. I place "epistemology" in scare quotes to signal a connotation that takes seriously Bernard Lonergan's suggestion that cognitional theory, which he considers properly basic to an analysis of the Dasein who understands, does something different from both epistemology and metaphysics (in his sense). Cognitional theory works out a—Lonergan might prefer to say *the*—structure of knowing based on what we can roughly designate as a phenomenology of insight. He calls it "generalized empirical method" in *Insight* ([1957] 1992), "transcendental method" and "intentionality analysis" in his more widely read *Method in Theology* (1972b). "What is happening when we are knowing?" ([1957] 1992, 16) is its guiding question. Epistemology, as it relates to his cognitional theory, is a concern with another question: "What is known when that is happening?" (17). Even if both questions seem to be concerned with a "what," the content of understanding, the first is more properly framed according to the phenomenological "how": How is knowing done? if you will. Lonergan surfaces, through description, the "unity-identity-whole" of the process, the consciousness that simply knows. To put it in the terms of this study, the question about the shape and function of cognizing is framed as intentionally subject-constitutive. That "what" is "whated" as a "how" to occasion in the reader an awareness of the "howness" of her knowing, to identify it in and for herself. In the second and third questions—the third, introduced ten years after *Insight*, took on the form of the second changed to "Why is doing that knowing?" (see [1957] 1992, 779, note f)—Lonergan means to elucidate this

"how" with respect to the "what." It is important to qualify this procedure with the phrase "with respect to" because, while the "what" comes into view, specifically in questions two and three, it is nestled in the "howness" of the entire program. Therefore, I suggest, cognitional theory, epistemology, and metaphysics, according to Lonergan's configuration, should be understood as fundamentally heuristic (see index entries "heuristic," "heuristic method," "heuristic structures" in Lonergan [1957] 1992 for the bigger picture).

One discovers this, of all places, at the *end* of *Insight*, namely, after covering cognitional theory, epistemology, and metaphysics. In chapter 19 of *Insight* one encounters Lonergan's "proof" of God, where a crucial distinction is made between intending "complete intelligibility" and knowledge of the unrestricted act of understanding, another name for God, knowledge of which pertains only to God (see Lonergan 1967; editorial note in Caputo 2004, xii, n3). Briefly, intending complete intelligibility is part and parcel of our being-in-the-world as knowers. It lies "at the root of all our attempts to mean anything at all" (Lonergan 1967, 259). It is the "how" in our intending "what," the source and end of which is in but beyond all that we grasp, the *unrestricted act* of understanding, the only being who has being itself as its essence (see Lonergan 1972a, 312). In other words, the "what" in Lonergan is welcomed through the door of the phenomenologically cognitional "how." One gathers this quite clearly in Lonergan's ([1967] 1988, 190, 202–204) response to Emerich Coreth, his (Coreth's) desire to make "explicit metaphysics" primary, a *Gesamt- und Gruntwissenschaft*. Lonergan, by contrast, argues for the primacy of what he openly calls "implicit metaphysics," the "subject as subject" raising and answering questions. This is interesting not only for gaining an understanding of the fundamental role of cognitional theory in Lonergan, but also because, in support of my claim that Lonergan puts the "what" in the service, so to speak, of the "how," he has no qualms calling cognitional theory "metaphysics."

This characterization has, of course, the Heidegger of *Being and Time* in mind, namely his distinction between the "how" and the "what" (see index entries "the 'who': das Wer" and "the 'what': das Was" in Heidegger [1927] 1962). I do this to underline the phenomenological character of Lonergan's cognitional theory and, I would add, his epistemology and metaphysics, even if that character appears strictly to apply to the first part of *Insight*, his cognitional theory. Of course, Heidegger's "how" in *Being and Time* is guided by a different set of questions, which some would argue grounds and even more radically problematizes gestures such as Lonergan's. See, for example, William J. Richardson's (1972) epic critique, to which Lonergan responded (1972a). Incidentally, I consider Jerome A. Miller's (1992) paired reading of Lonergan and Heidegger to be a creative alternative to Richardson's. In any case, the length to which I have gone to characterize this matter means to lay bare the understanding that if enecstatic philosophizing is referenced equivocally in the text as "epistemology," this is meant to be taken guardedly. It does not fully or strictly capture the configuration of enecstasis, nor does it represent the understanding of the practice taken seriously in its formation, namely, Lonergan's. This is important to note since the momentum is building in the text, distinguishing the context of Lonergan's desideratum from my own.

5. *Geschichtlichkeit* is Wilhelm Dilthey's term. "Dilthey and his fellow philosophers wrestled with the problem of temporality, i.e., the problem that no phenomenon and no approach to it can be seriously studied without an awareness of the historicality [*Geschichtlichkeit*] of human life and consciousness" (Jeanrond 1991, 53). "Historicality" encapsulates for me the basic ethos of continental philosophy. It is not altogether ignored by analytic philosophers of religion. However, their typical modus operandi suggests that priority is given to logic and argumentation and not to the constitutive determinations of the historicality frame. See chapter 5 of *Being and Time* for Heidegger's exposition of historicality "resolved to foster the spirit of Count Yorck in the service of Dilthey's work" ([1927] 1962, 455).

6. My use of the term "historicality" here does not suggest that Geertz's "cognitivist" approach excludes it. As a close reader of the hermeneutical and phenomenological traditions, Geertz was more than aware of what this consciousness entails. To my mind, there are stages of appreciation of historicality as encapsulated by systems of thought indebted to the continental tradition. Geertz's signals an appreciation, as his comments about Asad suggest, that by and large rejects the poststructuralist reception.

7. Examples from other traditions, with similar structures of authority, would fit equally well to demonstrate Asad's main problem with the cognitive approach.

8. See chapter 2 where, following Asad, I categorize Geertz's anthropology in terms of a "secular liberal strategy of confining religion" (in the social-scientific stream, albeit phenomenological) as opposed to a "liberal Christian strategy of defending religion" (overtly theological, albeit phenomenologically influenced as well). Both are normative stances with different aims. Whereas Asad's analysis of Geertz may suggest a different strategy on Asad's part, my sense is that Asad's discourse is a mixture of both, methodologically speaking, as he critiques the surface impartiality of strategies of confinement. While defending religion is to be kept separate from anthropology of religion, which I take to be Asad's stance, the strategy for doing so is not altogether absent from Asad's critique.

9. That is also why earlier I write that Asad's approach represents *a dimension* of the historicality frame, not a complete embodiment of it.

10. Since it may not be obvious, I should probably qualify this statement. By object-constitutive, I do not mean anything negative. For instance, what I consider to be enecstatic programs have an object-constitutive tendency (see chapter 2, for example, where I state this explicitly in deference to the programmatic objectives of the thinking in question). To use an old distinction, such an orientation focuses on the "whatness" of discourse while it implicitly cultivates or encourages the elusive "thatness" of subjective orientation. In the case of Asad's object-constitutive tendency the enecstatic is not obvious or—possibly better put—unannounced. That

is, it is a horizon eliminated or simply bracketed in critique. Asad does not seem to want to play theology in analysis, which is acceptable, of course. But to ask why this may be the case can surface relevant issues of fundamental importance that directly impact the scope and relevance of critique.

11. For a philosophical application (the so-called religious turn in philosophy), see Dominique Janicaud (2001). The controversy of the theological turn in philosophy (Janicaud) is not within a hundred miles of the controversy of normative reflection in religious studies (see chapter 8). A direct treatment of it here is avoided because I believe such a discussion is best broached when issues about method arise in specialized object-constitutive continental philosophy of religion. As I hope is clear, philosophy of religious studies, as I understand it, is more generalized when it comes to philosophy and methodology. Still, one would not be incorrect to surmise that my treatment of phenomenology of religion unequivocally sides with Janicaud's critics. The type of fluidity they imagine between phenomenology and theology resonates with my enecstatic aims.

12. See, for example, the important contribution of Francis Schüssler Fiorenza (2000).

13. I will discuss instances of this shortly. For more, see chapter 2 as well.

14. Stephen S. Bush (2012) distinguishes degrees of rejection in Sharf. Victor Sōgen Hori (2019) much more radically disarms Sharf's central claims concerning the impact of the reverse orientalism of D. T. Suzuki, among others. Suzuki, Sharf claims, invented a tradition, New Buddhism (Shin Bukkyo), rather than following one, "authentic" Chan/Zen. Hori shows that the Chinese Buddhist Electronic Text Association (CBETA) database suggests otherwise. The CBETA survey that Hori provides demonstrates "that D. T. Suzuki's conception of satori as a sudden experience has not been recently invented or manufactured. Although the modern philosophical terminology of *taiken* and *keiken* is not used in traditional Chan literature, [as Sharf rightly argues,] the character *wu*, [on the other hand,] read *go* or *satori* in Japanese, is used to refer to awakening as a sudden event. There are literally hundreds, perhaps thousands, of instances where someone is described as suddenly experiencing enlightenment. This is the 'traditional' way of conceiving of enlightenment in Chan/Zen. D. T. Suzuki did not invent that tradition" (Hori 2019, 55).

What Suzuki "invented" in support of the superiority of Japanese culture was based on the long-standing stereotype that Europe is logical while Asia is intuitive, inverting the original conclusion by arguing that that is why Asia, not Europe, is superior. He rallied to his defense the "experience" of satori in traditional Chan literature, transposing Western assumptions about European racial superiority to reflect the ideological convictions forged during the Meiji Restoration (78). Sharf has misdiagnosed the situation. He is fixed on the wrong object, namely, the introduction of a foreign notion—a Western-influenced phenomenological emphasis on religious experience—into authentic Buddhism, thereby inventing an offbeat tradition. Suzuki, as Hori points out, reflects tradition rather than invents it. Hori represents a mode of philosophy of religious studies I call "dialectic," the reversal of a false claim in mediating meaning. There is a "foundations" mode to it as well, which presses the issue of ideological investment. Why insist that Suzuki and company invent a tradition? Despite Hori's critique, what does such an emphasis reveal about Sharf's philosophical, perhaps even "religious," convictions? To what degree do they skew the data? And, as a result, to what degree can you or I follow him given our foundations? While important, this line of questioning is best left for another occasion. The principal aim in this chapter is to demarcate in general terms topics indigenous to philosophy of religious studies. But for more on the significance of these poles in philosophy of religious studies, "dialectic" and "foundations," see chapter 8.

15. James's methodological directives for psychology of religion, which are phenomenological in nature, are three: (1) mystical states are and have the right to be authoritative over those who have experienced them, (2) not to those who have not. The third directive speaks to both the critical function and epistemological potential of mystical states, namely, they "break down" the authority of strictly empirical judgments, offering insight into the possibility of other orders of truth to those viscerally open to them. See James ([1902] 1982, 585).

16. Joachim Wach (1967, 8, 10, 15), Gerardus van der Leeuw ([1938] 1986, 680, 683–689), and Mircea Eliade (1959, 88–89) made this point in different ways, in line with their programmatic objectives.

17. Consult, for example, the works in the references by Timothy Fitzgerald, Donald Wiebe, Robert A. Segal, Bruce Lincoln, and Russell T. McCutcheon.

18. Rodrigues and Harding (2009, 6–7, 10–11). In fairness, they qualify the last statement, writing that all theology, "in some measure, . . . is an exercise in apologetics" (10). I stand by what is in the text as a fair phrasing by dropping their intensifier "all."

19. A notable example from philosophy of religion is Charles Taliaferro (1998) who references R. G. Collingwood.

20. "As it has sometimes been put, one should attempt to be an outsider to one's own tradition (when studying it as a religious studies scholar), and an insider to other foreign traditions (those that one is studying)." And again, "one must strive to enter into a subjective experience of the tradition" (Rodrigues and Harding 2009, 11). More radical critics of the phenomenological tradition seek to problematize what to some is (pace Rodrigues and Harding's otherwise honorable attempt to appropriate such a procedure for a nonpartisan religious studies) fundamentally a phenomenological aim: to imagine what it is like to entertain an extraneous religious belief. Robert Segal (1983), in trying to topple the phenomenological edifice, argues that the very suggestion is approbative of theological aims. Wiebe (1983) regrets the metaphysics of the debate entirely.

21. Strenski cites Wiebe, who calls out McCutcheon (Wiebe's former student at the University of Toronto) for pitting a new "ideological agenda"—McCutch-

eon's "engaged, public intellectual"—over an old one, "religio-theological studies of religion" (2006, 340). The assumption of naturalism in the activity is no less meta-physical than that of the old rearguard.

22. This terminology is obviously technical and harks back to categories of Bernard Lonergan. See Lonergan (1972b, 125–133, 235–293). For an application of dialectic and foundations in the context of religious studies, see chapter 8.

23. Tyler Roberts has been doing his share to address this "new protectionism" in the scholarly tradition since at least 2004. His book *Encountering Religion: Responsibility and Criticism after Secularism* (2013) is a summation of his thoughts, envisioning a way forward. See, too, his chapter in Kanaris (2018) for a more recent development.

24. In chapter 2 I discuss an aspect of this thesis in conjunction with Paula Cooey (2002, 178), who relies on Kant to ascertain the "intentional [meaning] construction" of philosophical inquiry. She recognizes, as I do, that this is an important task of academic theology.

25. "Immediacy" and "mediacy" are philosophically loaded terms. Their function here is solely to illustrate a spatial relationship: an immediate normativity reserved for believers that objective scholarship sees itself as merely mediating. By discussing an "immediacy" peculiar to mediating scholarship—that is, "objective" scholarship—I am asking readers to entertain an equal current of normativity that runs through scholarly thinking.

26. See note 14 for Victor Hori's critique of Sharf, which probes more deeply than Bush the claims of Sharf about Zen Buddhism that seem to fuel his eliminativism. Hori's revalorization of "experience" for religious studies makes Bush's attempt quite modest by comparison. As I suggest in that note, the implication in Hori's gesture is indirectly (dialectically) enecstatic, an exposé of a specific scholarly inclination sullying the data. Were it more direct, the exposition would move from exposé to plaidoyer, how Chinese *wu*—which the Japanese *go* or *satori* of Zen Buddhism resembles—can inform the scholarly pursuit of the experience in question.

27. Refer to the preface for an explanation of my more idiosyncratic use of this term.

28. As will become increasingly clear, Lonergan is significant to my enecstatic aims (see my longish note 4). He has, in my opinion, identified in an unprecedented way the crucial, central role of self-possession—responsibility to self and other, if you prefer—in, specifically, the academic, intellectual enterprise. Careful readers will also note that my enecstatic aims, apropos of a philosophy of religious studies, differs from Lonergan's. The form of his project overlaps with themes that tend toward, but are not restricted to, the analytic mien (i.e., science). For reasons mentioned earlier, the context that my enecstatic accent seeks to service is saturated by issues hard-pressed to acknowledge projects as Lonergan's. Although I understand the antipathy—I would not have coined the

term "enecstasis" if I did not—I remain unconvinced that it should determine the relevance of application. In any case, this is a delicate balancing act, and I hope that my explanations, which begin to take shape in the text, become more satisfactorily nuanced. See chapters 6 through 8 for the protracted discussion.

Chapter 5. Derrida's Philosophy of Religion for Religious Studies

1. See the important study of Hent de Vries (1999).

2. It is interesting that Derrida (2002, 75) states that "it would have been madness itself to have proposed to treat religion *itself*, in general or in its essence. . . . Since the then common concern with the (re)appearance of religion, the phenomenon, Heidegger's semblance (*das Scheinbare, der Schein*), is: 'What is going on today with it, with what is designated thus? What is going on there? What is happening and so badly? What is happening under this old name? What in the world is suddenly emerging or re-emerging under this appellation?'" (75). This return, in other words, calls for deconstructive consideration, to summon that which is concealed in what reappears, religion "today," why that configuration should appear as such and what mechanism supplies its determinate response (*religio qua respondeo*). Both aspects will be considered in this chapter. In any case, such interest in religion looks to the announcement of the phenomenon, its appearance in the world, in terms of that which does not show itself but conceals itself in its appearance. Therefore, "to treat religion *itself*, in general or in its essence," is, for Derrida, to imagine religion outside its worldly context. This is to relate what is concealed in religion's disclosure to some worldless essence that stands apart from its appearance—"madness," as we saw. He indicts the various forms of religiosity that spearhead the return, but also the two poles of philosophy that rigorously tackle temporality, Husserl's "intuition of essences" through "free variation" and Heidegger's Dasein as time temporalizing its Being, being-in-the-world. I also mean to include, which incited this note in the first place, the posture in religious studies, whether phenomenological or new materialist, seeking the scholarly arbitration of this "essence" in seemingly disengaged ways. Derrida does not speak to this "madness" directly. Were he pressed, I imagine he would be circumspect, acknowledging the importance of scholarly productions. But this is also to say that I believe he would be circumspect about the tendency to enlist deconstruction to settle some ideological dispute in theory selection (see introduction, note 2).

3. "The detours, locutions, and syntax in which I will often have to take recourse will resemble those of negative theology, occasionally even to the point of being indistinguishable from negative theology. Already we have had to delineate that *différance* is not, does not exist, is not a present-being (*on*) in any form; and we will be led to delineate also everything *that* it *is not*, that is, *everything*; and

consequently that it has neither existence nor essence. It derives from no category of being, whether present or absent. And yet those aspects of *différance* which are thereby delineated are not theological, not even in the order of the most negative of negative theologies, which are always concerned with disengaging a superessentiality beyond the finite categories of essence and existence, that is, of presence, and always hastening to recall that God is refused the predicate of existence, only in order to acknowledge his superior, inconceivable, and ineffable mode of being. Such a development is not in question here, and this will be confirmed progressively. *Différance* is not only irreducible to any ontological or theological—ontotheological—reappropriation, but as the very opening of the space in which ontotheology—philosophy—produces its system and its history, it includes ontotheology, inscribing it and exceeding it without return" (Derrida 1982, 6, italics in original).

4. See Derrida (2002, 51, 54, 54n9, 55, 61, 85n31, 94, 96, 97, 97n42, 99) for an indictment of Heidegger's "Christian motifs." In a subsequent work, I should like to address an indictment brought against the *Verhaltenheit* ("modesty or respect, scruple, reserve or silent discretion that suspends itself in and as reticence" [Derrida 2002, 85n31] of both Derridean *religio*, messianicity, and what Derrida (2002, 96) describes as Heidegger's "ontological repetition . . . of a . . . markedly Christian tradition." I find this in the stirring proposals of Jean-Luc Marion (2012) starting with his celebrated *Dieu Sans L'Être: Hors-Texte* published in 1982 and translated into English in 1991, with a second edition in 2012 that includes a new preface from the author. Of course, I was keenly aware of Marion's work decades before I penned an earlier version of this chapter, in 2012. A prolepsis of why I, pursuant of a philosophy of religious studies, settled on Derrida, among others, instead of post-Derridean dignitaries as Marion was not available to me then. I can venture a rough sketch now as to why this may have happened. I completed a doctorate on Lonergan's philosophy of religious studies in 2000. Before and after 2002, when the dissertation was published, I published on works coming from poststructuralist quarters (mostly in France and mostly by Derrida and Foucault) severely criticizing basic claims resembling those of Lonergan's; the third part of this work, including the postscript, is the culmination of this development. Marion could have easily factored into this. His stance on the supposed onto-theo-logic of one of Lonergan's favorite thinkers, Thomas Aquinas, is a case in point. Marion (2012, xxx), incidentally, has reconsidered his position. Even if this might have "easily" been done, it would have been artificial or forced. Not only did I not possess the wherewithal to make the plausible connections, but I was also after a philosophy of religious studies weaned on Lonergan and others that could contribute to larger normative debates in the field. I was in the circle, neither puzzling over how to enter nor escape it (Heidegger [1927] 1962, 195). Derrida's *Verhaltenheit*, I believe, resonates more naturally in this pluralistic context of "human flourishing" than, say, explicit treatments of Christian motifs in highly

specialized continental philosophies of religion such as Marion's. However, I do wish to qualify this claim in the proposed future work wherein the specificities of *Christian* meaning-making are indeed very apropos surrounded as they are by different problematics. In this way, too, I hope to address some of the charges leveled at Derrida by Richard Kearney (2001, for instance) to further nuance the historical coincidences of thinker selection in my philosophy of religious studies.

5. This is only a convenient reference to the statement that couches a richer meaning: not only is there nothing outside the text but there is no referent outside a text, no arch-text or "pure" text, that exonerates the hegemony of a text that writes on behalf of this transcendental signified. One cannot point to something without thereby constituting that thing in its so-called pure essence.

6. "The concept of the sign, in each of its aspects, has been determined by this opposition throughout the totality of its history. It has lived only on this opposition and its system. But we cannot do without the concept of the sign, for we cannot give up this metaphysical complicity without also giving up the critique we are directing against this complicity, without the risk of erasing difference in the self-identity of a signified reducing its signifier into itself or, amounting to the same thing, simply expelling its signifier outside itself. For there are two heterogenous ways of erasing the difference between the signifier and the signified: one, the classic way, consists in reducing or deriving the signifier, that is to say, ultimately in *submitting* the sign to thought; the other, the one we are using here against the first one, consists in putting into question the system in which the preceding reduction functioned: first and foremost, the opposition between the sensible and the intelligible. The *paradox is* that the metaphysical reduction of the sign needed the opposition it was reducing. The opposition is systematic with the reduction. And what we are saying here about the sign can be extended to all the concepts and all the sentences of metaphysics, in particular to the discourse on 'structure.' But there are several ways of being caught in this circle. They are all more or less naive, more or less empirical, more or less systematic, more or less close to the formulation—that is, to the formalization—of this circle. It is these differences which explain the multiplicity of destructive discourses and the disagreement between those who elaborate them. Nietzsche, Freud, and Heidegger, for example, worked within the inherited concepts of metaphysics. Since these concepts are not elements or atoms, and since they are taken from a syntax and a system, every particular borrowing brings along with it the whole of metaphysics. This is what allows these destroyers to destroy each other reciprocally—for example, Heidegger regarding Nietzsche, with as much lucidity and rigor as bad faith and misconstruction, as the last metaphysician, the last 'Platonist.' One could do the same for Heidegger himself, for Freud, or for a number of others. And today no exercise is more widespread" (Derrida 1978, 281).

7. I bracket for purposes of my overview Derrida's use of χώρα as resisting and deconstructing Plato's system. See Caputo's (1997a, 87–96) discussion.

8. See Derrida 2002, 69, where Benveniste is quoted at length. The example is from a dialogue of Plautus that recounts an exchange between Ergasilus and Hegion about the return of the latter's son: "Is this a *promise* [*spondēn*]?—It's a *promise* [*spondeo*]. And I, for my part, promise you [*respondeo*] you that your son has arrived." Benveniste himself is not committed to the relation, *spondeo* with *respondeo* and consequently *religio*. But Derrida deconstructs Benveniste's stance based on an inconsistency in Benveniste that amounts to an admission of ignorance on Benveniste's part regarding the etymology of religion that he nonetheless couches in claims of knowledge. One is reminded of the early Derrida deconstructing Saussure who, evidently, could not embrace his own radical claim about the differential play of signs.

9. "Religion, in the *singular*? Response: 'Religion is **the response.**' Is it not there, perhaps, that we must seek the beginning of a response?" (Derrida 2002, 64); "But, **one still must respond**. And without waiting. Without waiting too long. **In the beginning** . . . 'we need a theme for this meeting in Capri' . . . . I respond, 'Religion'" (75).

10. However, the passage as quoted is bogus, rewritten by Quentin Tarantino, the film's director, for the film: "The path of the righteous man is beset on all sides by the inequities of the selfish and the tyranny of evil men. Blessed is he who, in the name of charity and good will, shepherds the weak through the valley of darkness, for he is truly his brother's keeper and the finder of lost children. And I will strike down upon thee with great vengeance and furious anger those who attempt to poison and destroy my brothers. And you will know my name is the Lord when I lay my vengeance upon you."

11. The connection to Kant here, who discusses radical evil in *Religion within the Limits of Reason Alone* (1793), not as an element of "dogmatic faith" (*parergon*) but as integral to "reflecting faith," is significant. Derrida's reference more or less suggests that Kant is so radically right about radical evil that his own "salvific" discourse is contrary to Kant's own intentions (i.e., not immune to it). Hence, he (Kant) can make the claim with a clear conscience that the Christian religion is the only truly moral religion.

12. The immunity of outbidding philosophies is not the same thing as autoimmunity, which I do not discuss here. Perhaps an example of autoimmunity in philosophic discourse would be Heidegger's flirtation with National Socialism, which, I believe, is always already a danger of any philosophy (given none of us live with the luxury of hindsight) and not necessarily something inherent in ontology.

13. See the important translator's note 29 in Derrida (2002, 82). See also note 11 on the notion of "radical evil." Derrida disengages Kant's notion from its specifically Christian meaning identifying it as the possibility and outcome of the structure of faith. He does the same with Kant's notion of "reflecting faith" as the modality of deconstruction.

14. Chapters 1, 3, and 4 of the present work provide the needed background to understand the ramifications of this claim.

Chapter 6. Theorizing Religion Enecstatically: The Transcendental Gesture in a New Key

1. Winquist (1995, 31): "Truth is not found. It is a way of looking that masks the fluxes and flows of the will to power. The troping of truth in Nietzsche is a turn to the arbitrariness of the elements of language. He liberates the productive imagination in a celebration of the endless possibilities for world-making and for surpassing the rigidified experience of the human condition."

2. "*Différance* instigates the subversion of every kingdom. Which makes it obviously threatening and infallibly dreaded by everything within us that desires a kingdom" (Derrida 1982, 22). See chapter 5, which exploits Derrida's deconstruction as an important feature of enecstatic thinking.

3. See William A. Mathews's (2005) recent and thorough investigation of Lonergan's struggle with the "flight from understanding" leading up to and including *Insight*. This personal scuffle doubtless solidified in Lonergan the importance of the particular, intellectualist form in which he cast self-appropriation.

4. See Lonergan's *Method in Theology* (1972b), in which the relation of the four "levels of consciousness" (experience, understanding, judging, deciding) are developed in connection with numerous "differentiations of consciousness" and their individual "realms of meaning."

5. Lonergan, strictly speaking, views "epistemology" as a secondary task of what, after *Insight*, he recognized as a tripartite concern in the investigation of the phenomenon of consciousness. He linked this concern to three questions: What am I doing when I am knowing? (the task of intentionality analysis or cognitional theory); Why is doing that knowing? (an epistemological question); What do I know when I do it? (a question of metaphysics). See Lonergan ([1957] 1992, 16, 779 note f). My hunch is that Lonergan would consider Winquist's idiosyncratic preoccupation with ontology as based on a confusion between the primary and tertiary tasks of cognition and metaphysics, which leads Winquist to the erroneous view that Lonergan's phenomenology of experience biases the second. For more, see chapter 4, note 4.

6. This is something I have argued in the past in deference to an important work by Fred Lawrence (1981). See Kanaris (2003, 73–74).

7. Winquist (2003) provides an ontological retelling of the transcendental imagination in which he relies, naturally, on Heidegger. Tillich and Whitehead are others from whom Winquist gains much inspiration. See note 5 for an assessment from the point of view of Lonergan's philosophy.

8. For what follows on the question of judgment in the artistic and intellectual patterns of experience I am indebted to an email exchange with Mark Morelli of Loyola Marymount University. See also Morelli (2015) for a detailed exposition of Lonergan's patterns of experience in terms of "motifs" of conscious awareness.

9. See Lonergan ([1957] 1992, 126–162). See also Kanaris (2005a, 91–95), in which I consider the hypervigilance of Foucault's philosophy as an example of thinking dominated by an artistic pattern, as blindsided by a caricature of explanatory knowledge that mismanages the statistical appreciation of the nonsystematic, that is, as noncomplementary to the classical intrigue with the systematic. From the perspective of Lonergan's cognitional theory, Foucault precludes the potential intelligibility of events, social practices, which diverge nonsystematically from the ideal frequencies of history. This gives Foucault license to extend his genealogical insights to other forms in order to secure the manifold of events as forever coincidental. This is the obverse bias noted in the text regarding Lonergan as it pertains to artistic judgments vis-à-vis a dominant intellectual pattern that is explanatory. Winquist falls in line with this tendency but in connection with (transcendental) ontology rather than history. A complementarity that negotiates a predilection to the artistic or explanatory horizon is something cultivated in the context-relative sensibility of enecstatic philosophizing. Here I find Derrida's deconstruction helpful as a strategy rather than as a system whose implementation does not depend on a particular pattern with a determined outcome.

10. This is an important bridge to be developed in the proposed future work mentioned in chapter 5, note 4, namely, the move from a subject-constitutive treatment of object-constitutive concerns à la enecstatic philosophy of religious studies to a subject-constitutive development of specific object-constitutive concerns of continental philosophy of religion. Of course, engagement with developments in comparative analytic philosophy of religion, implicit and explicit elements of enecstasis evidenced by it, is encouraged.

11. See the postscript for another angle on this question of the artistic.

12. Raschke's valorization of popular culture as conveying the *differend* does not necessarily legitimate the moral or ontological character of the "sign-performances" of popular culture. "It reframes their purpose, primarily in terms of the categories of regimentation, subversion, 'ceremonial' articulation, and ideological oscillation" (Raschke 1990, 678–679).

13. This is not to say, of course, that I fully embrace Descartes's philosophy. I am content with Lonergan's assessment, which points out that Descartes's discovery of the "I think," the *res cogitans*, has 'enduring significance" ([1957] 1992, 436) as does his *res extensa* for "elementary knowing" (448, 799 note p), that is, the properly basic field of all sentient life. Where Descartes goes wrong is in juxtaposing the "I think" and the so-called "'already out there now real' stripped of its secondary qualities and of any substantiality distinct from spatial extension"

(438). Lonergan, in his common clarity of prose, sums it up thus: "Cartesian dualism had been a twofold realism, and both the realisms were correct; for the realism of the extroverted animal [described earlier as 'elementary knowing'] is no mistake, and the realism of rational affirmation ['I think'] is no mistake. The trouble was that, unless two distinct and disparate types of knowing were recognized, the two realisms were incompatible. For rational affirmation is not an instance of extroversion, and so it cannot be objective in the manner proper to the 'already out there now'" (439). Heidegger levels a somewhat similar charge but in a different direction supported by his primary difficult task: the question of the meaning of Being. Among Descartes's mistakes is to equate the Being of Dasein with "constant presence at hand" ([1927] 1962, 129), an error to which Descartes is led thanks to the presupposition that the only genuine access to the Being of the "I" and the "world" is through knowing (*Erkennen*) "in the kind of knowledge (Erkenntnis) we get in mathematics and physics" (128). For a hermeneutical consideration of the enecstatic, elemental meaning, in Descartes indirectly influenced by Lonergan more than Heidegger, see the postscript.

Chapter 7. Enecstatic Philosophy of Religious Studies: A Sidelong Bow to Self-Appropriation

1. See chapter 3 for another, more general characterization of these two species of philosophizing religion.
2. See chapter 6 for the "delicate nature" of the contingencies surrounding Lonergan's objectification in the ether of philosophy (i.e., the continental tradition).
3. Lonergan (1972b, 20, 53, 105–106) enumerates the "transcendental precepts" along the lines of the transcendental notions of attentiveness, intelligence, reasonableness, responsibility, and love. Thus: be attentive, be intelligent, be reasonable, be responsible, be in love.
4. Chapter 8 provides examples of this.

Chapter 8. The Normative Impetus of Enecstatic Philosophy of Religious Studies: Dialectic and Foundations

1. See Pals (1987, 263–265).
2. See, for example, P. D. Chantepie de la Saussaye (1891, 9–10), G. van der Leeuw ([1933] 1986, 2:687–688), M. Eliade (1959, 88–89), and J. Wach (1967, 1–2).
3. See Rodrigues and Harding (2009, 6–12, 44–48). See also chapter 4.
4. See Kanaris (2002, 144). My aim is not to revitalize accusations, such as George Lindbeck's (1984), that Lonergan is an "experiential-expressivist," which single-handedly ties him to liberal Protestantism and the phenomenological tradition. I agree with Philip Boo Riley (1994) and Charles C. Hefling (1988)

that the charge is unfair. However, it is Lonergan's manner of engagement, normalizing a description of religious consciousness, that underlies the association I make in the text. See Wayne Proudfoot (1985, 120–148) on the logical priority of the grammar of religious experience as opposed to the phenomenological prioritization of psychological descriptions that aim to evoke the experience (see also chapter 2 for an outline of Proudfoot's position). It boots nothing, too, to admit that Lonergan may have been ill-advised to use Rudolf Otto and Friedrich Heiler in his model of religion, as Riley (1994, 242–243) does. Here, it is moot to nuance how unique Lonergan's model is, if only for the reason that an enecstatic philosophy of religious studies can readily accommodate the programmatic aims of Lonergan's model. More anon.

  5. For readers unfamiliar with Lonergan, it may be helpful to point out a close correlation between what Lonergan calls common sense and the everyday *they-self* of Dasein that Heidegger ([1927] 1962, 167) distinguishes from the *authentic Self*. However, in Lonergan common sense is an amalgam of undifferentiated and post-differentiated states whose inauthenticity *and* authenticity depends on the degree to which it is unencumbered by "an aberration of understanding," an unconscious scotosis and a resultant blind spot, "a scotoma" (Lonergan [1957] 1992, 215l see postscript, note 16). In other words the *they-self* of *common* sense is not, in Lonergan, a reference to perpetual "falling," estranged Dasein from itself, to put it once again in Heidegger's terms. Still, inauthenticity qua an aberration of understanding is always already fecund in common sense due to its strong tendency to confuse truth with presence-at-hand (*Vorhandenheit*), its experienced more-than-merely-already-out-there-now, namely, present-at-hand (*vorhanden*). See Heidegger ([1927] 1962, 48n1).

  6. However, Lonergan's rhetoric, as John Angus Campbell (1993, 8) points out, is constitutive rather than persuasive, by which he means to distinguish it from modern forms of rhetoric that use argument and style as "a psychological inducement to persuasion devoid of cognitive import." This is Smart's approach, however unwitting. See also Kanaris (2002, 27–29).

  7. "Anyone can do research, interpret, write history, line up opposed positions" (Lonergan 1972b, 268).

  8. They are: linguistic, literate, logical, methodical (stages); cognitive, efficient, constitutive, communicative (functions). See Kanaris (2002, 136–144).

  9. Incidentally, this, as well as my critique, applies to contemporary reiterations such as Craig Martin's (2022), unavailable at the time I penned this chapter. See introduction, note 2.

  10. A quick look at Strenski's understanding of what it means "to bring religion back in" (to religious studies) will reveal that his level of engagement with religion bears an uncanny resemblance to religious journalism. It is interesting to note, too, how he seems to have missed Smart's prognostications about Extended Religious Studies/Theology, since Strenski relies on Smart as an example of what thinking religion should mean. Extended Religious Studies/Theology, as

we have seen, does more than report the view of others. It goes without saying that enecstatic engagement is remote from Strenski's offering. See also chapter 2, note 2.

11. The connection of language to the process of extending Enlightenment critical thinking to the problem of representation is, I hope, an obvious one. In referencing Heidegger, I provide an important source (for my purposes anyway) of this subsequent extension. It is no accident that Foucault says Heidegger was his most important influence, let alone how central he is to Derrida's deconstruction.

12. See Wiebe (1984) on Segal, Strenski (2006, 339–341; 2015, 243–244) on McCutcheon, and the debate between Pals, Segal, and Wiebe (1991). In terms of the functional specialties themselves, their denotation in my philosophy of religious studies is broader than the connotations in *Method in Theology*.

13. See Sheila Greeve Davaney (2002, 148), who echoes my concern. Mark C. Taylor (1998) and John Milbank (1990, 3) seem to voice distinct versions of such an understanding.

14. See Roberts (2004, 2005, 2006, 2009, 2013).

15. Some may wonder why Ricoeur is not featured in this study since, one could argue, his concerns overlap more directly with Lonergan's, certainly more so than Derrida's (chapter 5). The principal, if banal, reason for this speaks to the idiosyncratic, autobiographical nature of this study, which I discuss in the postscript. Ricoeur's thought simply did not factor (at least consciously) into the trajectory leading to enecstasis. Moreover, featuring Ricoeur would involve me in an additional apologetics of Ricoeur's phenomenological gesture in the face of the artistic, deconstructive tendenz. It was enough to focus on the problematic of invoking Lonergan, whose notion of self-appropriation directly impacted enecstasis. This is also why Winquist was the more obvious choice since he read, inter alia, both Derrida and Lonergan closely.

16. Had Eliade been clearer about his *history* of religion as *Heilsgeschichte* in a mediated phase, which is to say, more than phenomenological eidetic vision (more mediating-phase-like)—best represented by van der Leeuw—the ire Eliade inspired may not have been as intense. And yet his program may not have been as thought-provoking had he been clearer.

17. Eliade looks to the "archaic" in his discourse of resistance—hence McCutcheon's (1997, 28–50) identification of it as a politics of nostalgia. Roberts, more eclectically, looks to a variety of conflicting perspectives, from negative theology to genealogy, from deconstruction to psychotheology, and so forth. Lonergan's model of religious experience in the context of philosophy of religious studies should probably be viewed from this vantage point. That is what I meant earlier by associating it with what to some is problematic about such models in religious studies. I believe the issue is obviated when contextualized along these lines. For the most thorough comparison of the work of Lonergan and Eliade that I know, see John D. Dadosky (2004).

18. This marks off Roberts's and my intentions from, for instance, the "academic theologies" of Davaney (2002) and Cooey (2002). The latter want to do something theologically specific, if pluralistic with religious concepts in a liberal arts environment.

19. The alternative is to appeal to what Roberts (2004, 154) calls "a kind of cultural hermeticism," which he rightly notes doesn't exist but is nevertheless deployed by new materialists for "protective purposes, to forestall exposure to certain kinds of questions and criticism—to keep the 'data' from talking back."

20. The context is the modernist crisis in Catholic theology. Lonergan was asked late in his career if he was deliberately careful treating sensitive issues such as religious experience during the crisis. He responded: "Well, you never want to be stupid. . . . In other words, you don't deliberately mislead people who are not bright, or allow them to mislead themselves" (Lonergan 1982, 123).

Conclusion

1. I am grateful to Merold Westphal for a correspondence in which he offers a taxonomy of the field.

2. See chapter 5, note 4, for a possible foreshadowing of it.

3. See Carrette (2010, 277) who makes this guarded but important point regarding poststructuralism: "I will maintain that post-structuralism to some extent develops the critique of the Enlightenment—even in its suspicion of such thinking—by extending the critical platform of knowledge to the problem of representation. It arguably rests in the longer philosophical tradition of epistemology." Enecstasis is intended as a constructive response to this situation.

Postscript

1. "C'est notre image—au miroir de l'absolu littéraire—qui nous est renvoyée. Et cette vérité massive qui nous est assénée: nous ne sommes pas sortis de l'époque du Sujet" (Lacoue-Labarthe and Nancy 1978, 27).

2. It is significant that Lonergan ([1957] 1992, 20), in his principal work on the subject, *Insight: A Study of Human Understanding*, states explicitly that he is writing not only from a moving viewpoint but also about a moving viewpoint. The subject as subject for Lonergan is, generally put, a formal precept to help one negotiate one's own dark struggle with the flight from understanding (9).

3. As I hope to have made clear in the preceding chapters, in my estimation, the cognitional approach of Lonergan and the deconstructive strategy of Derrida are, contrary to what one is programmed to think in this so-called

postmodern age, complementary *in this regard*. Both destabilize the myth of the given at work in representational thinking, albeit from different motifs of reflection and with different aims.

4. I do not wish to suggest that Beckett's language finds no application to the other forms of thinking with which I started. I only mean to suggest that the language in *The Unnamable* about "thinking" and "mind" connects more naturally with the assumptions in and context of the *Meditations*.

5. The first, *Malloy*, and the second, *Malone meurt*, were published originally in French in 1951.

6. All references to *The Unnamable* are from the English e-book edition, which has no page numbers and, as in the original French, no chapters. See Beckett ([1953] 2012).

7. See James Martell's (2011) illuminating gloss on Derrida's cryptic treatment of Beckett, Badiou (2003), and Žižek (2019).

8. I will return to this point later as different from what enecstasis seeks to address. To understand this in connection with Badiou would be to flag how his evaluation provides a means—certainly not the only means—to negotiate Beckett's foundational stance, for instance, how subjective involvement is responsibly managed along the lines of a mathematized ontology distinguishing "being" from "event." As I have argued, this is a separate philosophical issue. Identifying elemental meaning and gauging it vis-à-vis one's own being-in-the-world includes, of course, conversation with another's sense of it. But that is not the same thing as recognizing for and in oneself what the elemental meaning in question is and whether another's reaction to it is one's own and determining why or why it is not. This is crucial in agential self-possession, especially when engaging the elemental form of normative claims, however patterned, whatever their motifs.

9. By saying this I do not mean to denigrate attempts that tend to model such an approach. The contributions of Wesley J. Wildman (2010, 2018) are notable in this regard. Wildman is on the hunt for a comprehensive philosophy of religion, a "religious philosophy" that is both "multidisciplinary" and "comparative." Among his principal objectives is to mitigate "competing philosophic ideals" in the field that, in complicated ways, inspire the skepticism that exists concerning the viability of philosophy of religion in the modern academy. The attempt is ambitious and welcome to academics guided by the arguably "analytic" aspirations of the venture as a whole, as well as to administrators wary of religiously partisan forms of the tradition. Wildman's religious philosophy functions under a different set of concerns from what I am calling philosophy of religious studies. As I've argued, tasks such as his are the right of each specialist deciphering the relevance and application of a personal orientation vis-à-vis their primary difficult concern. That is, the issue is a separate one, subsequent to what enecstatic philosophy of religion fundamentally addresses. To put it more pointedly, Wildman protracts, while reforming, the tradition that manages religion in terms of truth claims. In

this sense it is philosophy of religion in the traditional sense, albeit wider in scope when it comes to religious traditions and multidisciplinary inquiry. Philosophy of religious studies, on the other hand, services a broader community, that of religious studies, which approaches the religious phenomenon with different philosophical assumptions characteristically much more general in scope and orientation.

10. As mentioned earlier, artistic thinking is shorthand for an intellectual mood many identify as "poststructuralism," which formulates elemental meanings such as I have been tracing in Beckett. It is supported by the linguistic turn too often nominated by the counterproductive cipher "postmodernism." I follow Carrette (2010, 277), who advises against confusing poststructuralism with postmodernism, especially in that serious consideration of the former moves "the discussion away from simple charges of relativism and anti-modernism." Poststructuralism "to some extent [extends] the critical platform of knowledge to the problem of representation. It arguably rests in the longer philosophical tradition of epistemology" (Carrette 2010, 277).

11. See Lonergan's (1972b, 254–257) discussion of "ordinary meaningfulness" and "original meaningfulness," which is an interesting gloss that sidesteps this thorny issue from the perspective of a phenomenology of cognition.

12. I say "devotional" to distinguish it from its possible relationship to mystical consciousness that gravitates to nontheistic unobjectified experience. See Kilbourn (2005, 87–88), who notes that "*The Unnamable* comes closer than perhaps any other modern novel to a 'replication' of the theological apophatic text," which also indulges in *apomnesis* or forgetfulness of self.

13. This nuance explains, at least to me now, years after inheriting McEvenue's concerns, why he felt similarly about Derrida and why we were at odds about him. His antipathy toward Derrida regards the latter's foundational stance, whose elemental meaning is expressed conceptually—in McEvenue's sense of the difference between "elemental" and "conceptual." McEvenue rejects Derrida for different reasons than he does Beckett; however, these reasons are at bottom an evaluation of the elemental meaning implied in the stance of Derrida, whose instrumentality I call artistic thinking. It's a stance that resonates with the Beckettian experience of the world (see Kilbourn 2005). McEvenue negotiates this by eliminating a Derridean obstruction to a properly basic premise of his hermeneutics, namely, that "divination" of elemental meaning (to invoke an apt term of the father of hermeneutics) is not only possible but necessary (see McEvenue 1990, 17, 57–58, 179n40; 1994, 16, 29, 80n). He is, of course, within his epistemic rights to argue this. However, he tackles this matter as an exegete who must demonstrate the dividends in applying his approach to a body of literature, not as a philosopher negotiating experiences of the world that contravene otherwise insightful approaches. Polymorphic consciousness is a delicate affair, especially when weighed in search of a philosophy of religious studies (see chapters 6 and 8 in this connection)

14. The imagery is taken from Pierre Legendre (as described by Saint-Germain 2013, 150–151) in a discussion of the father-son relation pictured in book 2 of Virgil's *Aeneid*.

15. I am, of course, aware that enecstasis is a latticework of ideas. I have assembled this latticework from a canon that functions, not despite it, but because of it. I am explicit about this in the work. However, just as parents are not disqualified from parenthood because they themselves are offspring, so too enecstasis cannot be dismissed as suspect because it relies on a particular history.

16. In Lonergan's terms, this provision is post-systematic, a modified common sense greatly impacted by the numerous differentiations of consciousness, political, social, scholarly, and so forth. See Kanaris (2002, 136–138).

17. From my point of view, not even object-oriented ontology (OOO), an interesting and relative newcomer to the debate, has preempted the notion of the subject in its emphasis on the fundamental role of objects in knowledge. The speculative realism out of which it grew has not, in my estimation, adequately addressed fundamental issues arising from the heritage, namely, transcendental philosophy. I aim to develop this explicitly in subsequent publications. Suffice it to say that the objectivity of truth that supporters of OOO wish to champion is indeed independent of the subject but, as Lonergan (1974, 70) has noted, ontologically resides in the subject: "Intentionally it goes completely beyond the subject, yet it does so only because ontologically the subject is capable of an intentional self-transcendence, of going beyond what he feels, what he imagines, what he thinks, what seems to him, to something utterly different, to what is so."

18. I am thinking here of developments in philosophy by thinkers such as Alain Badiou, Quentin Meillassoux, François Laruelle, Graham Harman, and Slavoj Žižek, and in religious studies by scholars such as Bradley B. Onishi, Steven M. Wasserstrom, Benjamin Schewel.

References

Asad, Talal. 1993. "The Construction of Religion as an Anthropological Category." In *Genealogies of Religion: Discipline and Reasons of Power in Christianity and Islam*. Baltimore: Johns Hopkins University Press.

———. 2001. "Reading a Modern Classic: W. C. Smith's 'The Meaning and End of Religion.'" *History of Religions* 40, no. 3 (February): 205–222.

Barnes, Michael. 2002. *Theology and the Dialogue of Religions*. Cambridge: Cambridge University Press.

———. 2010. "Religious Pluralism." In *The Routledge Companion to the Study of Religion*, 2nd ed., edited by John R. Hinnells, 407–422. London: Routledge.

Badiou, Alain. 2003. *On Beckett*. Edited and translated by Alberto Toscano and Nina Power with an introduction. Clinamen Press.

———. 2015a. *Le Séminaire Parménide: L'être 1—Figure ontologique 1985-1986*. Texte établi par Véronique Pineau. Paris: Librairie Arthème Fayard.

———. 2015b. *Le Séminaire Heidegger: L'être 3—Figure du retrait 1986-1987*. Texte établi par Isabelle Vodoz. Paris: Librairie Arthème Fayard.

Beckett, Samuel. [1953] 2012. *The Unnamable*. Edited by Steven Connor. London: Faber and Faber.

Braun, Willi. 2000. "Religion." In *Guide to the Study of Religion*, edited by Willi Braun and Russell T. McCutcheon, 3–20. London: Cassell.

Braun, Willi, and Russell T. McCutcheon, eds. 2000. *Guide to the Study of Religion*. London: Cassell.

Buber, Martin. [1923] 1986. *I and Thou*. Translated by Ronald Gregor Smith. New York: Scribner.

Burrell, David. 1986. "Lonergan and Philosophy of Religion." *Method: Journal of Lonergan Studies* 4, no. 1 (March): 1–5.

Bush, Stephen S. 2012. "Are Religious Experiences Too Private to Study?" *Journal of Religion* 92, no. 2 (April): 199–223.

Cady, Linell E. 2002. "Territorial Disputes: Religious Studies and Theology in Transition." In *Religious Studies, Theology, and the University: Conflicting*

Maps, Changing Terrain, edited by Linell E. Cady and Delwin Brown, 110–125. Albany: State University of New York Press.

Campbell, John Angus. 1993. "Insight and Understanding: The 'Common Sense' Rhetoric of Bernard Lonergan." In *Communication and Lonergan: Common Ground for Forging the New Age*, edited by Thomas J. Farrell and Paul A. Soukup, 3–22. Kansas City: Sheed and Ward.

Cantwell Smith, Wilfred. 1959. "Comparative Religion: Whither—and Why." In *The History of Religions: Essays in Methodology*, edited by Mircea Eliade and Joseph M. Kitagawa, 31–58. Chicago: University of Chicago Press.

———. 1962. *The Meaning and End of Religion*. New York: Macmillan.

Capps, Walter. 1995. *Religious Studies: The Making of a Discipline*. Minneapolis: Fortress Press.

Caputo, John D. 1997a. "Khôra: Being Serious with Plato." In *Deconstruction in a Nutshell: A Conversation with Jacques Derrida*, edited by John D. Caputo, 71–105. New York: Fordham Press.

———. 1997b. *The Prayers and Tears of Jacques Derrida: Religion without Religion*. Bloomington: Indiana University Press.

———. 2000. "For Love of Things Themselves: Derrida's Hyper-Realism." *Journal for Cultural and Religious Theory* 1, no. 3 (Fall). https://jcrt.org/archives/01.3/caputo.shtml.

———. 2004. Foreword to *In Deference to the Other: Lonergan and Contemporary Continental Thought*, edited by Jim Kanaris and Mark J. Doorley, vii–xiii. Albany: State University of New York Press.

———. 2018. "Radical Theologians, Knights of Faith, and the Future of the Philosophy of Religion." In *Reconfigurations of Philosophy of Religion: A Possible Future*, edited by Jim Kanaris, 211–236. Albany: State University of New York Press.

Carrette, Jeremy. 1999. *Religion and Culture: Michel Foucault*. Selected and edited by Jeremy R. Carrette. New York: Routledge.

———. 2000. *Foucault and Religion: Spiritual Corporality and Political Spirituality*. New York: Routledge.

———. 2010. "Poststructuralism and the Study of Religion." In *The Routledge Companion to the Study of Religion*, 2nd ed., edited by John Hinnells, 274–290. London: Routledge.

Chantepie de la Saussaye, Pierre Daniel. 1891. *Manual of the Science of Religion*. Translated by Beatrice S. Colyer-Fergusson. London: Longmans, Green.

Cooey, Paula M. 2002. "The Place of Academic Theology in the Study of Religion from the Perspective of Liberal Education." In *Religious Studies, Theology, and the University: Conflicting Maps, Changing Terrain*, edited by Linell E. Cady and Delwin Brown, 172–186. Albany: State University of New York Press.

Crites, Stephen. 1996. "The Pros and Cons of Theism: Whether They Constitute the Fundamental Issue of the Philosophy of Religion." In *God, Philosophy, and Academic Culture: A Discussion between Scholars in the AAR and the APA*, edited by William J. Wainwright, 39–46. Atlanta, GA: Scholars Press.

Crockett, Clayton. 2001. *A Theology of the Sublime*. London: Routledge.

———. 2007. *Interstices of the Sublime: Theology and Psychoanalytic Theory*. New York: Fordham University Press.

———. 2013. *Deleuze Beyond Badiou: Ontology, Multiplicity and Event*. New York: Columbia University Press.

———. 2017. *Derrida After the End of Writing: Political Theology and New Materialism*. Fordham University Press.

Crowe, Frederick E. 1992. *Lonergan*. Collegeville, MN: Liturgical Press.

Dadosky, John D. 2004. *The Structure of Religious Knowing: Encountering the Sacred in Lonergan and Eliade*. Albany: State University of New York Press.

Davaney, Sheila Greeve. 2002. "Rethinking Theology and Religious Studies." In *Religious Studies, Theology, and the University: Conflicting Maps, Changing Terrain*, edited by Linell E. Cady and Delwin Brown, 140–154. Albany: State University of New York Press.

Davidson, Arnold I. 1995. "Introduction: Pierre Hadot and the Spiritual Phenomenon of Ancient Philosophy." In Pierre Hadot, *Philosophy as a Way of Life: Spiritual Exercises from Socrates to Foucault*, edited by Arnold I. Davidson, 145. Malden, MA: Blackwell.

Dawkins, Richard. 2001. "Science Discredits Religion." In *Philosophy of Religion: Selected Readings*, 2nd ed., edited by Michael Peterson, William Hasker, Bruce Reichenbach, and David Basinger, 509–512. Oxford: Oxford University Press.

de Vries, Hent. 1999. *Philosophy and the Turn to Religion*. Baltimore: Johns Hopkins University Press.

Derrida, Jacques. 1978. "Structure, Sign, and Play in the Discourse of the Human Sciences." Translated by Alan Bass. In *Writing and Difference*, 278–294. London: Routledge.

———. 1982. "Différance." Translated by Alan Bass. In *Margins of Philosophy*, 1–27. Chicago: University of Chicago Press.

———. [1993] 1994. *Specters of Marx: The State of the Debt, the Work of Mourning, and the New International*. Translated by Peggy Kamuf. New York: Routledge.

———. 1997. "The Villanova Roundtable: A Conversation with Jacques Derrida." In *Deconstruction in a Nutshell: A Conversation with Jacques Derrida*, edited by John D. Caputo, 3–28. New York: Fordham Press.

———. 2002. "Faith and Knowledge: The Two Sources of 'Religion' at the Limits of Limits of Reason Alone. In *Acts of Religion*, edited by Gil Anidjar, 42–101. New York: Routledge.

El-Tobgui, Carl Sharif. 2020. *Ibn Taymiyya on Reason and Revelation: A Study of Darʾ taʿāruḍ al-ʿaql wa-l-naql*. Edited by Emilie Savage-Smith, Hans Daiber, and Anna Akasoy, vol. 3. Islamic Philosophy, Theology and Science. Texts and Studies. Leiden: Brill.

Eliade, Mircea. 1959. "Methodological Remarks on the Study of Religious Symbolism." In *History of Religions: Essays in Methodology*, edited by Mircea Eliade and Joseph M. Kitagawa, 86–107. Chicago: University of Chicago Press.

Fiorenza, Francis Schüssler. 2000. "Religion: A Contested Site in Theology and the Study of Religion." *Harvard Theological Review* 93, no. 1 (January): 7–34.

Fitzgerald, Timothy. 1999. *The Ideology of Religious Studies*. New York: Oxford University Press.

Flew, Anthony. 1971. "Theology and Falsification: A Symposium." In *Philosophy of Religion*, edited by Basil Mitchell, 13–15. Malden, MA: Blackwell.

Ford, David F. 2007. *Shaping Theology: Engagements in a Religious and Secular World*. Oxford: Blackwell.

———. 2010. "Theology." In *The Routledge Companion to the Study of Religion*, 2nd ed., edited by John R. Hinnells, 93–110. London: Routledge.

Foucault, Michel. 1999. *Religion and Culture*. Edited with an introduction by Jeremy R. Carrette. New York: Routledge.

———. 2005. *The Hermeneutics of the Subject: Lectures at the Collège de France 1981–1982*. New York: Palgrave Macmillan.

Freiberger, Oliver. 2019. *Considering Comparison: A Method for Religious Studies*. New York: Oxford University Press.

Fulford, Amanda, and Áine Mahon. 2018. "A Philosophical Defence of the Traditional Lecture." *Times Higher Education*. https://www.timeshighereducation.com/blog/philosophical-defence-traditional-lecture.

Geertz, Clifford. 1966. "Religion as a Cultural System." In *Anthropological Approaches to the Study of Religion*, edited by Michael Banton, 1–46. London: Tavistock.

Gregson, Vernon. 1985. *Lonergan, Spirituality, and the Meeting of Religions*. Lanham, MD: University Press of America.

Griffiths, Paul J. 1997. "Comparative Philosophy of Religion." In *A Companion to Philosophy of Religion*, edited by Philip L. Quinn and Charles Taliaferro, 718–723. Cambridge, MA: Blackwell.

Hadot, Pierre. 1995. *Philosophy as a Way of Life: Spiritual Exercises from Socrates to Foucault*. Edited with an introduction by Arnold I. Davidson. Oxford: Blackwell.

Harman, Graham. 2011. *The Quadruple Object*. Winchester: Zero Books.

———. 2018. *Object-Oriented Ontology: A New Theory of Everything*. London: Penguin Random House.

Hart, Ray. 1991. "Religious and Theological Studies in American Higher Education: A Pilot Study." *Journal of the American Academy of Religion* 59, no. 4 (Winter): 715–827.

Hefling, Charles C. 1988. "The Meaning of God Incarnate according to Friedrich Schleiermacher; *or*, Whether Lonergan Is Appropriately Regarded as 'A Schleiermacher of Our Time,' and Why Not." *Lonergan Workshop* 7: 105–177.

Heidegger, Martin. [1927] 1962. *Being and Time*. Translated by John Macquarrie and Edward Robinson. Oxford: Blackwell.
———. 1977. *The Question concerning Technology and Other Essays* Translated by William Lovitt. New York: Harper & Row.
———. [1949] 1992. "The Way Back into the Ground of Metaphysics." In *Primary Readings in Philosophy for Understanding Theology*, edited by Diogenes Allen and Eric O. Springsted, 248–262. Louisville: Westminster/John Knox Press.
Hori, Victor Sōgen. 2019. "D. T. Suzuki and the Invention of Tradition." *Eastern Buddhist* 47, no. 2: 41–81.
James, William. [1902] 1982. *The Varieties of Religious Experience: A Study in Human Nature*. New York: Open Road Integrated Media.
Janicaud, Dominique et al. 2000. *Phenomenology and the "Theological Turn": The French Debate*. New York: Fordham Press.
Jay, Martin. 2005. *Songs of Experience: Modern American and European Variations on a Universal Theme*. Berkeley: University of California Press.
Jeanrond, Werner. 1991. *Theological Hermeneutics: Development and Significance*. Houndsmill, Basingstoke: Macmillan.
Kanaris, Jim. 1997. "Calculating Subjects: Lonergan, Derrida, and Foucault." *Method: Journal of Lonergan Studies* 15, no. 2 (Fall): 135–150.
———. 2002. *Bernard Lonergan's Philosophy of Religion: From Philosophy of God to Philosophy of Religious Studies*. Albany: State University of New York Press.
———. 2003. "Lonergan and Contemporary Philosophy of Religion." In *Explorations in Contemporary Continental Philosophy of Religion*, edited by Deane-Peter Baker and Patrick Maxwell, 65–79. Amsterdam: Rodopi.
———. 2004. "To Whom Do We Return in the Turn to the Subject? Lonergan, Derrida, and Foucault Revisited." In *In Deference to the Other: Lonergan and Contemporary Continental Thought*, edited by Jim Kanaris and Mark J. Doorley, 33–52. Albany: State University of New York Press.
———. 2005a. "A Space for Difference: Appraising Foucauldian Hypervigilance." *Method: Journal of Lonergan Studies* 23, no. 1 (Spring): 75–100.
———. 2005b. "Bernard Lonergan, SJ (1904–84): A Theologian of Change and Judgment." *Theology Today* 62: 330–341.
———. 2013. "Enecstasis: A Disposition for Our Times?" In *Polyphonic Thinking and the Divine*, edited by Jim Kanaris, 97–104. Amsterdam: Rodopi.
———. 2016. "Jim Kanaris on 'What Does Philosophy of Religion Offer to the Modern University.'" Philosophyofreligion.org, February 25, 2016. http://philosophyofreligion.org/?p=443953.
———. 2018. "The Enecstatic Jig: Personalizing Philosophy of Religion." In *Reconfigurations of Philosophy of Religion: A Possible Future*, edited by Jim Kanaris, 173–188. Albany: State University of New York Press.

―――. 2023. "Enecstasis: An Outrageous Proclamation of Subjectivity." *Science et Esprit: Revue scientifique spécialisée en philosophie et en théologie* no. 1 (January–April): 67–78.

Katz, Steven. 1983. "The Conservative Character of Mysticism." In *Mysticism and Religious Traditions*, edited by Steven Katz, 3–60. Oxford: Oxford University Press.

Kaufmann, Walter. 1974. *Nietzsche: Philosopher, Psychologist, Antichrist*. 4th ed. Princeton, NJ: Princeton University Press.

Kearney, Richard. 2001. *The God Who May Be: A Hermeneutics of Religion*. Bloomington: Indiana University Press.

Kilbourn, Russell. 2005. "*The Unnamable*: Denegative Dialogue." *European Joyce Studies* 16: 63–89.

Lacoue-Labarthe, Philippe, and Jean-Luc Nancy. 1978. *L'absolu littéraire: Théorie de la littérature du romantisme allemand*. Paris: Éditions du Seuil.

Lakatos, Imre. 1970. "Falsification and the Methodology of Scientific Research Programmes." In *Criticism and Growth of Knowledge*, edited by Imre Lakatos and Alan Musgrave, 8–101. Cambridge: Cambridge University Press.

Lawrence, Fred. 1981. "The Modern Philosophic Differentiation of Consciousness: Or, What Is the Enlightenment?" *Lonergan Workshop* 2: 231–279.

Lease, Gary. 2000. "Ideology." In *Guide to the Study of Religion*, edited by Willi Braun and Russell McCutcheon, 438–450. London: Cassell.

Leeuw, Gerard van der. [1933] 1986. *Religion in Essence and Manifestation*, vol. 2. Translated by J. E. Turner. Princeton, NJ: Princeton University Press.

Lindbeck, George A. 1984. *The Nature of Doctrine: Religion and Theology in a Post-liberal Age*. Louisville: Westminster John Knox Press.

Lincoln, Bruce. 1996. "Theses on Method." *Method and Theory in the Study of Religion* 8 (3): 225–227.

―――. 2000. "Culture." In *Guide to the Study of Religion*, edited by Willi Braun and Russell T. McCutcheon, 409–422. London: Cassell.

―――. 2005. "Theses on Method." *Method and Theory in the Study of Religion* 17, no. 1: 8–10.

―――. 2012. *Gods and Demons, Priests and Scholars: Critical Explorations in the History of Religions*. Chicago: University of Chicago Press.

Lonergan, Bernard. 1967. "Response to Father Burrell." *Proceedings of the American Catholic Philosophic Association* 41: 258–259.

―――. 1972a. "Bernard Lonergan Responds." In *Language Truth and Meaning*, edited by Philip McShane, 306–312. Dublin: Gill and Macmillan, and Notre Dame: University of Notre Dame Press.

―――. 1972b. *Method in Theology*. London: Darton, Longman & Todd.

―――. 1974. *A Second Collection: Papers by Bernard J. F. Lonergan, S.J*. Edited by William F. J. Ryan and Bernard J. Tyrell. Toronto: University of Toronto Press.

———. 1982. *Caring about Meaning: Patterns in the Life of Bernard Lonergan*. Edited by Pierre Lambert, Charlotte Tansey, and Cathleen Going. Montreal: Thomas More Institute.

———. [1967] 1988. *Collection*, vol. 4 of *Collected Works of Bernard Lonergan*. Edited by Frederick E. Crowe and Robert M. Doran. Toronto: University of Toronto Press.

———. [1957] 1992. *Insight: A Study of Human Understanding*, vol. 3 of *Collected Works of Bernard Lonergan*. Edited by Frederick E. Crowe and Robert M. Doran. Toronto: University of Toronto Press.

———. 1993. *Topics in Education: The Cincinnati Lectures of 1959 on the Philosophy of Education*, vol. 10 of *Collected Works of Bernard Lonergan*. Edited by Robert M. Doran and Frederick E. Crowe Toronto: University of Toronto Press.

———. 1994. "Philosophy and the Religious Phenomenon." *Method: Journal of Lonergan Studies* 12, no. 2: 125–146.

———. [1985] 2017. *A Third Collection*, vol. 16 of *Collected Works of Bernard Lonergan*. Edited Robert M. Doran and John D. Dadosky. Toronto: University of Toronto Press.

Marion, Jean-Luc. 2012. *God Without Being: Hors-Texte*, 2nd ed. Translated by Thomas A. Carlson, with a foreword by David Tracy, and a new preface by Jean-Luc Marion. Chicago: University of Chicago Press.

Marsh, James L. 2014. *Lonergan in the World: Self-Appropriation, Otherness, and Justice*. Toronto: University of Toronto Press.

Marsh, James L., John D. Caputo, and Merold Westphal, eds. 1992. *Modernity and Its Discontents*. New York: Fordham University Press.

Martell, James. 2011. "Derrida on Beckett or the Painful Freudian Mark." *Mosaic: An Interdisciplinary Critical Journal* 44, no. 2: 95–108.

Martin, Craig. 2022. *Discourse and Ideology: A Critique of the Study of Culture*. London: Bloomsbury Academic.

Masuzawa, Tomoko. 2005. *The Invention of World Religions: Or, How European Universalism Was Preserved in the Language of Pluralism*. Chicago: University of Chicago Press.

Mathews, William A. 2005. *Lonergan's Quest: A Study of Desire in the Authoring of Insight*. Toronto: University of Toronto Press.

McCutcheon, Russell T. 1997. *Manufacturing Religion: The Discourse on Sui Generis Religion and the Politics of Nostalgia*. New York: Oxford University Press.

———. 2001. *Critics Not Caretakers: Redescribing the Public Study of Religion*. Albany: State University of New York Press.

McEvenue, Sean. 1990. *Interpreting the Pentateuch*. Collegeville, MN: Liturgical Press.

———. 1994. *Interpretation and Bible: Essays on Truth in Literature*. Collegeville, MN: Liturgical Press.

Micheelsen, Arun, and Clifford Geertz. 2002. "'I Don't Do Systems': An Interview with Clifford Geertz." *Method and Theory in the Study of Religion* 14, no. 1: 2–20.

Milbank, John. 1990. *Theology and Social Theory: Beyond Secular Reason*. Oxford: Basil Blackwell.

Miller, Jerome A. 1992. *In the Throe of Wonder: Intimations of the Sacred in a Post-Modern World*. Albany: State University of New York Press.

Moore, Christopher J. 2004. *In Other Words: A Language Lover's Guide to the Most Intriguing Words around the World*. London: Bloomsbury. E-pub.

Morelli, Mark D. 2015. *Self-Possession: Being at Home in Conscious Performance*. Chestnut Hill, MA: Lonergan Institute, Boston College.

Murphy, Richard. 1999. *Theorizing the Avant-Garde: Modernism, Expressionism, and the Problem of Postmodernity*. Cambridge: Cambridge University Press.

Nehamas, Alexander. 1998. *The Art of Living: Socratic Reflections from Plato to Foucault*. Berkeley: University of California Press.

Nietzsche, Friedrich. [1882] 1974. *The Gay Science*. Translated by Walter Kaufmann. New York: Vintage Books.

———. [1889] 1998. *Twilight of the Idols*. A new translation by Duncan Large. Oxford: Oxford University Press.

———. [1883–1891] 1999. *Thus Spake Zarathustra*. Translated by Thomas Common. Mineola, NY: Dover.

Nussbaum, Martha. 1997. *Cultivating Humanity*. Cambridge: Harvard University Press.

Olafson, Frederick A. 1993. "The Unity of Heidegger's Thought." In *The Cambridge Companion to Heidegger*, edited by Charles B. Guignon, 97–121. Cambridge: Cambridge University Press.

Onishi, Bradley. 2018. *The Sacrality of the Secular: Postmodern Philosophy of Religion*. New York: Columbia University Press.

Pals, Daniel L. 1987. "Is Religion a Sui Generis Phenomenon?" *Journal of the American Academy of Religion* 55, no. 2 (Summer): 259–282.

Pals, Daniel L., Robert A. Segal, and Donald Wiebe. 1991. "Axioms without Dogmas." *Journal of the American Academy of Religion* 59, no. 4 (Winter): 703–713.

Pannenberg, Wolfhart. 1991. *Systematic Theology*, vol. 1. Translated by Geoffrey W. Bromiley. Grand Rapids, MI: William B. Eerdmans.

Pratt, Mary Louise. 2008. *Imperial Eyes: Travel Writing and Transculturation*, 2nd ed. London: Routledge.

Proudfoot, Wayne. 1985. *Religious Experience*. Berkeley: University of California Press.

Prus, Wawrzyniec Jack. 2016. "Materializing Religion: The New Materialism in Religious Studies." Master's thesis, McGill University.

Quinn, Philip L. 1996. "The Cultural Anthropology of Philosophy of Religion." In *God, Philosophy, and Academic Culture: A Discussion between Scholars in the AAR and the APA*, edited by William J. Wainwright, 47-58. Atlanta, GA: Scholars Press.

Raschke, Carl. 1982. "Religious Pluralism and Truth: From Theology to a Hermeneutical Dialogy." *Journal of the American Academy of Religion* 50, no. 1 (Spring): 35-48.

———. 1990. "Fire and Roses: Toward Authentic Postmodern Religious Thinking." *Journal of the American Academy of Religion* 58, no. 4 (Winter): 671-689.

———. 1999. "Theorizing Religion at the Turn of the Millennium: From the Sacred to the Semiotic." *Journal for Cultural and Religious Theory* 1, no. 1 (Winter): 1-9.

———. 2001. "The Deposition of Signs: Postmodernism and the Crisis of Religious Studies." *Journal of Cultural and Religious Theory* 3, no. 1 (Winter). https://jcrt.org/archives/03.1/raschke.shtml.

———. 2005. "Derrida and the Return of Religion: Religious Theory after Postmodernism." *Journal of Cultural and Religious Theory* 6, no. 2 (Spring): 1-16.

———. 2012. *Postmodernism and the Revolution in Religious Theory: Toward a Semiotics of the Event*. Charlottesville: University of Virginia Press.

Ricoeur, Paul. 1981. "The Task of Hermeneutics." In *Paul Ricoeur: Hermeneutics and the Human Sciences: Essays on Language, Action and Interpretation*, edited by John B Thompson, 43-62. Cambridge: Cambridge University Press.

Riley, Philip Boo. 1994. "Religious Studies Methodology: Bernard Lonergan's Contribution." *Method: Journal of Lonergan Studies* 12, no. 2 (Fall): 239-249.

Richardson, William J. 1972. "Being for Lonergan: A Heideggerian View." In *Language Truth and Meaning*, edited by Philip McShane, 272-283. Dublin: Gill and Macmillan, and Notre Dame: University of Notre Dame Press.

Roberts, Tyler. 1998. *Contesting Spirit: Nietzsche, Affirmation, Religion*. Princeton, NJ: Princeton University Press.

———. 2004. "Exposure and Explanation: On the New Protectionism in the Study of Religion." *Journal of the American Academy of Religion* 72, no. 1 (March): 143-172.

———. 2005. "Rhetorics of Ideology and Criticism in the Study of Religion." *Journal of Religion* 85, no. 3 (July): 367-389.

———. 2006. "Between the Lines: Exceeding Historicism in the Study of Religion." *Journal of the American Academy of Religion* 74, no. 3 (September): 697-719.

———. 2009. "All Work and No Play: Chaos, Incongruity and Différance in the Study of Religion." *Journal of the American Academy of Religion* 77, no. 1 (March): 81-104.

———. 2013. *Encountering Religion: Responsibility and Criticism after Secularism*. New York: Columbia University Press.

———. 2018. "Reverence as Critical Responsiveness: Between Philosophy and Religion." In *Reconfigurations of Philosophy of Religion: A Possible Future*, edited by Jim Kanaris, 189–209. Albany: State University of New York Press.
Rodrigues, Hillary, and John S. Harding. 2009. *Introduction to the Study of Religion*. London: Routledge.
Said, Edward W. 1978. *Orientalism*. New York: Vintage Books.
Saint-Germain, Christian. 2013. "Owing Life—Surviving Your Father." In *Polyphonic Thinking and the Divine*, edited by Jim Kanaris, 149–155. Value Inquiry Book Series, vol. 257. Amsterdam: Rodopi.
Santner, Eric L. 2001. *On the Psychotheology of Everyday Life*. Chicago: University of Chicago Press.
Schopen, Gregory. 1991. "Archaeology and Protestant Presuppositions in the Study of Indian Buddhism." *History of Religions* 31, no. 1 (August): 1–23.
Segal, Robert A. 1980. "The Myth-Ritualist Theory of Religion." *Journal for the Scientific Study of Religion* 19, no. 2 (June): 173–185.
———. 1983. "In Defense of Reductionism." *Journal of the American Academy of Religion* 51, no. 1 (March): 97–124.
———. 1992. *Explaining and Interpreting Religion: Essays on the Issue*. New York: Peter Lang.
———. 2001. "In Defense of the Comparative Method." *Numen* 48 (3): 339–373.
Segal, Robert A., and Donald Wiebe. 1989. "Axioms and Dogmas in the Study of Religion." *Journal of the American Academy of Religion* 57, no. 3 (Fall): 591–605.
Sharma, Arvind. 1995. *The Philosophy of Religion: A Buddhist Perspective*. Delhi: Oxford University Press.
Sharf, Robert H. 1993. "The Zen of Japanese Nationalism." *History of Religions* 33, no. 1 (August): 1–43.
———. 1995. "Buddhist Modernism and the Rhetoric of Meditative Experience." *Numen* 42, no. 3 (March): 228–223.
———. 1998. "Experience." *Critical Terms for Religious Studies*, edited by Mark C. Taylor, 94–115. Chicago: University of Chicago Press.
Shatz, David. 2003. "The Biblical and Rabbinic Background to Medieval Jewish Philosophy." In *The Cambridge Companion to Medieval Jewish Philosophy*, edited by Daniel H. Frank and Oliver Leaman, 16–37. Cambridge: Cambridge University Press.
Simmons, J. Aaron. 2011. *God and the Other: Ethics and Politics after the Theological Turn*. Bloomington: Indiana University Press.
Smart, Ninian. 1996. "Some Thoughts on the Science of Religion." In *The Sum of Our Choices: Essays in Honour of Eric J. Sharpe*, edited by Arvind Sharma, 15–25. Atlanta, GA: Scholars Press.
Smith, Jonathan Z. 1978. *Map Is Not Territory: Studies in the History of Religions*. Leiden: Brill.

———. 1982. *Imaging Religion: From Babylon to Jonestown*. Chicago: University of Chicago Press.
Spiro, Melford E. 1966. "Religion: Problems of Definition and Explanation." In *Anthropological Approaches to the Study of Religion*, edited by Michael Banton, 85–126. London: Tavistock.
Stead, Christopher. 1994. *Philosophy in Christian Antiquity*. Cambridge: Cambridge University Press.
Storm, Jason Ānanda Josephson. 2021. *Metamodernism: The Future of Theory*. Chicago: University of Chicago Press.
Strenski, Ivan. 1998. "Religion, Power, and the Final Foucault." *Journal of the American Academy of Religion* 66, no. 2 (Summer): 345–368.
———. 2006. *Thinking about Religion: An Historical Introduction to Theories of Religion*. Malden, MA: Blackwell.
———. 2010. *Why Politics Can't Be Freed from Religion*. Malden, MA: Wiley-Blackwell.
———. 2015. *Understanding Theories of Religion: An Historical Introduction to Theories of Religion*. Malden, MA: Blackwell.
Taliaferro, Charles. 1998. *Contemporary Philosophy of Religion*. Malden, MA: Blackwell.
Taylor, Charles. 1997. "The Politics of Recognition." In *New Contexts of Canadian Criticism*, edited by Ajay Heble, Donna Palmateer Penee, and J. R. (Tim) Struthers, 98–131. Peterborough, ON: Broadview Press.
Taylor, Mark C. 1998. Introduction to *Critical Terms for Religious Studies*, 1–19. Chicago: University of Chicago Press.
Taylor, Vincent E. 2005. "Theorizing Religion II." *Journal for Cultural and Religious Theory* 6, no. 3 (Fall): 1–6.
Vahanian, Gabriel. 2003. *Praise of the Secular*. Charlottesville: University of Virginia Press.
Vroom, Hendrik M. 2006. *A Spectrum of Worldviews: An Introduction to Philosophy of Religion in a Pluralistic World*. Amsterdam: Rodopi.
Wach, Joachim. 1967. "Introduction: The Meaning and Task of the History of Religions (*Religionswissenschaft*)." In *The History of Religions: Essays on the Problem of Understanding*, edited by Joseph M. Kitagawa, 1–19. Chicago: University of Chicago Press.
Walmsley, Gerard. 2008. *Lonergan on Philosophic Pluralism: The Polymorphism of Consciousness as the Key to Philosophy*. Toronto: University of Toronto Press.
Wasserstrom, Steven M. 1999. *Religion after Religion: Gershom Scholem, Mircea Eliade, Henry Corbin at Eranos*. Princeton, NJ: Princeton University Press.
Westphal, Merold. 1996. "Traditional Theism, the AAR and the APA." In *God, Philosophy, and Academic Culture: A Discussion between Scholars in the AAR and the APA*, edited by William J. Wainwright, 21–28. Atlanta, GA: Scholars Press.

———. 1997. "The Emergence of Modern Philosophy of Religion." In *A Companion to Philosophy of Religion*, edited by Philip L. Quinn and Charles Taliaferro, 111–117. Cambridge, MA: Blackwell.

Wiebe, Donald. 1984. "Beyond the Sceptic and the Devotee: Reductionism in the Study of Religion." *Journal of the American Academy of Religion* 52, no. 1 (Spring): 157–165.

———. 1991. *The Irony of Theology and the Nature of Religious Thought*. Montreal: McGill-Queens University Press.

———. 2000. *The Politics of Religious Studies*. New York: Palgrave Macmillan.

———. 2019. *The Science of Religion: A Defence—Essays by Donald Wiebe*, edited, introduced, and critiqued by Anthony J. Palma. Leiden: Brill.

Wildman, Wesley J. 2010. *Religious Philosophy as Multidisciplinary Comparative Inquiry: Envisioning a Future for the Philosophy of Religion*. Albany: State University of New York Press.

———. 2018. "Reforming Philosophy of Religion for the Modern Academy." In *Reconfigurations of Philosophy of Religion: A Possible Future*, edited by Jim Kanaris, 253–269. Albany: State University of New York Press.

Williams, Rowan. 2002. *Writing in the Dust*. Grand Rapids, MI: William B. Eerdmans.

Winquist, Charles E. 1980. "The Subversion and Transcendence of the Subject." *Journal of American Academy of Religion* 48, no. 1 (March): 45–60.

———. 1995. *Desiring Theology*. Chicago: University of Chicago Press.

———. 2003. *The Surface of the Deep*. Aurora, CO: Davies Group.

Žižek, Slavoj. 2019. "A Literary Fantasy: The Unnameable Subject of Singularity." *The Philosophical Salon*. https://thephilosophicalsalon.com/a-literary-fantasy-the-unnameable-subject-of-singularity/#_ednref1.

———. 2020. "Slavoj Zizek—The Real Explained." Grebmops, August 15, 2020, YouTube video, 5:21. https://www.youtube.com/watch?v=jA8tn89-exk.

Index

a-venir, 84, 142
aesthetics, 19, 49, 96
agency, 11, 25, 73, 89, 127, 135, 143, 145, 147, 159, 164n9
agential self-possession, 11, 12, 14, 21, 36, 69, 72, 74, 77, 104, 118, 129, 140, 153–154, 156, 173n28, 184n8. *See also* enecstasis
anthropology, 26, 45, 57–62, 70–71, 72, 78, 170n8
   cognitive emphasis in, 26, 57–61, 170n7
   cultural, 45. *See also* Geertz, Clifford; Asad, Talal
   symbolic. *See* Geertz, Clifford
aporia, 151
   in the study of religion, 28, 35, 148, 166n14
   in the work of Derrida, 82
Asad, Talal, 26, 31, 57–62, 64, 66, 70, 163n2, 170nn6–10
atheism, 45. *See also* New Atheism
Augustine, 58, 59, 94
Axial Age, xi

Badiou, Alain, 18, 41, 145, 146, 184n8, 186n18
Barnes, Michael, 167n2
Beckett, Samuel, 28, 142–147, 150–153, 155–156, 159, 184n4, 184n8, 185n10, 185n13

being, 3, 7, 12–14, 20, 21, 32–34, 41, 45, 53, 63, 75, 79, 80, 82, 96, 97–98, 103, 104, 109, 110, 113, 118, 123, 131, 132, 136, 140, 143–145, 149, 150–152, 167n15, 169n4, 174nn2–3, 180n13, 184n8
belief, xi, 15, 26–27, 30, 40, 46–47, 52, 56–57, 63, 65, 66, 67, 69, 72, 73, 82, 83–85, 88, 89, 102, 126, 143, 172n20
Benveniste, Émile, 83, 177n3
bios theoretikos. *See* philosophy, as art of living/way of life
Braun, Willi, 35, 166n11
Buber, Martin, xiv, xvii
Burrell, David, 105, 106, 109, 113
Bush, Stephen S., 28, 29, 72, 171n14, 173n26

Cantwell Smith, Wilfred, 15, 20, 25–26, 30, 57, 164n8
Capps, Walter, 68
Caputo, John D., 5, 34, 79, 97, 164nn5–6, 169n4
care, 2, 12, 13, 30, 32, 36, 123, 127, 132, 136, 164n8. *See also* self-, care
Carrette, Jeremy, 36, 60, 61, 74, 108, 122, 168n3, 183n3 (Conclusion), 185n10
Cartesian, 2, 28, 29, 97, 145, 151, 153, 155–156, 180n13
   post-, 73, 89, 141

199

Chantepie de la Saussaye, Pierre Daniel, 180n2 (chap. 8)
Cicero, 83
cogito, 30, 32, 143, 144, 145, 151, 152
common sense, 116–117, 118, 141, 142, 144, 181n5
communism, 94
Connor, Stephen, 145
consciousness, 6, 8, 14, 15, 28, 29, 33, 54, 56, 63, 69, 80, 95, 96, 98–102, 103, 106, 107, 108, 109, 110, 113, 118–119, 120, 125, 126, 133, 136, 142, 150, 168n4, 170n5, 178nn4–5, 181n4, 185n12, 186n16
  effective historical, 8, 114, 133
  polymorphic, 99–102, 106, 119, 185n13
construction, 68, 75, 108, 135, 176n6
  intentional, 19, 31, 49, 52, 70, 108, 112–114, 120, 123–124, 132, 173n24
  of meaning, 16, 26–27, 58, 70
  of subjectivity, 108
Cooey, Paula, 19, 31, 34, 49, 52, 53, 167n19, 173n24, 183n18
Crites, Stephen, 40
critical responsiveness, xii, 125, 128, 164n5, 168n2
criticism, xii–xiii, 67, 125, 126
  Roberts's outline of, xii–xiii
Crockett, Clayton, 164n6
culture, 6–7, 19, 28, 31, 34, 36, 45, 46, 49, 65, 72, 89, 125, 129, 132, 148, 153, 156, 168n3
  academic, 31, 45
  modernist, 166n15
  popular, 20, 50, 51, 103, 179n12
  postmodern, 17, 18

Dasein, 2, 12, 13, 20, 21, 32, 79, 123, 164n8, 174n2

Davaney, Sheila Greeve, 34, 48, 49
Dawkins, Richard. *See* New Atheism
de Vries, Hent, 18, 19
deconstruction, x, 17, 18, 35, 49, 77–89 passim, 98, 102, 121, 133, 161n2, 162n3 (chap. 1), 163n4, 174n2, 177n13, 179n9, 182n11
definitions, 26, 68, 71, 107, 109, 133
  nominal, 12
  real, 12
Dennett, Daniel. *See* New Atheism
Derrida, Jacques, 5, 6, 11, 18, 33, 34, 35, 48, 75, 77–98 passim, 94, 96, 98, 123, 133, 142, 145, 146, 147, 155, 164n4, 165n2, 167n16, 174nn2–3, 175n4, 176nn6–7, 177nn8–9, 177n11, 177n13, 178n2, 179n9, 182n11, 182n15, 183n3 (Postscript), 185n13. *See also* deconstruction
Descartes, René, 79, 104, 142–147, 150, 153, 156, 179n13. *See also* Cartesian
desert, the, 82. *See also* Χώρα
desire, xiii, 84–86, 88, 94, 97, 102, 108, 154
dialectic, xii, xiii, 26, 44, 68, 95, 97, 115–129 passim, 136, 141, 157, 161n1 (Preface), 162n1 (Introduction), 164n6, 165n9, 172n14, 173n22
difference, 4, 5, 14, 15, 80, 100, 101, 141, 176n6, 185n13
  ontological, 13, 32, 33, 96
différance, 79, 174n3, 178n2
Dilthey, Wilhelm, 170n5
discourse, 14, 17, 18, 33–34, 47–50, 53, 55, 61–64, 66, 70, 71, 73, 74, 79, 80, 86, 87, 95, 102, 103, 104, 108, 111, 114, 120, 121, 125, 126, 133–134, 140, 142, 150, 153,

161n2, 170n8, 170n10, 176n6, 177nn11–12, 182n17
academic, 17, 63, 146
descriptive/analytic, 26, 31, 62–64, 72, 108, 111–112, 114, 116, 124, 132
prescriptive/mystical, 62–64, 66, 70, 124
object-constitutive, ix, 57, 60, 61–62, 64, 69, 73–74, 108, 109, 110, 111, 113, 117, 121, 122, 124, 126–127, 131, 133–136, 157, 158, 159
religious, 26, 47, 50, 62, 70, 79, 86, 89, 111, 116, 125, 126 127
subject-constitutive, 57, 69, 71, 73–75, 109–114, 121, 124, 127, 128, 131–134, 157, 158, 164n7, 165n9, 168n2, 179n10
theological, 17–19, 48–49, 59, 71, 112
theoretical, 93
discours théorique. See theoretical discourse
dualism, 28, 29, 180n13

Eco, Umberto, 86
ecstasis, 2, 12, 13, 14, 20–21, 32, 104, 110, 136–137
ego, 47, 79, 95
ekstasis. See ecstasis
ekstatikón, 13
El-Tobgui, Carl Sharif, 165n5
Eliade, Mircea, 19, 24–27, 30, 36, 46, 66, 112, 116, 126, 172n15, 182nn16–17
emancipate, emancipation, emancipatory, 42, 80, 125
empirical, empiricist, 6–8, 15, 16, 39, 47, 55, 65, 96, 108, 112, 113–114, 128, 154, 156, 161n2
enecstasis, xiv, 2–7, 8, 11–36 passim, 40, 48, 54, 71, 74–75, 77–89, 93, 104, 106, 110, 111–114, 123–129, 131–137, 140, 142, 143, 145, 146–147, 150, 151, 152–159, 162n3, 163n2, 163n4, 164nn6–7, 165n9, 166n12, 168nn2–3, 169n4, 170n10, 171n11, 173n26, 173n28, 178n2, 179nn9–10, 180n13, 181n4, 182n10, 182n15, 183n3 (Conclusion), 184n8, 186n15
Enlightenment, 69, 79, 182n11
critique of, 107, 122, 137
post-, 26, 31, 58, 59, 60, 70
epochē, 53, 74, 116, 153, 163n2
essentialism, essentialist, 19, 25, 26, 46, 161n2
event, 33, 42, 50, 171n14, 179n9, 184n8
evil, x, 43, 86, 143, 150, 177n10
radical, 86, 84, 177n11
experience, 1, 2, 29, 32, 50, 85, 96–98, 99, 100–101, 103, 132–133, 136, 143–147, 153, 158, 178n1, 178nn4–5, 185nn12–13
artistic pattern of, 7, 101, 179n8
as category in religious studies, 23, 28, 36, 62–66, 72, 136, 173n26
intellectual pattern of, 7, 3, 101, 179n8
mystical, 75, 103, 113, 172n15
religious, 28, 61, 74, 100, 107, 114, 116, 120, 124, 171n14, 181n4, 182n17, 183n20

faith, 15, 18, 20, 25, 26, 31, 36, 42–43, 47, 51, 74, 102, 128, 132
Derrida's notion of, 77–87, 89, 177n11, 177n13
feeling, 42, 62, 63, 124
Feuerbach, Ludwig, 43, 45
Fitzgerald, Timothy, 57, 162n2
Flew, Anthony, x
Ford, David F., 70, 71, 167n2
Foucault, Michel, 2, 5, 6, 30, 32, 34, 36, 47, 58, 61, 64, 73, 74, 96,

Foucault, Michel *(continued)* 99, 133, 145, 158, 161n2, 175n4, 179n9, 182n11
foundations, xiii, 6, 31, 40, 75, 112, 115–129 passim, 131, 157, 162n2 (Introduction), 164n6, 165n9, 172n14, 172n22
Freiberger, Oliver, 164n9
Freud, Sigmund, 44, 58, 61, 96, 103, 176n6
Fulford, Amanda, 140, 141, 158
future, 39, 84–85, 88, 142

Geertz, Clifford, 26, 57–61, 66, 70, 71, 170n6, 170n8
Gefühl. See feeling
Geschichtlichkeit. See historicality
ghost, 43, 94–95
globalatinization, 79, 81, 82
God, god(s), x, 4, 16, 18–19, 20, 31, 34, 42–43, 44, 45, 49, 50, 55, 58, 63, 72, 75, 79, 80, 81, 82, 83, 86, 93, 97, 100, 102, 104, 105, 109, 113, 117, 120, 128, 132, 143, 149, 150, 163n2, 165n5, 166nn5–6, 169n4, 175n3
Goddess, 16, 31, 49
grace, 36
Griffiths, Paul, 17, 166n9

Hadot, Pierre, 53–54, 73, 93, 94, 99, 158
hard core, 64–65, 68, 70
Harding, John S., 65–66, 172n18, 172n20
Harman, Graham, 41, 165n3, 186n18
Harris, Sam. *See* New Atheism
Hawkes, Terence, 107
Hefling, Charles C., 180n4 (chap. 8)
Hegel, G. W. F., 4, 42, 43, 45, 81, 95, 152, 153, 166n6, 166n8

Heidegger, Martin, xiii, 2, 6, 11–14, 20, 21, 24, 32, 33, 34, 41, 48, 73, 79, 81, 86, 95, 103, 104, 110, 123, 124, 125, 133, 136, 142, 147, 165n2, 169n4, 170n5, 174n2, 175n4, 176n6, 177n12, 178n7, 180n13, 181n5, 182n11. *See also* Heideggerian, post-Heideggerian
hermeneutics, 20, 26, 28, 96, 125, 148, 170n6, 185n13
of affirmation, 125
creative, 25, 26
romantic, 28
of suspicion, 96
Hick, John, 167n2
history, 7, 24, 45, 49, 78, 82, 95, 118, 179n9
of the concept of religion, 111, 136
effective, 28, 150, 158
of philosophy, 2
of philosophy of religion, 24, 29–30, 40, 132
of religious studies, 35, 164n7, 167n2
historicality, 57, 58–60, 166n8, 170nn5–6
historicism, 47, 49, 126
historicist, 16, 25, 116
Hitchens, Christopher. *See* New Atheism
holy, 86–87, 94–95
Hori, Victor Sōgen, 171n14, 173n26
Hume, David, 42, 98, 166n8
Husserl, Edmund, 5, 174n2

ideology, 11, 20, 47, 50, 59, 112, 134, 151
critique, xii, 108–109, 110, 114, 164n8
immunity, 86–87, 88, 177n12
auto-, 86–87, 177n12
discursive, 86–87

ineffability, 62, 63, 64
intellectus agens, 165n3
interstice, 2, 36, 82, 83, 89, 153, 164n5

James, William, 25, 63, 64, 66, 172n15
Janicaud, Dominique, 171n11
Jay, Martin, 48
Jemeinigkeit, 12, 36
judgment, 101, 141, 151
justice, 82, 84–86, 88

Kant, Immanuel, 4, 13, 31, 32, 41, 42–43, 44, 49, 81, 94, 95, 96, 97, 166n8, 173n24, 177n11, 177n13. *See also* Kantian, post-Kantian
Katz, Steven, 63–64, 122
keiken, 171n14
Kilbourn, Russell, 185n12
knowledge, 7–8, 15, 20, 27, 28, 31, 32, 35, 41–43, 52, 57, 60, 64, 65, 77, 83, 85, 88, 93, 96, 101, 106, 107, 120, 122, 125, 137, 149, 165n1, 166nn7–8, 177n8, 179n9, 180n13, 183n3 (Conclusion), 185n10, 186n17
  acquisition of, xiv, 3, 133
  of God, 105, 166nn5–6, 169n4
Khōra, 81, 123, 164n6. *See also* Χώρα

Lacan, Jacques, 151, 152, 153
Lactantius, 83
Lakatos, Imre, 64, 65, 107
language, 19, 29, 44, 49, 50, 79, 85, 108, 123, 124, 142, 143, 148, 166n14, 178n1, 182n11
  excess of, 20, 50
  game, 43
  non-agential, 22
  religious, 56, 62, 81
  theological, 20
  theory of, 55, 107

langue. *See* language
Lease, Gary, 166n11
Levin, David, 51
Levinas, Emmanuel, xiv, 18, 84, 96
liberal
  Christian, 26
  democracy, 87, 95
  education, 31, 34
  secular, 26, 170n8
  theology, 42
  values, 34
Lincoln, Bruce, 35, 67, 116, 128, 163n2
Lindbeck, George, 180n4 (chap. 8)
logic, 43–44, 55, 64, 68, 73, 86, 87, 89, 101, 121, 132m 170n5, 181n8
logocentrism, 35, 80, 98, 101
logos, 82
Lonergan, Bernard, 6–8, 13, 14, 74, 94, 97–104, 105–114, 116–123, 126, 127, 136, 139, 141, 147, 162n4, 168n4, 173n22, 173n28, 175n4, 178nn3–5, 178n7, 179nn8–9, 179n13, 180nn2–3 (chap. 7), 180n4 (chap. 8), 181nn5–7, 182n15, 182n17, 183n20, 185n11, 186nn16–17. *See also* self-appropriation
Lyotard, Jean-François, 33, 51, 103

Macquarrie, John, 13
Mahon, Áine 140, 141, 158
Marsh, James L., 97, 121, 162n3
Martin, Craig, 161n2
Marx, Karl, xiii, 44, 45, 58, 61, 94, 95, 153
Marxists, 47, 87
  Marxian alliance, 95
masters of suspicion, 79, 153
Masuzawa, Tomoko, 162n1 (chap. 1), 167n2

McCutcheon, Russell T., 15, 16–17, 19, 25, 27–28, 29, 31, 33, 35, 36, 47, 48, 50, 67, 108, 122, 127, 163n2, 172n17, 182n12
McEvenue, Sean, 148, 149, 150, 151, 153, 185n13
meaning(s), 7, 12, 13, 15, 25, 31, 52, 58, 74–75, 80, 89, 96, 98, 100–101, 108, 110, 116–117, 118, 120, 121, 129, 162n2 (Introduction), 172n14, 178n4, 185n11
 conceptual, 148–150, 157, 185n13
 construction of, 16, 26, 27, 58, 70, 120, 124, 173n24
 elemental, 146, 147–157, 162n5, 166n12, 180n13, 184n8, 185n13
 production of, 47
 religious, 24, 34, 64, 75, 113, 120, 123, 126, 176n4, 177n13
mechanism, 34, 58, 174n2
 of autoimmunity, 87
 coping, xi
Meillassoux, Quentin, 41, 186n18
meráki, x, 3, 6
Messiah, 84–84
messianic, messianicity, messianisms, 82, 84, 85, 89, 175n4
metaphysics, 4, 13, 20, 32, 65, 66, 67, 79, 80, 98, 116, 124, 132, 156, 165n4, 168n4, 172n20, 176n6, 178n5
 Kantian, 95
 naturalist, 122
 reductionist, 27
method(s); methodology, methodological x, xii, xiii, 4–8, 15, 23, 24–29, 30, 31, 34, 47, 53, 60, 65, 66, 67, 70–72, 74, 75, 88, 94, 100, 101, 107, 108, 112, 113, 114, 116–120, 123, 126, 131, 132, 134, 135, 145–147, 154, 157, 159, 164n9, 165n4, 168nn3–4, 170n8, 171n11, 172n15, 178n4, 181n8, 182n12
foundationalist, 11, 32, 33, 73, 98, 128, 133, 136, 155, 166n8
 meta-, 6, 113, 131, 134, 145, 157
 nonfoundationalist, 74, 166n8
 transcendental, 5, 6, 8, 94–95, 99, 103–104, 105–106, 111, 116, 118, 141, 168n4
modern, modernist, modernity, xvii, 2, 8, 11, 19, 41, 55, 57, 70, 75, 78, 81, 93, 98, 99, 100, 101, 107, 123, 126, 132, 133, 150, 166n15, 171n14, 181n6, 183n20, 184n9
 meta-, 161n2
mondialatinisation. See globalatinization
Moore, Christopher J., 3, 161n1
Morelli, Mark D., 127, 162n4, 179n8
Murphy, Richard, 18
mysticism, 63, 64

Nehamas, Alexander, 3, 30, 73, 158
New Atheism, 79
New Buddhism, 171n14
Nietzsche, Friedrich, 4, 11, 23, 24, 30, 31, 32, 34, 35, 36, 43, 44, 45, 61, 73, 81, 86, 95, 100, 102, 103, 110, 124–125, 158, 167n15, 176n6, 178n1
nirvana, 16, 31, 49, 72, 109, 140
noetic intuition, 93, 94
normative; normativity, xi, xiii, 16, 26, 40, 46, 55, 56, 62, 64, 66, 69–72, 89, 108, 109, 110, 111, 112, 113, 114, 115–129 passim, 150, 154, 155, 157, 158, 163n2, 163n4, 167n16, 170n8, 171n11, 173n25, 175n4, 184n8
nous, 165n5
numinous, 17, 46, 47, 51, 124
Nussbaum, Martha, 128, 158

object, xi, xii, xiii, 12, 15, 17, 18, 20,
    26, 27, 28, 36, 41, 45, 51, 53,
    63, 69, 71–72, 73–74, 82, 88,
    93, 98, 100, 102, 103, 107, 108,
    116–119, 121, 126, 135, 154,
    158, 163n2, 168n3, 186n17.
    See also discourse object-
    constitutive; subject, subject-
    object dichotomy; subject,
    subject-object relation
objectification(s), 103, 109, 119, 127,
    180n2 (chap. 7)
objectivism, 46
objectivity, 14, 16, 30, 44, 46, 49, 53,
    65–66, 74, 89, 93, 98, 122, 142,
    143, 145, 173n25, 180n13
object-oriented ontology, 41, 186n17
Onishi, Bradley B., 164n6, 168n2,
    186n18
ontic, 3, 7, 14, 21, 110, 123, 125, 136,
    142
    reflection, 12, 14, 74, 104, 111
ontology, xii, 2–3, 13, 18, 21, 32, 41,
    48, 67, 81, 161n2, 177n12, 178n5,
    179n9, 184n8
ontotheological, 41, 175n3
orientalism, 57, 88
    reverse, 171n14
Other, otherness, xi, 3, 7, 20, 33, 50,
    69, 73, 74, 81, 82, 83–85, 103,
    104, 111, 140, 141, 146, 151–152,
    157, 166n7, 173n23
Otto, Rudolf, 25, 46, 63, 66, 181n4
outbid, outbidding, 81, 86, 87, 89,
    133, 146, 177n12

Pals, Daniel, 48, 182n12
Pannenberg, Wolfhart, 165n5
paradox, 152, 176n6
Parmenides, 41
parole. See voice

personalism, xiv, 20, 25, 74
    aporia of, 35
phenomenology, x, 6, 80, 95, 98, 142,
    168n4, 178n5, 185n11
    anti-, 16, 29, 48
    neo-, 163n2
    personalist, 29, 30
    post-, 16–19, 29, 33, 48, 114
    of religion, xiv, 4, 5, 11, 14–16, 19,
        21, 23, 25, 26, 28, 30, 33, 47–50,
        60, 63, 65, 72, 114, 115, 120, 124,
        127, 156, 171n11
philosophy
    analytic, ix, 4, 8, 23, 24, 29, 43, 44,
        45, 56, 57, 59, 60, 61, 62, 107,
        132, 133, 135, 174n28
    as art of living/way of life, 4,
        53–54, 73, 93, 99
    continental, ix, 4, 23, 29, 44, 45, 55,
        57, 60, 61, 64, 88, 95, 96, 103,
        104, 107, 132, 133, 156, 166n8,
        167n17, 168n2, 170nn5–6, 180n2
        (chap. 7)
    departments of, 45, 51, 52, 55, 132,
        167n17
    French, 55, 132
        poststructuralism, 95
    German, 55, 132
        idealism, xi, 62
        romanticism, 29
    Heideggerian, 11, 12, 14, 32, 48, 79,
        82, 96, 110
        post-, 2, 11, 14, 21, 74, 77, 94
    idealist, 80, 95, 96, 107, 133
    Kantian, 87, 95, 96, 98, 100, 165n3,
        166n8
        post-, 43, 44
        pre-, 43, 45
    of language, 29
    postmodern. *See* postmodern,
        postmodernism, postmodernity

206 | Index

philosophy *(continued)*
  poststructuralist. *See* poststructuralism, poststructuralist
  pre-Socratic, 41
  rationalist, 55, 97, 142
  realist, 44, 56, 107
    anti-, 161n2
    hyper-, 5–7
    non-, 44, 56, 107
    speculative, 41
  of religion, ix, 39–75 passim, 105, 107, 184n9
    analytic, 39, 44–45, 51, 52, 55, 59, 75, 105, 107, 108, 156, 170n5, 179n10
    continental, ix, 39, 46–48, 51, 55, 59, 70, 75, 105, 132, 135, 156, 171n11, 176n4, 179n10
  transcendental. *See* transcendental
Plato 30, 81–82, 139–140, 146, 154
pluralism, 167
  philosophical, 100, 101
pluralist, pluralistic, 16, 49, 98, 167n2, 175n4, 183n18
Poincaré, Henri, 69
positional, positionality, 110, 114, 127, 136, 151
  counter-, 110, 111, 114, 122
postmodern, postmodernism, postmodernity, xi, 5, 11, 16, 17, 18, 20, 33, 35, 88, 89, 97, 101, 113, 123, 161n2, 167nn15–16, 184n3, 185n10
poststructuralism, poststructuralist, 14, 23, 59, 60, 101, 106, 107, 122, 123, 126, 133, 145, 158, 161n2 (Introduction), 168n3, 170n6, 175n4
power, xiii, 28, 36, 44, 57–61, 64, 78, 97, 108, 135, 178n1
problem of representation, 57, 60, 61, 73, 107, 122, 128, 137, 168n3, 182n11, 185n10

Proudfoot, Wayne, 62, 63, 64, 66, 72, 124, 181n4
psychology, 19, 39, 42, 49, 172n15

Quinn, Philip L., 45, 46, 48

Raschke, Carl, 17, 18, 20, 23, 33, 34, 39, 40, 50–51, 103, 162n3 (chap. 1), 164n6, 167n16, 179n12
rational, rationality, 6, 7, 42, 43, 98, 100, 109, 114, 145, 153, 180n13
  transrational, 44
re- (prefix), 83
reality, 7, 28, 56, 70, 96, 97, 100, 116, 117, 139, 142, 151, 152, 163n2
reason, 42, 43, 73, 77, 82, 97, 101, 132, 142, 143, 177n11, 180n3 (chap. 7)
reductionism, reductionist, 15, 26, 27, 41, 46, 58, 61, 112, 94, 99, 107
reflection, 12, 18, 19, 21, 24, 33, 34, 41, 49, 50, 52, 69, 70, 71, 72, 75, 77, 84, 85, 89, 106, 131, 158, 165n9, 167n17
  ontic, 12
  normative, xi, 46, 64, 118, 120, 124, 125, 163n2, 171n11
  theological, 28, 42, 115, 121, 124
  transcendental, 11, 33
reflexive; reflexivity, xii, xiii, 5, 23, 24, 27–29, 33–34, 40, 48, 69, 73, 103, 108–10, 112, 114, 118, 122, 131, 135–136, 148, 164n9. *See also* Self, -reflexive, -reflexivity
relationality, xvii, 32, 71, 74, 108, 111, 135, 151
relegere, religare, religio, 83
religion
  Abrahamic, 81, 115, 165n5
  act of, 83–86
  Buddhism; Buddhist, 16, 17, 28, 50, 72, 83, 103, 125, 171n14, 173n26
  Catholic, 7, 8, 45, 183n20

Index | 207

Christian; Christianity, 45, 52, 58–60, 63, 70–71, 79, 81, 82, 83, 84, 86, 87, 125, 165n2, 170n8, 175n4, 177n11, 177n13
comparative, xi, 4, 25, 29, 30, 45, 46, 52, 55, 69, 115, 164n9, 166n9, 179n10, 184n9
departments of, 45, 51, 55
Donatist, 58
historians of, 24
Islamic, 81
Jewish, 52, 83
monotheism(s); monotheistic, 50, 82, 87
nontheistic, 103, 185n12
phenomenology of. See phenomenology, of religion
Protestant, 26, 42, 115, 180n4 (chap. 8)
philosophy of. See philosophy, of religion
Reformed, 45
return of, 78, 86, 174n2
sui generis, 11, 15, 17, 35, 111, 115
Religionswissenschaft, 15, 24. See also religious studies
religious studies
  constructivism in, 63
  enecstatic philosophy of. See enecstasis
  new materialism in, 18, 29, 30, 36, 61, 122, 123, 125, 127, 135, 161n2
  protectionism in, 17, 29, 47
  self-authorizing discourse in, 33, 47, 50, 89, 102, 112, 116, 128, 163n4
respondeo, 83, 174n2, 177n8
revelation, 42, 82, 149, 165n5
Ricoeur, Paul, 3, 13, 95, 125, 182n15
Riley, Philip Boo, 180n4 (chap. 8)
Roberts, Tyler, xii–xiii, 17, 18–20, 30, 33, 36, 50–51, 80, 102–103, 108, 124–128, 162n2 (Introduction), 164nn5–6, 164n8, 166n13, 168n2, 173n23, 183nn18–19
Robinson, Edward, 13
Rodrigues, Hilary, 65–66, 172n18, 172n20

sacred, 17, 86, 103, 164n6
sacrifice; sacrificial, 87
Said, Edward, 57, 61
Santner, Eric L., 20, 28, 50, 51
satori, 171n14, 173n26
Schleiermacher, Friedrich, 25, 42–43, 45, 62–63, 66, 166n6
secular, secularism, secularity, 52, 58, 59, 60, 61, 70, 100, 125, 168n2, 170n8
Segal, Robert A., 16, 66, 107, 166n11, 172n17, 172n20, 182n12
self-
  appropriation, 6–8, 74, 94, 99–104, 105–114 passim, 123, 127, 136, 162n3 (Introduction), 178n3, 182n15
  awareness, 28, 74, 75, 77, 88, 89, 126, 158, 166n7, 168n3
  care, xii, 2, 36, 133
  fashioning, 32, 34
  reflexive, reflexivity, 29, 33, 48, 110, 114, 131, 136, 148
  transcendence, 158, 186n17
semiotics of representation, 17, 34
Sharf, Robert H., 28, 29, 31, 64, 72, 171n14, 173n26
Sharma, Arvind, 167n18
Shatz, David, 165n5
Shin Bukkyo. See New Buddhism
Sigmund, Freud, 44, 58, 61, 103, 176n6
Simmons, J. Aaron, 95
singularity, xiv, 2, 5, 11, 18–19, 20, 21, 32, 33, 50, 80, 85, 103, 123, 128, 143, 151–152
  of the self/selfhood, xiv, 7, 8, 13, 20, 73, 104, 123, 132, 133, 141, 142

Smart, Ninian, xiv–xv, 48, 67, 113–114, 118–119, 121, 163n2, 181n6, 181n10
Smith, Jonathan Z., xi, xii, xiii, 35, 111, 112, 122
Socrates, 41–42, 165n1
Söderblom, Nathan, xv, 113
Sorge. See care
souci de soi, 5, 36
specter; spectrality. See ghost
spirit, 3, 77, 95, 166n7
  methods of, 32
spiritual, 36, 102, 125, 133
  exercise, 30
  practice, 110, 121
Spiro, Melford, 12
spondeo, 83, 177n8
Stead, Christopher, 165n5
Storm, Jason Ānanda Josephson, 161n2
Strenski, Ivan, 27–28, 67, 122–123, 163n2, 172n21, 181n10, 182n12
subject, xiii, 2, 29, 68, 69, 71, 73, 74, 80, 106, 107–108, 123, 133, 142, 143, 145, 146, 147, 150, 152, 153, 157, 169n4, 183n2 (Postscript), 186n17. See also discourse, subject-constitutive
subject-object dichotomy, 26
subject-object relation, 14, 108
subjective, subjectivity, 11, 12, 14, 16, 20, 21, 28, 33, 65, 66, 68, 72, 74, 75, 93, 96, 97, 98, 99, 106, 108, 109, 110, 116, 120, 122, 123, 125, 133, 135, 136, 141, 148, 151, 154, 157, 158, 164n5, 170n10, 172n20, 184n8
Subjectum. See subject
Sunyata, 16, 31, 34, 49, 50, 109
Suzuki, D. T., 171n14
symbol(s), symbolic, symbolism, 12, 15, 16, 19, 24, 25, 27, 31, 49, 52, 58, 59, 60, 61, 70, 112, 151, 152

Taliaferro, Charles, 44, 167n18, 172n19
Tao, 16, 31, 49
taiken, 171n14
temporal, temporality, 13, 82, 102, 170n5, 174n2
Tertullian, 83
testimony, 83
theism, 45
theodicy, 55
theology, x, 1, 14, 15, 16, 18, 19, 24, 31, 33, 39, 40, 48, 54, 59, 60, 62, 65, 66, 67, 71, 72, 75, 79, 88, 89, 94, 97, 103, 104, 106, 107, 108, 109, 114–118, 121, 123, 125, 132, 165n5, 166n6, 167n2, 171nn10–11, 172n18, 183n18
  academic, 4, 8, 11, 16, 17, 31, 34, 48–49, 52, 71, 108, 173n24
  crypto-, 24, 116, 124
  negative, 71, 174n3
  philosophical, 4, 8, 29, 31, 40–44, 48–49, 51, 52, 55, 132, 134–135, 164n5
  postmodern, 97, 102
  radical, 34, 164n5
  secular, 70
théorétique vie. See philosophy, as art of living/way of life
theoria, 93–94
theory; theorizing, x, xiv, xv, 16–19, 27, 33, 35, 39, 46, 50, 53, 55, 57, 89, 93–95, 100–104, 105, 106, 107, 108 109, 111, 113, 114, 116, 117, 119, 124, 136, 149, 157–159, 161n2, 167n16, 168n4, 174n2, 178n5
thinking, x, 2–3, 5, 8, 16, 18, 24, 29, 36, 40, 41, 51, 59, 63, 70, 73,

78, 82, 85, 96, 98, 100, 103 142, 143, 144, 148, 150, 163n2, 164n6, 165n4, 166n8, 167n17, 167n1, 173n25, 184n4
  artistic, 31, 73, 102, 110, 112, 123, 147, 162n5, 179n9, 182n15, 185n10, 185n13
  basic, 106, 109, 114, 117
  critical, xii–xiii, 47, 133, 182n11. See also critical responsiveness; criticism
  enecstatic, 4, 103, 133, 178n2. See also enecstasis
  engaged, 32
  representational, 2
  religious, 25, 42, 43, 50, 122
  transcendental, xii, 2, 5, 6, 8, 11, 29, 33, 73, 89, 93–104 passim, 105, 106, 110, 111, 116, 118, 128, 132, 133, 136, 141, 145, 164n8, 168n4, 176n5, 178n7, 179n9, 180n3 (chap. 7), 186n17
  hyper-, 32, 134, 142
  signified, 80
tradition(s), ix, x, xii, xiii, 2, 4, 5, 15, 17, 25, 35, 45, 53, 56, 57, 60, 61, 62, 64, 65, 67–72, 73, 75, 77, 79, 81, 82, 84, 87, 94, 102, 103, 104, 107, 111, 113, 114, 122, 124, 131, 132, 133, 135, 148, 157, 162n2 (Introduction), 166n8, 170nn6-7, 171n14, 172n20, 173n23, 175n4, 180n2 (chap. 7), 180n4 (chap. 8), 183n3 (Conclusion), 184n9, 185n10
  analytic. See philosophy, analytic
  continental. See philosophy, continental
  first-order, 60, 68–71, 164n8
  second-order, x, xii, xiii, 5, 68–72, 111, 121, 163n3, 164n6

transcendence; transcendent, 21, 36, 41, 42, 57, 74, 82, 97, 116, 117, 120, 121, 128, 163n2 157n15. See also self-, transcendence
triumphalism, 95
truth(s), 41, 42, 59, 60, 61, 66, 71, 83, 86, 96, 99, 101, 102, 108, 112, 118, 121, 132, 139, 140, 146, 148, 149, 166n9, 172n15, 178n1, 181n5, 184n9, 186n17

Vahanian, Gabriel, 94
van der Leeuw, Gerard, ix, xv, 113, 172n16, 180n2 (chap. 8), 182n16
value(s), xii, xiii, 7, 19, 31, 34, 47, 49, 52, 53, 65, 69, 73, 86, 87, 118, 121, 141, 149
voice(s), 1, 74, 75, 114, 123, 136, 143, 145, 154
Voltaire, 81, 86
Vroom, Hendrik M., 167n2

Wach, Joachim, 172n16
Walmsley, Gerard, 99–100, 101
Wasserstrom, Steven M., 19, 168n2
Westphal, Merold, 43, 97, 166nn6-8, 183n1
Wiebe, Donald, 66–67, 116, 166n11, 172n17, 172nn20-21, 182n12
Wildman, Wesley J., 184n9
Williams, Rowan, 125–126, 127
Winquist, Charles E., 6, 8, 18, 19, 33, 50, 94–104, 136, 178n1, 179n9, 182n15
Wisdom, John, x
Wittgenstein, Ludwig, 45, 94, 95, 107
Wolterstorff, Nicholas, 43, 166n8
world(s), 7, 20, 27, 30, 42, 44, 50, 52, 73, 77, 78, 81, 82, 97, 100, 107, 118, 120, 121, 140, 143, 144, 152, 153, 157, 158, 174n2, 178n1, 180n13

world(s) *(continued)*
 being-in-the-world, 75, 113, 169n4, 184n8, 185n13
wu, 171n14, 173n26

Χώρα, 81–83, 85, 176n7; see also *Khōra*

Žižek, Slavoj, 18, 145, 151–153

www.ingramcontent.com/pod-product-compliance
Lightning Source LLC
Chambersburg PA
CBHW020653230426
43665CB00008B/419